J. B. YEATS

Letters to his son W. B. Yeats and others

J. B. YEATS

LETTERS TO HIS SON W. B. YEATS AND OTHERS
1869–1922

edited with a memoir by
JOSEPH HONE

and a preface by
OLIVER ELTON

Secker & Warburg
London
In association with the
Arts Council of Great Britain

First published in Mcmxliv
by Faber and Faber Limited
Second impression May Mcmxliv
This edition first published in England 1983 by
Martin Secker & Warburg Limited,
in association with the Arts Council of Great Britain
54 Poland Street, London W1 V 3DF

ISBN 0-436-59205-3

Printed in Great Britain by
St Edmundsbury Press, Bury St Edmunds, Suffolk

PREFACE

In 1887, Yeats with his family settled in Bedford Park, there to remain until 1902. It must have been as happy a refuge as England—which Yeats would cheerfully call 'your villainous old country'—could offer to the Irish wanderers. This leafy oasis, lying west of Hammersmith, of red villas built by Norman Shaw, was a self-contained settlement, with a school, a church, and a single general store. Many artists, writers, and teachers lived there; few of them were well off, and some were poor; but there was no lack of good-looking children, perhaps imprudently begotten, to be seen about the roads. There was a talking society called the 'Calumet', much favoured by Yeats, without forms or fixed quarters, where all things were discussed in a free spirit. His own house was a great rallying-point—a transplanted slip of Old Ireland; and thither my wife and I, newly married, who had come to the Park in the winter of 1888–9, soon found our way. In 1890, we left for the North, but I was often in the place afterwards. It is all long ago; and these notes are composed from memories of many occasions.

Yeats was still barely fifty. With his grey head (in harmony with a loose grey suit), he would have looked older but for his large bright eyes, changeful and ever-watchful. Mrs. Yeats, as I knew her, was a silent, flitting figure. She came from the fairy shores of Sligo, and Yeats would speak of her as the right kind of mother for a poet and dreamer. He would also speak much of her kinsman, George Pollexfen, the astrologer, and of his accurate and prophetic horoscopes. The poet, William Yeats, in 1889 published his *Wanderings of Oisin*; containing 'Down by the Salley Gardens', 'Kanva', and other poems which are still untouched by time. But in our evening gatherings, he spoke less of poetry than of things occult—spiritualism, or the gifts of Madame Blavatsky, or the esoteric significance of certain colours as beheld in dreams. Miss Yeats (Lily) the elder sister, was already aware of psychic gifts, though she did not speak of them to the company; but, even in company, she could at times retreat into a world of waking visions, and in this way re-people scenes of the past with 'forms more real than living man'. Miss Elizabeth Yeats ('Lolly') did not, so far as I know, claim these powers. She had much practical capacity as a teacher and craftswoman; and was afterwards in Ireland to train girls of the people for her Cuala Press, just as her sister did for beautiful embroidery

5

work. The sisters, good hostesses, were concerned to draw out the company, and to smooth over the few sharp corners in the political talk. Jack Yeats, the artist, was mostly a listener. He too had his dreams, as we know; they were of fairs and roadsides and country folk and horses—all real, and yet with an air not quite of this world.

All this dream-element, be it said, was in the background, unobtruded. The conversation was rapid and cheerful. If it were too rapid or buzzed too loudly, Yeats would hold his peace and wait for a pause; and then he might pour forth, without effort or study and without rhetoric, and in his soft flexible voice, a stream of his peculiar eloquence. The voice is now silent; but for the same play of mind and fancy, the same pure good English and naturally good rhythm, we have but to turn to Yeats's letters. They are just like his talk, and flow on with hardly an erasure. I think that the best prose of William, the poet, must owe some of its ease and simplicity to his father.

The political temperature was very high during the years 1887–1891. They covered the rule of the Unionists, for the first Home Rule Bill had been defeated in 1886; Parnell's action against *The Times*, and the exposure of Pigott; the contemptuous alliance of Parnell with the Liberal minority; his fall, late in 1890, and his abandonment by Gladstone; the break in the Irish party, and his death in 1891. Yeats, anti-English in all his traditions and convictions, was not only a Home Ruler, but strong for Parnell as against the dissidents, and against Gladstone. But there was one occasional visitor, already an historical figure, who would scarify, impartially, all parties, English and Irish; and, in particular, the parliament-men, the men of compromise.

This was the old Fenian leader, John O'Leary (always, in that company, 'Mr.' O'Leary). He was now (1890) only sixty years old; but seamed, and grey, and bearded, after nine years spent in an English prison. He had been released on condition of quitting Ireland, and had retreated to Paris; but by the Amnesty Act of 1885, being now judged harmless, had been re-admitted, and had come to England; he was afterwards to return to Ireland for the rest of his days. I have read that there is an admirable portrait of him by Yeats in the Dublin Gallery; and William Yeats, in a poem enumerating 'beautiful lofty things', speaks of 'O'Leary's noble head'. (I felt very young when the old man chanced to speak of the past; remembering how my father had taken me, a child of six, to see the breach in the wall of Pentonville gaol, blown out by the Fenians. I think O'Leary himself was then in Portland.) One of his remarks comes back to mind:

Preface

how the British gaolers would only give him Bibles to read, and had always denied him the works of Shakespeare.

Another visitor, without whom the evening would seem incomplete, was Frederick York Powell, the historian, the unprofessor-like professor. His magnificent laughter warmed the hearts and raised the spirits of the company. All his learning was quickened by a rich intelligence; but he dispersed his powers, and left no great historical monument of his own. In 1906 the Clarendon Press published my memoir of Powell, with selected letters; and I rejoice that Mr. Hone is including the pages in which Yeats portrays him. There is no better account of Powell, and Yeats is here at his very best.

There were many others in the circle: John Todhunter, the poet, perhaps best known for *Aghadoe*, with its slow lingering tune; Joseph Nash, the black-and-white illustrator, noted for his drawings of ships; Harry Paget, another good illustrator, and a portrait-painter—a boxer too, and thought to be 'the strongest man in the Park'. But, I will name only one more, whose gay talk and beautiful deep voice filled the room with her vitality. This was Mrs. Emery, on the stage 'Florence Farr' (her unmarried name), the brightest, the most unsentimental, of good companions. She had played Rebecca in Ibsen's *Rosmersholm* successfully. Afterwards, she took to chanting—a craft between speech and singing, and accompanied her voice with the dulcimer. Once she came with William Yeats to perform in our Liverpool University; and after giving his 'Little Red Fox' and other good things, she startled the house with a magnificent rendering of one of the world's great poems—'By the waters of Babylon . . .' Mrs. Emery, under an impulse noted by William Yeats in his verses *All Souls' Night*, migrated to Ceylon to teach in a native school, and there died, in 1917.

In March, 1907, I was in Dublin, and for a fortnight, under Yeats's auspices, saw much of the Irish intellectuals, going often to the Abbey Theatre, then in its glory; and meeting Lady Gregory, George Russell (AE), George Moore, 'Seumas O'Sullivan', Miss Susan Mitchell and many others. The storm aroused by Synge's *Playboy of the Western World*[1] was just subsiding; William Yeats and Lady Gregory and the actors had steered it through triumphantly, in the Abbey Theatre; but the dispute was still on every tongue. A scholar of a later generation, Dr. Una Ellis-Fermor, has written a close, appreciative study of *The Irish Dramatic Movement* (1939). It is not my topic here, though the figures of the Fays and of

[1] The play was performed first in January 1907.

7

Sarah Allgood are fresh in memory, like their beautiful utterance of prose —the prose of Synge, of Lady Gregory, and of William Yeats. So, too, is the presence and the speech of AE, who needs no praises here. We walked out once by moonlight, and talked and corresponded about dreams (which *he*, of course, would in no case rationalise) and I saw his visionary paintings on his walls. As for Yeats himself, he was now once more at home, in his natural *milieu*, painting, pencil-drawing, friends and personages and politicians, with redoubled fervour, in his Dublin studio. He could take pride in the now established fame of William, as a poet, a playwright, and an inspirer of the theatre; the admitted chief, already, of living Irish men of letters.

The atmosphere of unending, mocking, fencing, glancing, talk quickened all Yeats's powers. Ceaselessly, humorously, and with rare exceptions tolerantly, he brooded on the scene and on the people. England seemed a long way off, though he was ever ready to hold forth on the 'Englishman', a theme that was also to pervade his letters from overseas. *The* Englishman, in his eyes, came to be a type (Tory, class-proud, official, public schoolboy, self-centred, etc.); but he made many a concession to our poetry, and also to our common people. He was, then, very much at home in Dublin, and yet he was restless. Not even here could be his abiding city. Life was difficult, financially and otherwise; and I was not surprised when I heard that, like myriads of his fellow-countrymen, like the migrating birds, he was flying to the West.

In December, 1907, accompanied by Miss Yeats, he stayed with us in Liverpool, in high spirits, for they had taken tickets to New York; yet somewhat distraught. There had been many efforts to keep him back; and afterwards he was often pressed, and even tempted, to return, but in the end he always resisted, refusing, unlike the birds, to change his mind. I think he was impelled, first of all, by the racial instinct, *vis a tergo*, to quit the homeland, still under alien rule, blistered with internal strife and evil memories, and ever oppressed by the difficulty of living. Another impulse, *vis a fronte,* was, I judge, his inextinguishable curiosity; the passion for a new life that would provide a new spectacle of men and women and manners; and perhaps a new hope, perhaps a living for the artist. The hope, as all his letters show, was more than realised. Life in America, though often hard, and sometimes very lonely, was deeply enjoyed by Yeats. The kindness and politeness that always greet a stranger who comes with introductions soon warmed, in his case, into affection and admiration. He lectured and talked, drew and painted, and wrote home profusely. But I must not continue, or I should seem to be catching his bent —though not his gift—for analysis. As he and his daughter sailed, we watched them from the landing-stage, and my wife said 'He will never come back'. His soft hat and white beard vanished slowly as they waved to us. He too watched, and wrote a few years later: 'I hope Mrs. Elton is quite well. The last thing to disappear in the mist of distance at Liverpool was the tuft that ornamented her hat. It is now a little blurred in my mind, in which also the mists are gathering. I am getting elegiac.'

NOTE

My thanks are due to Jack B. Yeats and Miss Lily Yeats, the owners of the copyright in J. B. Yeats's letters; and for further help in making this volume I am indebted to Mrs. W. B. Yeats who provided me with the letters to and from the late W. B. Yeats, and to the various other persons to whom the letters now published are addressed.

The ten letters from W. B. Yeats are reprinted by permission of Michael B. Yeats, Ann Yeats and the Oxford University Press.

CONTENTS

NOTE. The letters are *to* the persons named except in a few cases, where it is expressly stated that they are *from* them. In the text the name of the recipient appears at the head of the group of letters written to him, but not on subsequent letters in the group.

Contents

Contents

Contents

Contents

Contents

Contents

Contents

Contents

J. B. YEATS

Letters to his son W. B. Yeats and others

MEMOIR OF
JOHN BUTLER YEATS

Most of those through whom Ireland has been known to the modern world, and a majority of the Irish national leaders, from 1700 until the change came with Mr. de Valera and James Joyce,[1] have been what is now called Anglo-Irish. Swift, Berkeley, Burke, Grattan, Synge, Yeats, Bernard Shaw and the rest can be so grouped together, on the one hand, because they bear non-Gaelic names, and on the other, because their religious origins separate them, not only from the Catholic Irish but also from the Presbyterian population of Scots origin in Ulster. The term Anglo-Irish has therefore some value of convenience, but is misleading in many ways, especially as used by political and religious propagandists, who wish to discredit the great figures of Protestant (episcopalian) Ireland by identifying them with the Plantations and so with records of confiscation and oppression. In fact, landlordry, whether Norman, Cromwellian or mixed Irish, can claim credit for comparatively few of Ireland's famous sons. Neither Swift nor Berkeley was born in a great house; Goldsmith came from a country rectory; Burke was the son of a lawyer, Wolfe Tone of a coachmaker; Grattan's father was a Recorder, Thomas Davis's an Army surgeon; Bernard Shaw's ancestor was a lawyer in Kilkenny; and these men were not only born in Ireland but educated there, not at Eton, Oxford and Cambridge, where since the seventeenth century Irish rank and riches have chiefly sent their young.

The list could be extended to include the family of the subject of this memoir, one of the most distinguished in art and letters of our time. 'We have always been in much the same station,' John Butler Yeats once wrote with some pride. His father and grandfather were clergymen; further back the Yeatses were a minor dynasty of Dublin merchants. The name Butler was inherited from a great-grandmother, a Mary Butler who in 1773 married Benjamin Yeats 'at the house of Gideon Tabuteau of Portarlington'. She was a small landowner, and on her mother's side inherited French blood from an immigrant naturalised under Cromwell; to this ancestry J. B. Yeats used to attribute the subsequent evangelicism of his family, also its good manners. Her son, after winning prizes at

[1] Born in the same year, 1882. Both mirror the return of Ireland to the scholastic temper.

23

Trinity College, Dublin, was content to pass most of his life as Rector of Drumcliffe in the wild and remote parish of Drumcliffe in Sligo, where he was as much beloved by the poor Roman Catholics as by the sprinkling of prosperous Orange farmers and 'ascendancy' landlords who were his spiritual care. An old woman once praised him to his great-grand-daughter, Lily Yeats, as follows: 'My father was butler at the Rectory. Mr. Yeats always went about in creaking shoes and rattled his keys, so as to be sure not to catch anyone doing wrong.' The Drumcliffe Rector was a generous and open-handed man; but he succeeded in preserving his mother's estate in Kildare, which he passed on to his eldest son, the Rev. William Butler Yeats, Rector of the parish of Tullylish, Co. Down, where J. B. Yeats was born on March 16th, 1839.

John Butler Yeats was brought up in this Ulster parish, with many brothers and sisters. That they were a notably happy family is made evident in the fragment of autobiography which was published after his death at his daughter's press.[1] 'My father', Yeats there wrote, 'was my friend and counsellor, my mother my conscience. My father theorised about things and explained things and that delighted me . . . My mother never explained anything, she hadn't the theoretic faculty, but she had a way of saying "Yes, darling" or "No, darling", which, when put out, she would change into a hasty "Yes, dear" or "No, dear" that was sufficient for all purposes.' His father, red-headed and very tall, a good horseman and a racket-player, combined a wide charity and devotion to the poets, particularly to Shelley, with zeal for evangelical theology; a notable preacher, he was sent with another clergyman to speak in England on behalf of the Irish poor during the Famine years; and later, he caught the famine typhus while ministering to the dying. J. B. Yeats used to tell how he could remember him at this time sitting opposite to his mother at the table, doing secretary's work for some relief fund. She also would be writing, and when her husband had finished a sheet in his illegible hand, he would toss it across to have it copied. Outside the open window stood a girl watching the distant road for the coach to which, when it came in sight, she would call out, whereupon the letters were hastily sealed and handed to her that she might run down with them to the gate and fling the bag to the guard.

Another memory of childhood that J. B. Yeats carried, was that of sitting in the Tullylish Rectory in the evening, with his mother sewing, his father reading, the only light two tall candles in silver candlesticks on

[1] *Early Memories, Some Chapters of Autobiography*, Cuala Press, 1923.

the table, their snuffers and the tray between them. He, too, sat at the table reading Robinson Crusoe with such delight and excitement that he kept his hands under the table, so that his father and mother might not see how they were shaking. He was so young that to him Crusoe lived in a romantic strange place pronounced Island; the printed word could not be the spoken word, so familiar, island.

The red-headed rector's charity extended not only to the sick but to sinners. His dearest friend was Isaac Butt, who afterwards formed the first Home Rule party; a man of high culture and great political integrity, who ran after women and was always in debt.[1]

While still a very small boy, Yeats was sent to a kindergarten school in Liverpool, kept by three sisters;[2] afterwards he went with his three brothers to a boarding-school in the Isle of Man called the Atholl Academy, returning home but once a year, for six weeks in summer. The Scotsman who governed the school enforced the classics on his pupils by a system of terror, and did his conscientious best not to 'spoil' the child. Yeats was good at his work and got on well with the boys, among whom was a certain George Pollexfen from Sligo, who was to become his brother-in-law. In later life, when he recalled his schooldays, he would say that the tyranny of the master enabled the boys to maintain their individuality and a certain freedom and solitude, both absent from monkish establishments, such as are English public schools, where the boys form a democracy. 'We all talked and thought about our homes, and how natural, and everybody was an individual, either because of his own strength or because he partook of the individuality of the home.'[3]

It was his father's hope that he would become a famous mathematician because of some fancied resemblance to his uncle Thomas Yeats, from whom great things in this science had been expected; and he was top boy in the Academy in Euclid, as well as in classics. However, when he entered Trinity College, Dublin, in 1857, it was generally assumed that he would follow in the footsteps of his father and grandfather and take orders. But as soon as he began to study the foundations of belief, as set out in Butler's *Analogy*, he discovered without sense of loss that he could not accept the supernatural. He was attracted, he says, by some aspects of the Catholic Church, and one day he told an intellectual priest that he would become a convert but for this one difficulty. The priest hesitated for a moment, and then threw up his arms and shouted: 'No, impossible; we

[1] See letters 148, 158.   [2] See letter 171.   [3] *Early Memories*.

should collapse altogether.' A few weeks later Yeats was lunching with his best friend, John Dowden, a High-Churchman, afterwards Bishop of Edinburgh, and told him of what he said to the priest. 'What did he reply?' Dowden asked in great excitement. 'That without the supernatural we should collapse altogether.' 'Of course we would—of course we would', Dowden repeated in a musing grumbling kind of voice.[1]

Yeats still conformed to public opinion to the extent of going to church once every Sunday. The visitor to Dublin city and county to-day is surprised at the two cathedrals and at the number and size of the churches which are in the possession of the Irish Episcopalians, a minority of eight per cent in the population. They are at least half as many as the Roman Catholic churches—which were called 'chapels' when J. B. Yeats was a young man. It is significant of the decline in the Irish Protestant population, and of other things, that in J. B. Yeats's undergraduate days the Episcopalian churches were so crowded that young men, unable to find a seat, remained the whole service standing in the aisles. This suited J. B. Yeats. He chose a church at Kingstown down by the sea, where he could stand during the two hours of sermon at the door, half within and half without, so that while listening to the eloquent clergyman, he could at the same time soothe his spirit by looking towards the sea and sky.

In Ireland the movement against eighteenth-century laxity took the evangelical form, and there is an interesting page in J. B. Yeats's Memoirs in which he speaks of the effect of evangelicism on the 'Irish gentlemen'. He points out that in England it was the middle and lower classes which were chiefly touched by this influence, and it made them more commercial. Whereas in Ireland 'the wild men, described by Charles Lever, who cared for nothing except romance and courage and personal glory, now walked in the footsteps of their Lord and Master'. That is why it could be said in the middle of the nineteenth century that there was 'no gentleman like the Irish gentleman'.[1]

After Yeats's rejection of a clerical career the law was spoken of. His father's friend, Isaac Butt, M.P., Q.C., at that time still the rising hope of the Irish Tories, a favourite of Disraeli's and Professor of Political Economy at Trinity College, would have been prepared to forward the young man's interests at the Bar. But secretly J. B. Yeats wished to be an artist. Paper had been very dear when he was a child, but he had been so fond of sketching that he used to draw on the margins that his mother cut for him from *The Times*. At the horrible school in the Isle of Man there had

[1] *Early Memories.*

been an excellent drawing-master—a son of Mark Lemon, an editor of *Punch*—who had encouraged him to develop his artistic talent.

Though at Trinity College, Dublin, one heard little of art, the University was full of brilliant young men, figures thirty years later in the last efflorescence of the Ireland of Burke and Goldsmith. Mahaffy, Tyrrell, Edward Dowden, George Fitzgerald (who first indicated some of the stranger hypotheses of modern physics), Thomas Allingham, brilliant brother of the poet William, were among Yeats's contemporaries, along with others who were later to occupy great administrative and judicial positions in Ireland and the Empire. Trinity inspired respect rather than affection, but Yeats made some good friends at College. The brothers Dowden, Edward and John, belonged to his company, and of his fellow students in the Law School he liked, and was liked by, several who were afterwards to become High Court Judges and drive in carriages and pairs.[1] George Fitzgerald, of whose poetical mind he has written, was twelve years younger, and he made his acquaintance some years after leaving the University. Years later he painted the portraits of Judges Holmes, Madden, Fitzgibbon, Monroe; Madden, the Shakesperian scholar,[2] he painted with Mrs. Madden, and it is somewhat typical of the mishaps of his career that the frame-maker happened to send this portrait to the house on the very day that Madden was making his second marriage.

Towards the close of his undergraduate years Yeats was much with his mother's brother, Robert Corbet, a rich man, who lived close to Dublin in an eighteenth-century house, with towers added and large gardens, called Sandymount Castle. Corbet was an amiable, sociable man who entertained interesting people and collected pictures; perhaps his nephew's desire of art was further stimulated by this association. This was another happy period in Yeats's life. He was athletic, and would take immense walks through the night from Ladymount into the heart of the Wicklow Mountains to breakfast with relatives at Lough Dan. He shot, fished, and rode when the opportunity offered.[3] He made occasional visits to Sligo, where he stayed with his Uncle Thomas or with his Aunt Mary Yeats, who farmed some land at Ballincar, or at the house of William Pollexfen, a shipowner, and the father of his school friend, whose eldest sister he courted. In his last year at Trinity he studied the writings of

---

[1] See letter 164.

[2] Author of that excellent book, *The Diary of William Silence*.

[3] When in his old age he filled in a paper for *Who's Who* he wrote under 'Re-creation', 'would like a little fishing'.

John Stuart Mill and won a University prize in Political Economy. Some years later when he lived in London he went to the meeting at which Mill, accused of calling the British working man a liar, replied, 'I said so'.[1] Yeats admired this man, who wore no peacock's feathers, and allowed no self-emphasis to come between him and the truth. He became very argumentative on the liberal and humanitarian side. 'I wanted to quarrel with everyone', he says;[2] and his advocacy of Mill provided him with excellent opportunities for quarrelling, as Carlyle's influence then prevailed in Irish intellectual circles. Perhaps he was confirmed in his 'religion of humanity' by an experience in Dublin, when a medical student, John Todhunter, took him to the Cork Street Fever Hospital. The reform of Mary Aikenhead had not yet penetrated there, and he saw sights which he never forgot: the patients delirious and with their heads shaven, and the nurses with long floating veils and artificial flowers in their hair.

Upon his father's death in 1862 J. B. Yeats inherited the property in County Kildare which brought him in a few hundreds a year. The next year he married Susan Pollexfen, a good-looking girl with pale fine skin and deep-set eyes, and settled with her near his uncle at Sandymount. He did some 'devilling' for Isaac Butt, and was called to the Bar in 1866. To prove that he attended at the courts, his copy of Mill's *Some Unsettled Questions of Political Economy* (1844), is filled with sketches of legal figures of the period.[3] His lack of enthusiasm for his profession was, however, sufficiently ardent to be a source of vexation to his father-in-law. William Pollexfen was a fine old man but irascible, and his wife, a member of a west of Ireland trading family, named Middleton, was ambitious for her children. Middletons had raced from Customs officers in the old days, and William Pollexfen had driven his ships through wind and wave. They were people of simple faith, with a streak of iron, for whom the fear of God was the beginning of wisdom, and Yeats's theoretic habit, his perennial hopefulness and his avowed contempt for practical ends must have been a sore trial to them. Their anxieties were not relieved when, in 1867, he exchanged the law for art,

[1] At the elections of 1865, when Mill spoke in public for the first and last time.

[2] 'This,' he says, in *Early Memories*, 'was not due to Mill's teaching. Mill must have been most persuasive, while I in my crudeness must have been the least.'

[3] The autographed copy survives in the possession of a distinguished Irish bibliophile and poet.

and moved from Sandymount to 23 Fitzroy Road, London, with his wife, his two-year-old son (the poet) and an introduction to Doyle, the caricaturist, who died in the following year.

He first attended at Heatherley's famous school, where he studied with Samuel Butler, of whom years afterwards he wrote in *Irish and American Essays*, and with Sydney Hall. His apprenticeship was a long one; and it should have been longer, he used to say, but for the good feeling that made him desire to meet the wishes of the Pollexfens. He might have acquired 'skill' if he had not felt that he must earn money. His family increased to five, three sons (W. B. Y., Robert and Jack), and two daughters (Lily and Elizabeth or Lolly). In 1869, when he was thirty, he made his first visit to the Continent, where he saw the Dutch Galleries in the company of the future Bishop, John Dowden. Everyone in Holland took him for an Italian, so black was his beard and so olive-coloured his skin. In London, his principal friends were three artists, remarkable but unsuccessful men: the pre-Raphaelite J. T. Nettleship, the water colourist, George Wilson, and Edwin J. Ellis, a poet as well as a painter. Yeats, Nettleship, Wilson and Ellis named themselves the Brotherhood. They were literary, believed in the union of the arts, worshipped at the shrines of Blake and Rossetti; and nearly all Yeats's early pictures were poetic and imaginative. But of these first years in London not much is recoverable. Yeats said little of them in his fragment of autobiography, *Early Memories*, and his children were too young to remember. Moreover, the latter were frequently with the Pollexfens in Sligo, where there were several young aunts, as well as numerous servants, to look after them. Yeats was constantly harassed by financial difficulties, and his wife's delicacy made it difficult for her to manage a household. None of her children knew her well; she was never able to put her strong feelings into words. 'Inarticulate as the sea-cliffs were the Pollexfens', J. B. Yeats once wrote, 'lying buried under mountains of silence. They were released from bondage by contact with the joyous amiability of my family, and of my bringing up, and so all my four children are articulate, and yet with the Pollexfen force'.

Not all the Pollexfens were inarticulate. They could not express their emotions, but both George, whose chief interests were horses and astrology, and Mrs. J. B. Yeats, could tell a story very well.[1] Another of the sisters, Isabella Pollexfen, had a gift for art and went to Paris to work

[1] W. B. Yeats says in his autobiography that his mother told 'stories that Homer might have envied'.

in the studios of the famous Julian.[1] But Yeats, to whom conversation was already the chief end of life, could never reach the right side of his father-in-law, whom he found 'like Napoleon unamusable'. After a visit to the Pollexfens at 'Merville' he complains that 'Willie', who was getting on so well by being with his mother, is greatly disimproved by being at Merville. 'He will only develop by kindness and gentleness.' The second boy, Robert, is a more robust and active nature, and therefore less likely to be harmed by unintelligent treatment. Yet a little later, when Yeats himself tried to educate his eldest son, he was himself often guilty of hasty reproof and unconsidered speech. In after life he explained that glimpses of what he called Pollexfen apathy in the child had frightened him.

There are records of Yeats's doings in 1872 and 1873. A part of these years he spent in London keeping house with George Wilson,[2] his wife being absent in Sligo with the children. He had his first commissions in 1872, when he painted portraits of the great Herbert family of Muckcross, Killarney.[3] Then in March 1873 he was summoned to Sligo by the death from croup of his second son. The children's rooms overlooked the garden at Merville and one morning Lily was awakened by her grandmother's voice, high and strange, and full of tears, crying 'my little son, my little son,' then she heard a galloping horse, and someone said that Uncle Frederick had gone for the doctor without waiting to put a saddle on the horse. 'You will remember', Miss Yeats writes to me, 'that there is a galloping horse in Willie's last play, *Purgatory*. When I saw it at the Abbey, all round melted away, and I felt myself back nearly seventy years in my cot on that March morning, hearing the galloping horse off too late for the doctor for my baby brother.' J. B. Yeats remained at Merville for a while after Robert's death, and it was then that he commenced educating his elder son, and found that the deplorably backward child could enjoy *The Lays of Ancient Rome* and the romances of Walter Scott.

A year or two later Yeats was able to gather all his family around him again in London; first at North End and then at Bedford Park. He was still painting subject pictures under pre-Raphaelite influence, and of these his college friend John Todhunter, a wealthy man who lived in Bedford Park, bought a good number, the present whereabouts of which it has been impossible to discover. Nettleship, Wilson, and Ellis were still his close friends, and to these were now added Potter, the gifted painter of the 'Dormouse' and Farrar, an American landscape artist. Ellis's father,

[1] See letters 3 et seq.   [2] See letter 16.   [3] See letter 169.

Memoir

Alexander T. Ellis, wrote deep books on dialects, and one day W. B. Yeats and his sister Lily, aged about nine and eight, were invited to lunch with him at his house in Kensington, and he got them to talk. They afterwards learned that he was making mental notes of their language and accent, derived from their greatest friends, the old coachman and the young stable boy at their grandfather's in Sligo. It was easy enough to make Yeats's children talk, and they quickly became interested in their father's circle of friends, delighting particularly in Potter, a little man with a stutter, who was to die of neglect and starvation. (The touching note on him in the Tate Gallery Catalogue is by J. B. Yeats.[1])

Nettleship had turned away from pre-Raphaelitism, and had become an impressionistic lion-painter, and presently Yeats began to question the romantic style of his youth and to say that one must paint what is before one. A magnificent portrait of Isaac Butt, of which there is a copy in chalk in the Irish National Portrait Gallery, dates from this period. His chief trouble was indecision, often lasting for several months, and W. B. Yeats, in his *Reveries over Childhood and Youth*, has told of his father's painting a picture of a pond, from spring through all the seasons of the year, only giving it up when he had painted snow upon the heath-covered banks.

At the beginning of the eighties Yeats returned with his family to Ireland, where life at that time was less expensive than in London. He lived at first at Howth, near Dublin, and every week-day morning he and W. B. took the first train into the city—the one bound for his studio, the other for his school—talking of the poets on the way and at breakfast in the studio. For studio Yeats had a large room in an eighteenth-century house in York Street, the basement of which was occupied by the caretaker, a young married man. Later, he moved his canvases and paints to 7 Stephen's Green, a studio built for himself; but he was still at York Street in 1882, the year of the Phoenix Park murders, when he did many drawings of the big trial. He noticed that the caretaker's wife looked ill, and he asked her what was wrong; she said, 'Nothing', but shortly afterwards she came up to his room, and, taking a revolver from her apron, asked him to keep it in hiding for her. This he did, thinking that the poor woman feared that her husband was a member of the Invincibles (as probably he was).

Politically, Yeats was a heretic in those houses of College notabilities, judges, leaders of the Bar, where he was frequently invited to dine. He

[1] W. B. Yeats has given vivid descriptions of Nettleship and Ellis in *Reveries over Childhood and Youth*.

31

was a Gladstonian if not a Parnellite—he could never quite forgive Parnell for having deposed Isaac Butt from the Home Rule leadership! One regrets that he has not left an account of a party at Lord Justice Fitzgibbon's at Howth, when he met the witty Father Healy, a great pet in the best Unionist houses, and Lord Randolph Churchill, come to Ireland to say that 'Ulster would fight and Ulster would be right!'

'The Bird Market', a little masterpiece, was painted in the Stephen's Green Studio, as was also a large water-colour, one of his best pictures (now unhappily lost), of a beggar-girl. In cold weather Yeats used to bring in the newspaper boys to sit for him, and with them came the little girl, a feeble creature, afflicted with consumption; he painted at the far end of the room, letting the children sit on the floor near the fire and persuading them to talk, for he always strove to learn from his models. The children called him 'the man', and they called W. B. Yeats, who was constantly in the studio, 'Willie'. Miss Lily Yeats, however, was always known as Miss Yeats. 'I met Willie on the street', one of them said one day, and another answered, 'I met Miss Yeats on the bridge, and she smiled at me; if I had to face my God so she did!' 'The Bird Market' and another large water-colour, which looks like an oil-painting, were given to the Dublin Municipal Gallery by Dr. Fitzgerald, the oculist, a son of that Baron Fitzgerald, who at the time that Carlyle died, greatly pleased Yeats by calling out at a dinner-party: 'The great Sham is dead; what is to be done with the great Sham?'

Yeats painted, among others at this time, Dr. Fitzgerald's children, Sir Andrew Hart, the Vice-Provost of Trinity, Lord Justice Fitzgibbon, Judge Monroe, Judge Madden, Katherine Tynan, and Dowden's daughter, now Hester Travers Smith. He exhibited twice in the Royal Academy, in 1887 and 1889, and from 1880 onwards, fairly frequently, in the Royal Hibernian Academy, of which he became an Associate in 1892 and a Member some years later. Several of the above-mentioned portraits were very fine, but his work failed to earn him a great reputation, partly perhaps because of the absurdly small prices that he charged. His son has said of him: 'He was the most natural among all the fine minds that I have known'; and had his facility for expressing the wisdom and wit of his mind in conversation been less, more attention might have been paid to his painting.

In 1884 he left Howth with his family for a little red-brick house in Ashfield Terrace, Terenure, a Dublin suburb. Quite close but in a more fashionable street lived Edward Dowden, who was then engaged upon a book which all the reading world awaited—his *Life of Shelley*, in two volumes. W. B. Yeats has told in his autobiography how 'sometimes we were asked to breakfast, and afterwards my father used to tell me to read out one of my poems . . . Dowden was wise in his encouragement, never overpraising and never unsympathetic . . .' Yeats and Dowden were two of the six people in these islands who had sent an early message of admiration to Walt Whitman, and Dowden had been rebuked by the University authorities for presenting a copy of the *Leaves of Grass* to the College Library. But now Yeats had begun to criticise his learned and generous friend for timidity. Had Dowden not confessed that he had lost his liking for Shelley, and that he would not be writing the biography except for a promise made to the Shelley family? Yeats would now say that Dowden's brother, the Bishop, was the better man of the two, and that Dowden's cradle had been too much rocked all his life—by sisters, college porters and docile pupils. 'Oh', he said, when Dowden recommended George Eliot to W. B. Yeats's attention, 'she was an ugly woman who hated handsome men and handsome women.'

W. B. Yeats owed a great part of his early literary and philosophical education to his father, who imbued him with a love of Shakespeare, Balzac, and Blake, a distrust for the poetry of ideas, and for facile habits of belief and the achievements of the logician. A constant emphasis on the 'solitary' nature of the 'superior' man will be found in the Letters in this volume, and this 'pet' thought of J. B. Yeats's evidently sank deep into his son's mind, for it is constantly reflected in W. B. Y.'s poetry.[1] But while the family was still at Rathgar, W. B. Yeats broke away in certain respects from his father's influence; he found friends for himself, such as the old Fenian, John O'Leary, Katharine Tynan, and the theosophical AE. J. B. Yeats admired and delighted in the heroic O'Leary—than whom no one had ever a finer or more remarkable head—and he accused Protestant Dublin of being very ungracious towards so sweet a young poetess as Katharine Tynan, whose portrait he painted in 1887, contemporaneously with O'Leary's. But he never felt drawn towards mysticism or towards the (in Ireland) related movement back to mythology, and it is remarkable that, though a romantic painter at the start, he painted but one picture, 'King Goll'—the subject of one of

---

[1] For instance. 'And God stands winding his lonely horn.' (*Into the Twilight*).

'I mourn for that most lonely thing, and yet God's will be done.' (*His Phoenix*.)

'A lonely impulse of delight drove to this tumult in the clouds.' (*An Irish Airman*.)

his son's early poems—that recalls the 'Celtic' movement of the nineties and early nineteen-hundreds.

All hated the little house in Rathgar, and no one protested when in the summer of 1887, Yeats again renounced Dublin for London. At 58 Eardsly Crescent, Earl's Court, a great misfortune befell him; his wife had a stroke from which neither her mind nor her body ever recovered. Soon after this, the family found itself once more in Bedford Park, but in another house—3 Blenheim Road, and from here Yeats started to seek employment from editors and publishers as a black-and-white artist. He did work for Dent, for whom he illustrated a small-paged edition of the works of Defoe; and a series of his drawings for Tennyson's *In Memoriam* appeared in the *Leisure Hour*, the editor of which, Mr. Stevens, was his excellent friend and the first English editor to publish his son's verses. There were three illustrations to each of the Defoe volumes, and Dent remarked one day that all the illustrations, with the exception of Black Man Friday, bore a singular resemblance to the artist's daughter, Lily, who, indeed, had been the model for most of them. Times, however, were unfavourable for the black-and-white artist, owing to the improvements in photography, and Yeats's hope—Shorter's wife was a patriotic Irishwoman—that he might be employed by Clement Shorter on *The Sphere* was doomed to disappointment. In 1897 he returned to oil portraits, and in the following year again exhibited at the Royal Hibernian Academy. Mrs. Shorter came to Bedford Park to be painted by him; but few of his sitters were in a position to purchase their portraits, of which the finest in this period are those of Miss Lily Yeats and of Mrs. Melville Smith—for the latter he was rewarded by the gift of an old bicycle.[1] His wife's health worsened, and she died in 1900, by which time both his sons had left the parental roof. Jack, the artist, who had married early, lived in Devonshire. W. B. Y. divided his time between his rooms in Woburn Buildings, near Euston, and visits to George Pollexfen and Lady Gregory in the West of Ireland.

Yeats found relief from his sorrows and anxieties in the successes of his children and in new friendships, particularly in those with York Powell,

[1] The portrait of Mrs. Smith was shown at the Guildhall Exhibition of Irish artists in 1904, and reproduced in the catalogue. Professor Bodkin has singled it out for special reference in an article on J. B. Yeats. (*Dublin Magazine*, Jan. 1924.) Mrs. Smith (Nannie Smith) was one of the daughters of Farrar, the painter. See letters 16, 17.

Memoir

Oliver Elton and Henry Paget,[1] neighbours in Bedford Park and members of the 'Calumet', a conversation club founded by Monicure Conway, and consisting of twelve members living within easy reach of each other, who met at their respective houses every second Sunday at nine, and often did not disperse until three in the morning. Of Yeats's earlier London companions, Nettleship and E. J. Ellis were still in evidence—Ellis achieved some distinction by collaborating with W. B. Yeats in an interpretation of Blake's mythical writings—but it was 'the unprofessor-like Professor, York Powell' whom J. B. Yeats now placed on the highest pedestal.[2] Another interesting neighbour was young G. K. Chesterton, whose autobiography contains a delightful page on the Yeats household, as he knew it in the late nineties. All went to his wedding—Yeats adored weddings—and later, when the Misses Yeats had made their home in Ireland, they seldom visited England without staying for a few days with G. K. C. and his wife.[3]

Ireland in the opening years of this century looked like an interesting and attractive country in which to live. The Gaelic League and W. B. Yeats's intellectual movement bade fair to confer ideal benefits that would still the rage of party and sect and perhaps achieve that union of all Irish-born men, which, as Thomas Davis said, would (if ever it were accomplished) give Ireland 'the greatest and most varied material for an illustrious nationality, and for a tolerant and flexible character in literature, manners, religion and life, of any nation on earth'. In Dublin in particular it seemed that there had been excited a hope of improvement which would regain for the town a reputation for learning, taste, and genius as distinguished as it had possessed in the great epoch of the Irish Parliament, when the poor downtrodden artist and writer no longer pined in idleness and poverty.

Yeats was moved by the spirit of the times, and became as national as his son; like George Moore he found London intolerable during the South African war. His letters record his discontents; his quarrels with his friends at the 'Calumet' club and his vain search for pro-Boers (there should have been no scarcity of them in Bedford Park). A more practical motive for his return to Ireland (which took place in the summer of 1901) was provided by Hugh Lane, the famous connoisseur, who,

[1] See Preface.   [2] See letters 36, 39, 44.
[3] See letter 208. Miss Yeats writes that on one of her visits she noticed a priest 'stalking' Chesterton.

brought into the Irish movement at this time by Lady Gregory, invited him to do a series of portraits of leading personages in Irish literary and political life. In the autumn of 1901 an exhibition of pictures by him and by Nathaniel Hone was organised, seventy-two works in all, in a Dublin studio. Yeats showed forty-three of these. The catalogue contained an introduction, signed by Sarah Purser, and critical notes on Yeats and Nathaniel Hone were contributed by Professor York Powell and by George Moore, respectively.

For a time Yeats moved from one Dublin lodging to another. Then his daughters came over and joined Miss Gleeson's Dun Emer Industries, where Lily conducted the embroidery department—she had learned the craft under May Morris—and Elizabeth the hand-press.[1] Dun Emer was established near the village of Dundrum, and they took a house at Dundrum for themselves and their father, to which they gave the Gaelic name of Gurteen Dhas. Dundrum is about five miles from Dublin, and J. B. Yeats went every week-day to his old studio at 7 Stephen's Green. He usually walked the whole way, as did his daughter Elizabeth whenever she had occasion to go into town. But they never walked together, for they could not agree as to which was the shorter road. The father always arrived first, but it was suspected that he ran for a part of the way.

Yeats's health stood him in good stead; he was as handsome an old man as could be found in Dublin; he worked as hard as ever, and talked more brilliantly. His most notable work of this period (1900–7) included portraits of Miss Horniman, the Englishwoman who presented Dublin with the Abbey Theatre, and of other Abbey Theatre personages, such as W. G. Fay, Padraic Colum, Lady Gregory, and of George Moore, Standish O'Grady, Horace Plunkett, Mrs. Burke, and Timothy Harrington, Lord Mayor of Dublin. The portrait of the Lord Mayor is in the Dublin Mansion House; of the others several are in the hall of the Abbey Theatre, or have been acquired by the Irish National Portrait Gallery or by the Dublin Municipal Gallery.

He regarded young William Orpen, who used to come to teach in Dublin, as his chief rival; Orpen also was commissioned by Lane to do portraits of Irish celebrities, and Henry Lamb, A.R.A., has contrasted those glittering canvases with the natural girth and gravity of Yeats's portraits in the same galleries, 'qualities for a parallel to which one has to think of Courbet and Titian.' 'I think', writes Henry Lamb, 'that he stands, rather

[1] Later the Misses Yeats removed the hand-press and embroidery class to Dublin, and carried the work on there under the name of Cuala Industries.

more evidently than most, for so much more than he delivered, and it is in this sense that I place him in the highest rank. He is at the very opposite pole of that aspect, of vulgarity which has been defined (by whom?) as the excess of the means of expression over the content.' 'It is hard to analyse the great power he possessed,' says Professor Thomas Bodkin, Director of the Barbour Institute in Birmingham. 'He was not strikingly accomplished in the mere technique of painting, and his bent was intellectual rather than sensuous; according to him, "desire and not emotion is the substance of art" . . . His portraits of women are always full of respect and understanding. Some of his great men portraits, those of John O'Leary, and of Standish O'Grady, and of George Russell . . . have an air of mingled intimacy and dignity that no other portrait painter of modern times surpasses, unless, indeed, I may cite Gustave Ricard himself!' [1]

Fortune never came to J. B. Yeats; one of the reasons why he could never be a popular portrait-painter was his belief that 'there is no beauty unless we can discover some flaw or weakness';[2] another was his comparative lack of interest in all but the face of his sitter; another, that the meaning in his portraits so outran the expression. It is doubtful whether he ever struggled for adequate recognition; certainly nothing made him so unhappy as a commission from someone he did not like. But there were really very few people who failed on meeting him to inspire him sympathetically, and his drawings—blocked in with a soft pencil—were scattered everywhere in Dublin, as they had been in Bedford Park, for he drew everyone who interested him. A family that he singled out for special attention was that of George Hart, barrister, geologist, and botanist, who lived at Howth. Everything that George Hart knew, he knew accurately; therefore he was a Tory, and Yeats confesses 'I never uncovered before that ironic smile'. It was Yeats's greatest pleasure to spend his Saturday afternoons at Howth, talking to and sketching one or other member of the Hart family and marvelling at the incredible industry which Mr. Hart showed among his flowers and plants. In painting Ethel Hart,[3] the eldest daughter, as a young woman, he had what he once called 'his most difficult subject'. 'She had a fascinating precipitation of thought and action that recalled her mother,' he wrote, 'together with the

---

[1] *Dublin Magazine*, January 1924.

[2] It is worth noting that he never appears to have wished to paint the reigning Irish beauty, Maud Gonne, to whom his son's early love poetry is addressed.

[3] Now Lady Babington, wife of the Attorney-General for Northern Ireland.

beauty derived from both her father and mother'. 'I lived in that home many days, perpetually failing and perpetually hopeful.' [1] The family did not much mind, and the portrait in question disappeared after an auction. Naturally, it was with the writers and talkers of Dublin and with those associated with his son's literary movement that Yeats associated most. He was an independent critic of the leading figures of the period, as will be seen from his letters, and he even found fault with his son on occasions, though he was always the first to dash to the defence whenever W. B. was attacked by strangers.[2]

Never in his life was Yeats known to make a plan, and wherever he went it was always his inclination to stay. His family and friends were, therefore, not greatly surprised, when, after a visit to America with his daughter Lily at the beginning of 1908, he failed to return at the appointed time. His daughter, who had been showing her embroidery in New York, returned, and he promised to be back by an early boat. He continued to make that promise, and the weeks lengthened into years. Sometimes he would even fix the date of his sailing.

John Quinn of New York was partly accountable for the 'flight to the West'. Quinn was a successful company lawyer of distinguished appearance, Tammany by politics, whose enthusiasm for all things Irish seemed inexhaustible. No one before had ever bought so many Irish books and pictures. On his first visit to Ireland in 1902, he had commissioned J. B Yeats to paint portraits of John O'Leary and of George Russell (AE) for his collection;[3] and when the painter and his daughter arrived in New York, he spared no pains to make their visit attractive, and gave Yeats introductions to many 'promising' people. Later nothing that was not French and 'modern' seemed good to Quinn; he was carried away by a strong feeling of sympathy for France during the Great War, suffered some disillusion about Ireland, and was involved in many quarrels. To the Yeats family he remained an attached and loyal friend, though he disapproved of J. B. Yeats's indefinite sojourn in New York.

It would be repetitive to speak of Yeats's American life in detail, as so much is told in his letters in this volume, and to them I have attached explanatory notes. He lived first in various hotels, and finally settled at 317 W. 29th Street, a boarding-house kept by three French sisters, named

[1] See letters 90, 109, 165.   [2] See letters 47, 58.
[3] Yeats painted several portraits of both these men, but his versions for Quinn's collection are his best.

Petitpas. The boarding-house had a restaurant, and the excellently cooked dinner was at six, to suit the convenience of the actors and actresses, who chiefly patronised it. Sometimes a few quiet English came, and, presently, a number of Yeats's own friends made it a practice to see him by dining there once a week. In John Sloan's picture 'Petitpas', he sits, sketch-book in hand and cheroot in mouth, at the head of his particular table, surrounded by a group of eight listeners, men and women. His fame as the 'best conversationalist in New York' spread from that table.[1]

His continued optimism about his work, so apparent in his letters, his conviction, even at eighty, that he was on the verge of new advances, are very touching. When his elder son, whose attitude to him was more like a father's than a son's, was able to promise him his financial support, his comment was: 'Now, I shall be able to give up money-making; and acquire skill.' On another occasion he observed that he was unwilling to go home, because he did not care to play the rôle of father to a famous son—that in New York he could still feel like the head of an illustrious dynasty. A wit called him: 'The old man who ran away from home and made good,' and, on the whole, his career of fourteen years in America warranted the description. But it was his fate in New York, as it had been in Dublin and in London, to receive greater consideration as a critic, philosopher, and conversationalist, than as a painter. He seldom charged more than 250 dollars for a portrait, and, as he said, this was fatal to his prospects of establishing rich and fashionable connections. 'An old artist seeking work', he wrote in a moment of despondency, 'is like a ticket-of-leave man seeking for a situation—either might run away with the spoons.' And again: 'If I could only find out that someone had made a mistake about my age, how my heart would swell!' In November, 1910, he was represented at an exhibition of 'Independents' in New York, when one of his portraits of John O'Leary was shown along with Augustus John's portrait of Quinn, and during the next year he started a portrait of himself, commissioned by Quinn. He worked at this portrait until the end, convinced that it must be his masterpiece.[2] It was Quinn's opinion that finally he lost the power to paint in oils, but that his pencil-sketches

---

[1] He was so described in obituary notices in the New York press, where almost nothing was said about his painting.

[2] See letters 209, 210, etc. The portrait was done from his reflection in the mirror, and he wrote under it, 'Myself seen through a glass darkly'. Quinn gave it to W. B. Yeats after the artist's death. Sloan's 'Petitpas' portrait is in the Washington Art Gallery.

got better and better. Some of his last drawings, especially of himself, were perfect.

While in Ireland he had occasionally contributed to newspapers, and after arriving in New York, he formed hopes of being able to gain a livelihood by writings and lectures. He soon made acquaintances among literary men, such as Fred King, the dramatic editor of the *Literary Digest*, Van Wyck Brooks and Alan Seeger. Some of his essays were printed and well paid for in *Harper's Weekly* and in representative magazines, and were later collected in a book called *Irish and America* (1918), which came out both in New York and in Dublin. Two small volumes of extracts from his letters to W. B. Yeats were published in 1917 and 1920 by his daughter's hand-press, the one edited by Ezra Pound and the other by Lennox Robinson. His lectures, not confined to New York, were, as a rule, on homely subjects, such as 'How to bring up a Family', and often met with great success, but his stories seldom found a publisher, and it appears that W. B. Yeats hardly glanced at them.[1] There was a play, too, on which he set great hopes, but which his son condemned.[2] Towards the close his son and Quinn urged him vigorously to give up writing articles about women's suffrage, prohibition and the like, and to concentrate upon his memoirs. As they walked together, and Yeats told stories of his life and friends, Quinn would say, 'Now, that should go into your book in just those words.' Yeats did not like to be pressed, and perhaps felt that he had years and years to live, but he wrote some passages, and these were published after his death under the title, *Early Memories*, *A Chapter of Autobiography*. There are delightful things in this little book, but it is repetitive and unconstructed. If he had embarked upon a big book, he would have needed someone at his side to jog his memory, plan and edit— Padraic Colum, say, or Ernest Boyd, both in New York at the time, who were familiar with the background of his life.

After leaving Ireland, the only one of his children whom he saw again was W. B. Yeats, who came fairly frequently to America on lecture tours or with the Abbey; in 1920 he had the excitement of meeting a young daughter-in-law. He was the indefatigable correspondent of all his four children; after them, he perhaps wrote most to Oliver Elton and to Susan Mitchell, the Irish poetess, AE's secretary, both of whom were associated in his memory with the days at Bedford Park. In old age his handwriting became so minute that W. B. Y. always sent the letters to his typist before attempting to read them. Many of his letters to W. B. Y. from New York

[1] See letter 63.   [2] See letters 193, 195.

were written, on the latter's suggestion, with a view to ultimate publication. They were intended to expose his philosophy, and are more elaborated as a rule than the letters to other correspondents. But even in them
he does not refrain from amusing gossip and description of people and
events, and in all his letters of any length, one finds the rich and large, if
unmasterly, touch of his portraits. In the letters he does not attempt to be
masterly; how engaging are some of his impromptus: 'The Greek Temple
carved out of blancmange' seems just right for a letter. Notice also a
passage about Dowden and the canary.[1] He shows very acute insight into
the poetical motives of his son, and an insight remarkable in a man of his
generation and W. B. Y.'s own father. W. B. Y. wrote (unlike 'literary
men') because he had 'convictions which were desires and could not be
imprisoned in opinions', and elsewhere, he warns him against 'aristocratic
illusions, sacerdotalism, and the ferocious absurdity of the Overman'.
Though he confesses to a weakness for superstition, he has not much
sympathy for excursions into mysticism, and thinking perhaps of the
beautiful accuracy of his son's observation of natural beings, birds and the
smaller beasts,[2] he urges him to keep imagination wedded to concrete
fact. A favourite theme, whomsoever he may be addressing, is psychological characterisations of peoples (English, American and Irish). 'Samuel
Butler was the politest, the most ceremonious of men, but the sneer (of the
English upper-middle class) was there, all the more palpable because so
carefully veiled.' 'Why is the Englishman happy?' 'Because he thoroughly
enjoys liberty and believes in it—for himself alone.' But these characterisations were made *pour parler au monde* not *pour le juger*, and in such
passages Yeats was not playing up to the Irish-Americans whom he
knew to be often foolish. He had the Protestant Irishman's facility for
uncovering both English and Irish weaknesses; the besetting sin (he
says) of the English is selfishness, that of the Irish is spite. He can find
no fault with the Americans, except that their philosophy of life is false,
or at least inimical to poetry.

'Emotion is a pleasure and is a spendthrift, living for the moment; desire
looks far ahead and sees all the trapdoors that lead to sorrow. Whoever
experienced the feeling of affection and did not instantly remember
death? Desire has the lean-drawn side of the famished wolf, desire has
infinite curiosity and will summon to its aid all the powers of intellect and

[1] See letter 105.
[2] W. B. Y. was an entomologist in his boyhood.

knowledge; hence the multiplicity and complexity in the contents of poetry and art.'

On the vexed (if one may nowadays call it so) question of democracy, he appears to contradict himself frequently. Perhaps he fails to distinguish between true human democracy (such as he finds in Ireland and the Latin countries) and political international democracy. Modern aristocratic theories—for which his son showed some predilection—he always denounces at sight, but he tells us that government by the people is necessarily corrupt, and that the state is not the people.[1] Yet, although aware that liberty abides only in a few spirits, he has never the heart to refute American social optimism. 'Happiness for oneself and others' is the American ideal, and in one letter he records his conviction that it will be achieved.[2]

As a rule his thought starts from a consideration of the place of the artist and poet in life. For him the poet and artist are at the same time 'world-makers' and 'world forsakers', as in Arthur O'Shaughnessy's poem. He did not read books of philosophy, properly so-called, or of science, nor does he show much acquaintance with the history of thought. Thus, unlike his son, he does not look towards a recovery of myth by philosophy; as for the scientist he is merely a man whose business it is to discover nature for the practical purpose of controlling it.[3] 'The men of science', he says, 'hate and revile us, being angry with impotent rage, because we seem to live in profitless idleness . . . They always work in groups, many minds engaged on one task, whereas we live and work singly.' Nor, when he describes art as 'dreamland' and rejects philosophical and ethical poetry as contradictions in terms is this exactly Croce's theory of art as the dream (in the sense of the primary form) of the life of knowledge. 'The world is not vanity', he writes in another letter. 'God made it, it is reality, and art and poetry are vanity.' [4] 'We live by the illusions that the artist and poet have created.' 'A man loves his wife—is it the real woman he loves? He has long ceased to see that woman.' [5]

He became during his last days a voracious reader of the latest literature; fiction, history, biography, but he kept Shakespeare and Montaigne always at his side. 'Montaigne says' or 'Shakespeare was a *kind* man', were the familiar openings of his discourse. Among his books he had all the plays of Shakespeare printed in vest-pocket size in the finest type and

[1] See letter 243. [2] See letter 179. [3] See letter 137. [4] See letter 170.
[5] Elsewhere, however, he gives this original reason against divorce that a long lifetime is not long enough for two people to know each other.

with flexible morocco covers. He would stick one of the little volumes in his pocket and read it on the trains or street-cars, like a priest with the Missal of his Office. When Quinn was defending James Joyce's *Ulysses*, he happened to be reading *Timon of Athens*, and he quoted sentence after sentence from that play where the language was as broad as possible. One day, when they were speaking of George Moore, he said that he had read in a recent book of Moore's, that the prettiest love scene in any book was that between the plump serving-maid, Fotis, and Apuleius in *The Golden Ass*, when Fotis stirs the pot and Apuleius watches her as she stirs. He said that while he remembered reading Lucian's *Timon* and *The Dream of the Cock*, he had never happened to read *The Golden Ass*. Quinn sent him the book, and the next time they met it was lying open on the small table beside Yeats's chair. 'So you've read Apuleius,' Quinn said. 'Yes,' he said. 'It's delicious. I wonder how I missed finding it before. I agree with George Moore—for once. How well Apuleius handled the scene. He set down the facts—just the facts. That is why it is so charming.'

During his first years in New York, next to Quinn, Yeats's most valued friends were John Sloan, a Socialist who 'painted the war of the poor against the rich', and Miss Sloan, Mr. and Mrs. Simeon Ford, Charles Johnston and his Russian wife,[1] and Eric Bell, nephew of the English publisher,[2] whose early death was a great blow to him. He was very fond of Van Wyck Brooks, whom he knew from the beginning, and the poet, Alan Seeger, an occasional visitor at Petitpas, aroused his admiration.[3] In the later years, as Patriarch of Petitpas, he was interested in Captain Freeman, an eighty-year-old romancer who charmed him with the fable of a noble Irish ancestry;[4] in Allen Benson, the Socialist; in E. A. Boyd; in Zelinski, an Ukrainian; in Zimmern, the writer on Greek thought; in artists like Robert Henri (who named him the greatest painter of the Victorian age) and George Bellows; above all in Padraic and Mrs. Colum. Quinn made him known to many Irish-Americans, and, though he was often appreciative, as in the case of Judge and Mrs. Keogh,[5] he never became intimate with that world of lawyers and politicians. His own power of calling forth warm affection never failed; there was a lodger at Petitpas —a strange lonely man—of whom it was said that his only attachment was for the old painter. He had many women friends, young and old, such as Miss Squire, Mrs. Egerton Winthrop, Mrs. Martha Fletcher Bellinger, Mrs. Jeanne Roberts Foster, and he greatly enjoyed their atten-

[1] See letters 68, 83. [2] See letter 94. [3] See letter 150. [4] See letters 130, 133.
[5] See letter 61.

tions. Sloan remarked to him one day that short skirts were a failure, since there were so many ugly ankles in New York. 'I am surprised to hear you say that, Sloan,' he said gravely. 'I think they're all beautiful, and I'm glad I've lived to see them.'

Yeats's health, if not exuberant, remained good until the autumn of 1918, when he was attacked by pneumonia. He was a difficult patient, and quarrelled with his North of Ireland nurse; and when he became convalescent, refused to listen to Quinn's proposal that he should recuperate at Yama farms and then go back to Ireland. It was not in his mind never to return, but he objected to being hustled.[1] He would wait to 'see the warm days in New York'. 'When we get to Dublin,' he said to Colum, 'we'll paint the town red.' When the warm days came, going about as before, he was knocked down by a motor-car. Quinn, sending the family an account of the accident, said: 'Your father was, as usual, strolling through the traffic of New York like an Emperor in his garden.' A pleasing incident of his convalescence was a meeting with G. K. Chesterton, in whose philosophy (religious dogma aside) he discovered much that he could approve,[2] and Chesterton in a letter to the New York *Sun* on an 'Irishman now living in America', was enthusiastic in praise of the intellectual detachment of 'perhaps the best talker I ever knew'. 'He is not what is called orthodox; he might well be called sceptical. He has cultivated rather continental aesthetics than Catholic apologetics. It is solely by a serene insight into what his French teachers would call the *vraie vérité* that he sees the way the world ought to go, and pauses upon the phrase, "the return to the home".'

In further correspondence with the family (May, 1920), Quinn recorded an evening in his apartment, when Yeats was his guest along with Massingham, the editor of the *Nation*, Clement Shorter, Lawrence Godkin, and C. C. Burlingham, the Admiralty and international lawyer. The lawyer was amusing when he made fun of Quinn's Matisses and Picassos: of 'The Sleeping Muse' by Brancusi, and Massingham and Shorter passed over some much prized pieces of African sculpture with less notice than they would have given to Dresden shepherdesses in a lady's boudoir. Massingham's smile, when he talked of English politics, was full of a radical's conceit and wickedness, like the smile of a religious mystic, but he said nice things about Yeats when he had gone. 'How pregnant his questions are! And how much to the point his statements are!' and then, 'What a good listener he is!' Like Carlyle's Marquis de Mirabeau, Yeats was 'raying

[1] See letter 228.   [2] See letter 208.

out curious observations to the last'. Sometimes, no doubt, he was lonely. He renounced the theatre owing to his growing deafness. 'Oh, Quinn,' he would say, 'I don't enjoy the theatre now, and I will be happier down at my place, or in my room.' But he never spoke of loneliness and he read and saw his friends, or they visited him, and he worked at his portrait and made drawings of himself. Quinn described him as a most unselfish and unseeking man, who shrank from giving others any trouble. If he was lonely, he did not inflict his loneliness on his friends.

On Christmas Day, 1921, there was a party in E. A. Boyd's apartment, and Colum brought in a young man, named Edward O'Brien, who had been seeing a good deal of W. B. Y. in Oxford. Yeats asked many questions about his son, Mrs. Yeats and their two children. He talked a great deal of his own early married life, and he recalled W. B. Y.'s birth and his jealousy of the monthly nurse because she had the baby so much with her. Similarly, his letters were now full of allusions to long-dead relations and friends. In the last letter that he wrote to his daughter Lily was a sketch of the figures at Stonehenge by moonlight, 'very grand', to represent the impression that W. B. Y. had given of the Pollexfens in his autobiography.

Up to the end, he went to Quinn's apartment every Sunday. They remained however in disagreement, not only because Quinn thought he should go home. Quinn often told him that he was a sentimentalist—the last of the eminent Victorians—especially when he spoke of marriage.[1] Yeats's disregard of all the latest rules of health and diet, and his lack of interest in the advance of science also disturbed his progressively minded friend.

Yeats's last article was published in the *Freeman*, an Irish-American journal, and it dealt with his old Dublin memories. He recalled John O'Leary, head of the uncompromising Fenians, most unpractical of men, who had always a good word to say for Orangemen and for feudal landlords, and who made many good English friends, and he contrasted O'Leary's generosity of outlook with the attitude towards Ireland of the 'shop-keeping gang', which latterly had given Unionism its tone.[2] Then, he spoke of his boyhood in Ulster. 'How well I know the Belfast man in his fierce conviction that he is always right. I also know Dublin city citizens and their unsureness—sometimes plaintive, sometimes tragic—that would question everything, and their cynicism; and also that idleness

[1] See letters 130, 179.
[2] O'Leary used to say that there was never a cause so bad but it was defended by good men and for what seemed to them sufficient motives.

which is so diligent. That the soil of Dublin should come to New York ought to be the desire of every American citizen.'

One of his last outings was at a Poets' Evening at the MacDowell Gallery, when he stood upon the stage to recite his lines called *Autumn*, the 'slender, tottering man', recalled by John Weaver in an 'obituary' poem that appeared in *The World* a fortnight later. On January 27th, 1922, Mrs. Foster took him to buy some things for himself down town, and afterwards drove him and Quinn to the American Art Gallery to see the Kelkiian pictures, where he admired the Cézannes and Courbets. He said of a portrait by Corot: 'That's a poor painting as a portrait, but it's interesting nevertheless, for it's a portrait by a landscape painter. I'm always interested in portraits by a landscape painter. I remember seeing once a very striking portrait by Turner, a very fine thing indeed.' A self-portrait by Toulouse-Lautrec, set down in the catalogue as a portrait of Apa Godeski, evoked the comment: 'It's the portrait of a man who ought to have been guillotined.'

Though he had now only one good lung, he did not take cold, and the end did not come from pneumonia. On a day of a heavy blizzard he went walking, and greatly overtaxed his strength, and his heart was tired. He was kept comfortable by injections of morphine, and his brain remained clear. His friend, Mrs. Foster,[1] and Madame Jais, who had taken over the little hotel from the Petitpas sisters, looked after him with the greatest tenderness. He told anecdotes of Samuel Butler and of the Dublin painter, Miss Purser, jested in his high-pitched voice and quoted Montaigne: 'If the disease does not kill you, the doctor will.' He died on the morning of February 2nd, 1922. He was buried in the cemetery of the village of Chestertown, on the lower Adirondacks, where Mrs. Foster owned a vacant plot. There is a stone over his grave with the inscription: 'In memory of John Butler Yeats of Dublin, Ireland. Painter and Writer.'

[1] A poem by her on Yeats, 'Alas, for the wonderful yew forest', appeared in the *New York Times* (Feb. 6, 1922).

TO EDWARD DOWDEN

I

This and the next letter appeared in Extracts from Letters of Edward Dowden and his Correspondents (*London, Dent, 1914, pp. 43–44 and 47–48*), *and are reprinted here with acknowledgments to J. M. Dent and to the Executrix of the late Edward Dowden.*

> 23 Fitzroy Road
> (*1869*) Regent's Park

. . . These little poems I send you are by Miss Ellis, with one exception, the poem by Edwin Ellis on the sea, which was suggested by a picture of the sea, by himself. He makes designs with incessant activity. That you should meet him and his sister, and Nettleship of course, who is growing greater every day, is, and has been for a long time, my supreme wish. Ellis and I have a studio in conjunction. On the opposite side of the street lives Nettleship. They are both perfectly lovable men, although so different. They and all four,[1] are looking forward to your article on Walt Whitman. Nettleship some months ago paid very nearly his last three guineas for a copy which had not been bereaved of its indecencies. 'The Brotherhood' love him, Swinburne and Shelley. Wordsworth they abhor.—Yours ever—J. B. YEATS

The Ellis's read your articles with delight and talk about them. Your sonnet on the Apollo is much comfort to all. Nettleship often murmurs over the last line.

I wish you could come over for a few weeks. Would it cost much for you to come over and take lodgings for a few weeks near the British Museum? It is near us.

2

Dowden defended Wordsworth in a letter which W. B. Yeats in Reveries over Childhood and Youth *characterises rather unfairly as 'pained and solemn'. J. B. Yeats retained his prejudice against Wordsworth; but he was not sure later on of his love for Whitman, Shelley and Swinburne, and soon accused*

[1] 'All four', Yeats, Nettleship, Ellis, and Wilson, group of friends jestingly named 'the Brotherhood'—artists all. See *Memoir*, p. 29.

Swinburne in particular of precisely the excitement that he alleges in his next letter to be the feature of an insufficiently emotional nature.

23 Fitzroy Road, Regent's Park
Decr. 31st, 1869

My Dear Dowden—It seems to me that the intellect of man *as man*, and therefore of an artist, the most human of all, should obey no voice except that of emotion, but I would have a man know all emotions. Shame, anger, love, pity, contempt, admiration, hatred, and whatever other feelings there be, to have all these roused to their utmost strength, and to have *all* of them roused, (two things you observe), is the aim, as I take it, of the only right education. A doctrine or idea with Catholicity in it is food to all the feelings, it has been the outcome of some strong and widely developed nature, and every other nature is quickened by it. Art has to do with the sustaining and invigorating of the Personality. To be strong is to be happy. Art by expressing our feelings makes us strong and therefore happy. When I spoke of emotions as the first thing and last in education, I did not mean excitement. In the completely emotional man the least awakening of feeling is a harmony, in which every chord of every feeling vibrates. Excitement is the feature of an insufficiently emotional nature, the harsh discourse of the vibrating of but one or two chords. This is what Ellis also meant by 'violent and untiring emotion'.

With you intellect is the first thing and last in education. With us, with me at any rate, and with everybody who understands the doctrine, emotion is the first thing and last. In haste, yours ever—J. B. Yeats

TO MRS. J. B. YEATS

3

In the winter of 1872–3 J. B. Yeats remained working in London, while his wife and children visited at Merville, the big house of the Pollexfen relatives-in-law outside Sligo. He kept house in his family's absence with his friend George Wilson, the water colourist.

The following fragment of a letter to his wife is certainly of this period, while he was still studying under Poynter. The Lathrop who is mentioned in it was an American artist. J. B. Yeats met him in New York in 1908, and was pleased by his saying 'How pretty all your children were'. Brown is Oliver Madox Brown, the pre-Raphaelite wonder boy who died young. He fell in love with Isabella Pollexfen, J. B. Yeats's artistic sister-in-law, and wanted to follow her to Sligo, but J. B. Y. dissuaded him, thinking that he and the Pollexfens would not understand each other. Brown was at an art school in London with George Moore, who has left a remarkable description of him as a young genius in Hail and Farewell.

Ellis (Edwin J.) collaborated many years later with W. B. Yeats in the edition of Blake.

Mrs. Giles, a maternity nurse, was the mother of the children's nurse, Janey.

23 Fitzroy Road
(1872)

I hope you continue reading to the children; working and caring for children makes one anxious and careful of them, but amusing them makes one fond of them. The first week I was here every perambulator passing along the pavement used to make me start fancying it was the children and several times in the night I woke up thinking I heard them crying.

The taxes have come in and there will be the rent at Xmas—I paid £10 to Poynters.

I have Annie on board wages but at what rate I don't yet know—Have you any hints?

Hughes and Lathrop and Brown called here. Yesterday Wilson and I went to Chelsea to see Hughes and Lathrop, but they were out. Brown says 'Lathrop is a very decent little fellow if he was not so lazy'.

Tell me constantly of the children.

The Dudley is open. I have not seen it. Ellis and Nettleship had their pictures rejected by the New British Ex. in Bond St. to which they sent them after they had been refused by the Dudley.

I hope you let Isabella know these little bits of artistic gossip and such-like. Ask her to write to me. Your affectionate husband—J. B. YEATS

P.S. I am glad you are doing nothing. If you could be got to do this oftener—particularly when you have a cold beginning you would now be a strong woman.

My model has just gone. He was tipsy but I managed very well...If you were strong and in good spirits there are many things to laugh over ...

Mrs. Giles has arrived. She says you won't be well unless she goes and takes care of you—that is what you want.

4

The 'Willie' of this letter is W. B. Y. at the age of 7.

> *23 Fitzroy Road, Regent's Park*
> *Nov. 1, 1872*

... I think Willie was greatly disimproved by Merville. He was coming on from being so much with his mother and away from his grandfather and dictatorial Aunts. From his resemblance to Elizabeth,[1] he derives his nervous sensitiveness. I wish he could be made more robust—by riding or by other means—*not by going to school*. I was very sorry he could not have the pony more, but perhaps he might ride that donkey about which he used to tell me....

Tell Willie not to forget me.

5

> *23 Fitzroy Road, Regent's Park*
> *Jan. 30th, 1873*

... You will be surprised to hear that one of the tenants came over from Kildare to ask me about consenting to his buying a farm. Annie told me when I came home that a big red man who said he was a tenant had been twice and would be here again before six. My dismay and Wilson's delight were equal—an Irish tenant is not to be seen every day. He was much impressed by his bigness and hulking solidity. . . . Poynter will do Wilson and me good over the painting. He bullies me not a little and I am afraid even to murmur....

6

To this letter Miss Lily Yeats has attached the following note:

'Bobby *our little brother who died suddenly almost a month after this letter was written.*

'Johnny, *Jack (the artist).*

'*I think Papa used to meet Swinburne at the Robertsons. Young Robertson*

---

[1] One of the Pollexfen aunts, afterwards Mrs. Orr. She was gentle, kind and a woolgatherer. W. B. Y. has told of his rides on the pony in *Reveries over Childhood and Youth.*

who recited must have been Forbes Robertson, son of the Robertson at whose house they all met.

'*Writing of Swinburne reminds me that on the day of his death I met Willy (W. B. Y.) in O'Connell Street and said to him "Swinburne is dead." "I know," he said, "and now I am king of the cats".*'

O'Shaughnessy, presumably the poet Arthur O'S.

23 *Fitzroy Road, Regent's Park*
Feb. 6th, 1873

My dear Susan—I was very glad to get your letter which was full of unforced good humour, and glad to get *so good an account of Bobby*—he has sensibility—will love ideas and have enthusiasms and will go through more emotional experiences in a month than another in ten years.

I am glad to hear about Lolly.[1]

Take care of Johnny; his turning cross may forerun some ailment. You remember that was the way with Lolly.

I hope when you write again you will have something better to tell of your father. All your family's ailments begin in the mind. A sort of nightmare takes possession of them and then they lose their appetite and get ill.

I have been very busy the last few days with my designs getting ready for to-morrow night when we all go to Robertsons and shew them.

Robertson holds a sort of open evening every Friday when any friends may go—Joachim Miller is expected to-morrow—he is marrying a friend of theirs.

Swinburne used to be there very often.

O'Shaughnessy is often there—Cave Thomas the artist [also], we all like him.

Last time young Robertson recited very successfully a long poem.

We have had not much frost but plenty of snow. . . .

I hope you don't tease the Middletons too much about their love making as you will make them hate you. I am very glad you are continuing to improve in looks—take care of yourself and all will be well.—Yours affectionately—J. B. YEATS

7

The 'Willie' of this letter is J. B. Y.'s brother, William Butler, who had emigrated to Brazil at the age of 18, where he married and had children. He

[1] J. B. Y.'s younger daughter, Elizabeth.

became a prosperous stockbroker and died in 1899 in Rio. He is said to have been 'the life and soul of the town'.

Feb. 17th, 1873

. . . Willie is much disgusted with my untrimmed beard and hair and my hat and the dust and untidiness of my studio; he is respectability itself and has mutton chop whiskers. . . . He is stopping at Langham Hotel.—I dare not ask him here. He is far too respectable for us. He has already hunted up and looked at all my drawings. I wonder with what conception or feeling about them.

8

23 Fitzroy Road, Regent's Park
(post mark Feb. 21st, 1873)

. . . Nettleship was here this morning. He told me he had seen Poynter yesterday at one of the Metropolitan stations and that he had asked him did he not think I was doing wrong to work on so long at the school and at study instead of painting pictures. Poynter said 'No' and that all he knew was that I worked like a nigger and that I was making great progress. These were Poynter's words, according to N. Tell your mother. She thinks I have no commonsense and it will please you.

TO EDWARD DOWDEN

9

Howth, Co. Dublin
7th Jany. 1884

Could you send me Willie's MS. His railway ticket is up so that he is a prisoner at Howth and cannot go for it. If you rolled it up and put a stamp on it would it not come safely. He wants it for a rehearsal which is to come off immediately.

Of course I never dreamed of publishing the effort of a youth of eighteen. The only passage in it which seems to me finally to decide the question as to his poetic faculty is the dialogue between Time and the Queen.[1] There was evidence in it of some power (however rudimentary) of thinking, as if some day he might have something to tell.

[1] W. B. Yeats wrote his first poems in 1882, just before he was seventeen. Masses of his early work, which included a number of plays, remained unpublished.

I tell him prose and verse are alike in one thing—the best is that to which went the hardest thoughts. This also is the secret of originality, also the secret of sincerity. So far I have his confidence. That he is a poet I have long believed, where he may reach is another matter.

. . . His bad metres arise very much from his composing in a loud voice manipulating of course the quantities to his taste.

TO W. B. YEATS

10

[*This letter was written on the occasion of the appearance of* The Countess Cathleen *and Various Legends and Lyrics,* W. B. Yeats's *second book of poems.*

John Davidson, author of the review in the Daily Chronicle, *was a member with W. B. Y. of the Rhymers' Club. Irishman and Scot, Yeats and Davidson were often at each other's throats, being more full of 'blood and guts' (Davidson's phrase) than the other members.*]

3 Blenheim Road, Bedford Park, W.
2nd Sept. 1892

My dear Willie—Last night I sent you the *D. Chronicle* and the *Star*, the poison and the antidote.

Who could have written the *D. Chronicle* criticism? Was it Davidson—as a *tit* for your *tat*? The tats were provoking and rather unnecessary and since probably totally unexpected therefore the more bewildering and enraging to the fiery Scot. I would like to write and ask him if he wrote it and also whether he *really* thought so badly of the poems. Apart that is from the tit for tat business, the criticism was a very effective piece of coarse journalism, but by its nature only appealed to the merest vulgar and [is] not likely to do you or anybody any harm. I send you to-day's *Chronicle* and have marked a passage which will show that the good *Daily Chronicle* has returned to its sober senses.

I laughed very much and without any bitterness over the offending criticism and assuming Davidson to be the author liked him all the better. It is a good sign when a man does not know how to wound.

I showed it to-day to York Powell who of course entirely disagreed with it. He said beauty of diction and lyrical quality are exactly what distinguish 'The Countess Cathleen'.

When I showed York Powell your book he said he hated plays and would not read it. But he was into it at once as silent and busy as a bee buried in a flower—merely calling out from time to time—'This is very good'—'this is a great improvement', and several times over—'There are some fine lines here'. He never stopped till he had finished the whole book. He said then by way of general conclusion that you had learned to *compress*—and again that the whole book was full of fine lines.

York Powell thought the criticism in the *Star* extremely good and quite concurred in it. York Powell does not like the latter part of Cuchulain. He knew of a different ending and takes it as a personal matter that you departed from the authority he was familiar with.

Rose [1] has been away the last fortnight but returns this evening and to-morrow Lily turns up. . . .

Your Mother is very well for her and to my great *relief* and content has taken up once more *a book*—a novel by Emerson, husband of the pretty and interesting Mrs. Emerson we used to meet at Mrs. Benson's. It is a novel, all about Norfolk and is almost entirely in Norfolk dialect—it seems very good. York Powell to-day when sitting to me read it through and pronounced it to be, 'By Gum a splendid book' and 'as good as Zola'. It is called 'A son of the Flesh'.[2]

Jack was here the other day. He left us in the middle of the night in the rain and *walked* all the way to St. Pancras terminus to get a five o'clock morning train for Manchester so as to be at his office in good time. It seemed to me madness.—Yours affectionately—J. B. YEATS

I I

3 Blenheim Road, Bedford Park, W.
3rd Sept. 1898

. . . It is always a question how far an artist *needs a reception*—must he have this actually or, as when he looks to *future* fame, ideally? I myself think yes and *no*. You as a boy would go about (for some weeks) saying over and over to yourself 'Magna est veritas et prevalabit'. (I had told you the meaning of the words. You were only about six or seven—and knew no latin or English either.) Herein you were an artist and sought manifestly no listeners. When an artist finds he can catch a sympathiser and obtain a reception it is an added pleasure to be sought unweariedly;

---

[1] An Irish servant, who was with the Yeats family for forty years.
[2] Mrs. J. B. Yeats had been an invalid for several years.

only if his sincerity moult a feather by so much is his pleasure—the keenest portion of it—diminished.

12

3 Blenheim Road, Bedford Park
Sept. 16th, 1898

. . . York Powell has seen some warm friend of Oscar's. Oscar [Wilde] is in Paris and cannot work—whether it is reaction or collapse and he is in debt and cannot live within bounds. His friends are devoted to him. They tried paying him an income in weekly amounts, but it galled him too much—poor wretch.—

I used to think Powell on the subject of Oscar too granitelike, but now he is all compassion. Only with Powell it is always sooner or later: 'Cherchez la femme.'

The poor wife is offered for sacrifice—exasperating, tiresome, silly, etc. —as I dare say she was—her purely feminine charm being to Oscar nothing—his terrible passions having gone away elsewhere.

However, I am glad Powell is sympathetic and more than sympathetic. He was in France lately and regretted that he could not get to Paris to call on Oscar.

I am keeping quite well—and very confident—but it is impossible to sell anything, being the dead season. I should feel more tranquil if I thought there was any chance of Horace Plunkett's portrait.[1] I wonder whether his people liked the reproduction. . . .

13

3 Blenheim Road, Bedford Park
23rd Decr. 1898

My dear Willie—We are all much disappointed at your not coming over for Xmas. Besides it is possible to stay too long away in the peace of the country. Importunate friends are often a blessing in disguise. In the country many a fruitful moment is lost which in London would have been captured for ever. . . .

[1] Yeats painted the portrait of Plunkett, who was coming into prominence as an Irish reformer at this time.

Tell George how glad we were to get *the cheque*, and how *astonished*. . . .[1]

Last Saturday I dined with [D. S.] MacColl. I met Rothenstein[2] whom I liked greatly. He is wonderfully clever and amiable and pleasing to look upon. I felt so sorry I did not like his portrait of you. I fancy he is like Ellis[3] much too clever to have any delusion about his own work. He has I fancy little of the student about him, not sufficiently *sensitive*, and herein so different from MacColl—and will never be any *one thing* in particular, either artist or litterateur. Rather he will play many parts—gay and attractive; in light marching order; quickly concentrating his forces and quickly dispersing them. In fact I should think very like Ellis—tho' not without the *sensuous*—Ellis's great want as you pointed out.

We are having an exceedingly fine and mild Xmas.

We constantly hear from Jack who is building an addition to his house and working hard at his pictures for his February Exhibition.

There are no changes here. Mrs. Emery (whom I met last night at Pagets)[4] some weeks hence is going away to Switzerland. She sometimes turns up here. Susan Mitchell[5] has an amusing antipathy to her as I think you predicted. Susan like Chas. James Fox and many others among the great—lives on applause on affection on sympathy. Were she a Prima Donna popularity would be her darling—and Mrs. Emery will not be cajoled into the most momentary affection—'Of the millions I rule more or less &c.' . . .

Lolly working fewer hours has made £75 since last Sept. Yesterday she and Lily were sitting gloomily in front of the parlour fire when I brought them the cheque. *They opened their eyes.* Yours affectionately—J. B. YEATS

14

My dear Willie—I am very glad to hear of the contemplated debate at Historical Society. I never joined that Society though I often thought

[1] W. B. Y. was with his uncle George Pollexfen, the astrologer, in Sligo.
[2] Now Sir William Rothenstein.   [3] Edwin J. Ellis.
[4] Florence Farr, the actress, see p.7.
[5] A Sligo girl, noted afterwards in Dublin for her witty verses. She was a great favourite with Yeats and often stayed at Bedford Park.

about it, and I remember perfectly how now and again its debates used to have a real importance in College. Lecky of course was a constant speaker there. I kept to the undergraduate Philosophical from some impression that the hard-headed Philistine abounded too much in the historical. . . .

I saw Todhunter. He was evidently surprised to find how well your play went on the Stage. He said your speech immensely impressed Tyrrell.[1]

I hope at the historical that the Philistines may muster well and develop a strong attack as it will give you a better opportunity.

I saw Mrs. Emery.[2] She has the temerity to say that there are none or very few pretty girls in Dublin compared with London. She has no arithmetic. In London you see more pretty girls, because you see more people. For the same reason, if in a cantankerous mood you can see more ugly girls. The comparison should be made between at homes and social gatherings in London and at homes in Dublin—where the numbers are about the same, and drawn from the same class.

Mind you let me know how the Historical Society goes off.

Martyn [3] when he was here spoke about my doing his portrait over in Galway. If you see a chance I wish this could be brought off.

Believing my salvation to lie that way I have devoted the whole year and last year also to portrait painting.—(Remember that from 1890 to 1897 I never touched a paint brush, and altogether, unlike Miss Purser and others, I have never had full chances as regards painting.)

My portrait of Ashe King done and finished in *two mornings* is a vivid success, also of Susan Mitchell and Mrs. King. The Ashe Kings are trying to get me their brother and his wife—and I have begged them to try and get me even a photo to copy. I have in the past often copied Photographs both in colour and black and white. . . .

I am quite certain I would do a good thing of Martyn and not keep *him any time* . . . and now his name is floated on every wind. . . .

Photography is superseding black and white drawings being so much cheaper and better liked by the stupid people. . . . Wollen tells me

[1] R. Y. Tyrrell, the famous Greek scholar. The play was *The Countess Cathleen*; its performance in Dublin early in May inaugurated the Irish Literary Theatre. W. B. Y.'s speech at the banquet is immortalised on a page of George Moore's *Hail and Farewell*. In W. B. Y.'s account of the occasion (*Dramatis Personae*) Tyrrell is described as a 'Unionist though drunk'.

[2] Florence Farr, who had played in *The Countess Cathleen*.

[3] Edward Martyn, the Irish dramatist, who was in alliance with W. B. Y. and George Moore at this time.

everyone is complaining of want of work, and he curses Clement Shorter for it. . . .

I hope you had some luck in your fishing—Yours affectly—J. B. YEATS

15

3 Blenheim Road, Bedford Park
(1899) undated

My dear Willie—Some time ago York Powell asked me to get you to write to the poet Bridges explaining that you were too busy etc. to go down to see him. It seems that he was rather hurt that you never accepted his invitations to come and see him. He admires your work very much, and he is of course a good poet himself. *The tender-hearted Powell is concerned about it.*[1]

I hope your knee and heel are all right again. But indeed you ought to be careful as regards all rheumatic symptoms. You yourself as a boy had an attack of rheumatic fever. . . .

To-morrow I am to have a long sitting from Mrs. Clement Shorter,[2] and feel not a little anxious, as it draws towards the close the difficulties increase. In Shorter I have excited an expectancy and in Mrs. Shorter a possible impatience—in myself much confidence with fits sometimes of deadly sickening fear, the more so as I know how much depends on this particular effort. The situation is hemmed round with dangers. A few days ago Shorter happened to say his wife would not sit again for a week. I did not sleep that night till four in the morning. I was perfectly calm, perfectly cheerful but wide awake. One cannot take things at sixty as we do at thirty. . . .

My best hopes are all *clustered* around Mrs. Shorter's portrait. Shorter seems to me a very good fellow, and I fancy he is popular. His wife thoroughly believes in him . . . I am doing life size—a half length and she has your 'Wind in the Reeds' in her hand. Her dress is black with white lace, but low in front and with bare arms. The background is a deep blue which looks almost black. I am made most welcome and she professes to enjoy the sittings which probably she does, since she has a real pleasure in conversation.

[1] W. B. Y.'s acquaintance with Robert Bridges dated from 1897, when he stayed with him in Oxfordshire.

[2] Dora Sigerson, the Irish wife of Clement Shorter, bookman and editor of *Sphere*.

Shorter speaks of getting it into the New Galleries which I have no doubt he can accomplish with his far-extending business reach, even if its merits were nil—however I said I prefer the R.A. ...

I have almost ceased even to think about black and white work.

I never saw your address as published in O'Grady's paper. I had hoped you would send it to me. Remembering student life in T.C.D. I should have some enlightenment as to how it would take it.—Yours very truly—J. B. YEATS

16

3 Blenheim Rd., Bedford Park, W.
(*1899*)

My dear Willie—I send you a Chronicle. It is an interesting number because of Goethe and because of 'Modern Russian Realists'. I don't know what papers you see, or whether you see the Chronicle regularly.

I hope you are quite well and that you have no return of the rheumatic symptoms. If I were you I should be careful about them. They are always most serious things.

I am doing a portrait of Nannie Smith—and it is very good I think.[1] They are delighted with it. I find it impossible to sell any black and white drawings. I fancy my style is too heavy too laboured too oldfashioned. This being so I have been putting all my hopes on portrait painting and therefore have been glad to get Nannie Farrar to sit. She sits with the most cheerful alacrity and patience and is of course very pretty and dainty. Moreover she has lots of friends, well-to-do friends—so that a portrait of her is a portrait well placed. They are of course themselves not at all well off, but in their kindness have insisted on giving me a bicycle, which turns out to be a great success. The other one was so heavy, it was such labour to drive it along.

. . . This portrait of Nannie fills me with hope. That is the joy and temptation of the artist's life. We always know that one good portrait, one good picture will retrieve everything. Moreover, a good portrait is, everyone knows, not an accident—done once it can be done again and again.

Nannie's cousin, a millionaire young lady, returns from Paris on Tuesday on her way to America and the kind and ingenious Nannie is to make her see my portrait of her—out of which may arise *Events*.

---

[1] Mrs. Melville Smith (Nannie Farrar). See *Memoir*, p. 34.

To-morrow Jack returns to London from the Broads where he and wife have had a week's yachting at the expense of some friends. Jack will return at once to his Castle where Isaac intends to come and stay awhile.

There is no news except that this house has a new inmate, a grey cat, so playful and tender, such big eyes, such soft paws, and such claws, that only it *is a boy* I would have it christened Susan—after Susan Mitchell.—Yours affectionately—J. B. YEATS

Elton [1] has just been here. He is the most loyal and ardent friend of your work I know.

TO LILY YEATS

17

3 Blenheim Road, Bedford Park
(Summer) 1899

... There is no news and no luck to record. O. Elton insisted on paying me £4. 4. for the sketch. He is greatly pleased and so is old Mrs. Elton. I took special pains in getting the oldest boy's likeness, because I knew his grandmother's partiality for him. Herbert Smith (I think a most engaging lovable sort of being) has given me for Nannie's portrait what used to be Jack Stewart's bicycle. It is too small for me but I am trying to exchange it and my own for another one which Owers is offering me (Owers is the cycle man on the high road). I am absorbed in Nannie's portrait, and hope it will be an exhibition portrait—she and Smith are greatly pleased with it. ...

The heat here is still terrible, but your mother seems particularly well. Maria has the little grey cat in the room with her every night. She says it's company. ...

TO W. B. YEATS

18

3 Blenheim Road, Bedford Park
Monday (1899)

My dear Willie—I am most awfully grateful to you for the £5—and if you only knew how opportune its arrival is. We are now poorer by £50

[1] Oliver Elton.

Pamela Colman Smith

a year than we were, as last Xmas the firm gave us the last of the £500 bequeathed by your grandfather.[1]

I am however *extremely* hopeful. The practice I have had in portraits has not been without good results. I am perfectly convinced that a portrait *well placed* would go near curing all my maladies.

I hear from Ashe King [2] that Dr. Nicholl [3] is going to have his portrait done. I am now doing a portrait of that very pretty girl, Nannie Farrar (now Mrs. Smith) partly for practice, partly for renown—Nannie of course can't pay.

I have finished two black and whites which you would like—the titles are suggestive 'Love's Farewell' and 'A Haunted Chamber'. I have even thought of sending over to you 'Love's Farewell', as if you liked it you might be able to '*push it*' some where or other.

Pamela Smith and father are the funniest-looking people, the most primitive Americans possible, but I like them much. Pamela (Miss Smith her father always said even when addressing her) is bringing out a book of Jamaica folklore. Her work whether a drawing or telling of a piece of folk-lore is very direct and sincere and therefore original—its originality being its naïveté. I should feel safe in getting her to illustrate anything. She does not draw well, but has the right feeling for line and expression and colour. [Drawing.] Her dressing is not a decorative success. The bluest of blue dresses, you feel disposed to call it scarlet, blue seems in this connection such a mild word. She sits as above—the hat is straw, with great black cork feathers sticking up out of it. She looks exactly like a Japanese. Nannie says this Japanese appearance comes from constantly drinking iced water. You at first think her rather elderly, you are surprised to find out that she is very young, quite a girl. I would say of her as was said of Robespierre—she will go far because she believes in all her ideas, this time artistic ideas. I don't think there is anything great or profound in her, or very emotional or practical. She has the simplicity and naïveté of an old dry as dust savant—a savant with a *child's heart*.[4]

I tried to get them to stay for supper but they would only pay their visits and be gone. . . .

---

[1] William Pollexfen.   [2] Novelist and Irish correspondent of *Truth*.
[3] Editor of *British Weekly*.
[4] Pamela Colman Smith lived in London for many years and was associated with Gilbert Murray, Arthur Symons, W. B. Yeats and others in an endeavour to found a Theatre of Beauty. She was a delightful person full of talent, and on her mother's side was related to the author of the Brer Rabbit stories.

A Dream

Solitude reigns in Bedford Park. All are at the seaside—all that is of any account, like a North-American wigwam when the braves are out on the warpath.

Jack and wife are to be here next Thursday on their way to spend some time on the Broads, where Jack no doubt will find many subjects.—Yours affectionately—J. B. YEATS

19

Blenheim Park
undated (1899)

. . . I have no place to which I can invite a possible patron to come—besides which I *work* under the greatest difficulties. It was a fatal indecision which prevented my taking Oliver Elton's house—although I comfort myself by thinking that a Studio further into town is the real solution. Last year I paid off over £400 of old debts—if only I could have kept that £400.

Last night I had an amazing dream—I thought I was listening to a wonderful sermon by my father—he and I afterwards walked up and down an old garden and to all my delighted compliments he only answered 'it was very loosely constructed'. I remember constantly trying to get hold of the MS. that I might see his handwriting, which I have not seen for many years and which I have always wanted to see—my father was a man who excited strong affection. Afterwards came a lot of events causing to me great pleasure. A sort of dissolving view in which joy succeeded joy. At the end when all the rest had dispersed I found written on an unnoticed piece of paper the words, 'The apple tree has been made free'—and all seemed to be a consequence of my father's sermon—the text was a passage from some modern book or the Times newspaper. A dream like that is a good omen.

I am thinking of painting a picture, the subject The banquet of life—I will make a black and white drawing of it and perhaps some one would commission me to paint it. I would ask £50.

Lolly is in good health and has been doing well. She goes to France near Dieppe with Mrs. McMahon—her object to paint landscapes and acquire the French language.

I am sure this is the longest letter I ever wrote you.—Yours affectionately—J. B. YEATS

P.S. After the dream had departed I mused long on the words 'the apple tree has been made free' being still in that state of semi-consciousness which treats a dream as a series of realities and came to the conclusion that it meant the apple tree that was in Eden; which seemed to me a very tremendous and beautiful revelation.

Mrs. Hinkson [1] had already sent me the little paper with news of your play's success.

20

Monday (1900)
Care of Mr. Foale
Fugue, Strete, Dartmouth

My dear Willie—I am sorry to hear from Jack that you have been so very unwell. When I saw you at the Thompsons I thought that you looked very badly but had no idea that you had been undergoing so very unpleasant an experience as Jack describes.

It is beautiful here. I wish it were possible for you to come and occupy Jack's spare room. He was speaking about it yesterday. His house is extraordinarily nice and comfortable—Chippendale furniture etc. with pictures and art in a small thatched house among thick woods seems as if it were something quite new. I think you would like the place greatly. Cottie is as hospitable as possible and both have the gift of making life peaceable—A ticket (return) costs only 30/-.

We are stopping in an old farmer's. I find that he regards this war with growing disfavour—farmers like *slow methods*—this rushing into war to subdue 30,000 Boers, when by going to work more slowly etc. . . . not of course that he minds about the Boers—but there is the expense.

He tells me he is neither a liberal nor a tory—but that his mind had been much influenced some years ago by a retired Irish policeman Mr. 'Ogan—who told him all about the Landleague, etc.

When in London I met Mr. Martin and Miss Purser. We went together to see the Romneys which I learned to admire for the first time.

Lolly has got a grand cycle. She is at home with a girl friend to stay with her.

I suppose it would be quite impossible for you to come here now but if you could it would be pleasant *when we are all here*. I know of course your

---

[1] The poetess, Katharine Tynan.

intentions as regards going to Galway.—Yours affectionately—J. B.
YEATS

21

3 Blenheim Road
July 28, 1900

... My portrait of A. Symons was given by me to the Editor of Dome
last Wednesday, and he promised to let me know what the Editor thought
of its chances of good reproduction. The drawing itself is I think *much the
best I have ever done*. Symons was a most sympathetic sitter, these men who
do their work without friction have a sort of *calm resolve* about them
which acts pleasantly on one's nerves, whether you are their companion or
their painter. ... We had a Calumet on Sunday. Wollen just returned from
the war was here (it was at this house) but added nothing to our knowledge.
He asserts that Roberts and Kitchener are not on speaking terms. ... He
also said the war would go on to Xmas. However, he knows as little as any
of us. Probably he does know something of the seamy side of things.

22

3 Blenheim Road, Bedford Park, W.
Dec. 20th, 1900

My dear Willie—I was awfully sorry to waste your time so much—but
I never calculated on getting beyond an hour's sitting from B. O'Brien[1]—
and when I saw him willing to give me so much more time I had not
enough *unselfishness* (if you would call it so) to refuse the chance of making
a masterpiece. (For practical purposes it was quite good enough quite
early in the sitting) and I did not accept his suggestion of another day,
because I know from experience these sketches have to be done at one
heat—another day would have meant a fresh sketch.

... As regards *Herod* [Stephen Phillips's popular poetic play], I think
very much as you do as regards the poet's part, the words, etc., but I do
think that the staging of the play, which you tell me is on this occasion the
merest commonplace, gave *opportunities*, which tho' all missed, *are still
opportunities*.

I think Leader the great champion Philistine who vulgarises everything
he touches yet nevertheless *he can give space and height*—(his work even in

[1] Secretary of the London Irish Literary Society and biographer of Parnell.

this is all glittering commonplace)—so that from his studio a pupil might come who would be the greatest of all landscape painters.

The other evening watching that play untouched by all its gaudy rhetoric, the mere grouping of the figures was to me so effective that I wondered the players themselves did not invent a dialogue that would have set themselves and everybody else on fire.

All this means that in my humble opinion the stage and its traditions are still of value.

I am just reading 'The Shadowy Waters' with great enthusiasm. Don't forget to send a copy to

W. Stevens,[1]

Norfolk Villas,

Woodford, Essex

and put your inscription in it. He is really so broadminded and loves ideas more than anybody I ever met. There is also plenty of strength and concentration in the old fellow and he is as receptive as York Powell.—Yours affectionately—J. B. YEATS

Long ago I called Leader the *artist* of *the expected*.

23

The Calumets were the Club in Bedford Park, of which Oliver Elton and York Powell were members. (See Preface.) John O'Leary, the old Fenian, had paid one of his rare visits to London.

3 Blenheim Road, Bedford Park
London (1901)

. . . O'Leary was here on Sunday and was in great form. The Calumets were delighted—he discoursed the whole time with great astuteness, avoiding dangerous subjects. He is not without the wisdom of the serpent. I tried several times to roll in the apple of discord, but they all looked as if they did not see it. O'Leary told me that not for twenty years has he been so happy as this war has made him. He looks much better than when he arrived. I think, poor old fellow, he has been moderating his whiskey consumption. It is the awful dreariness of his life that makes the poor old fellow take to evil courses!

[1] Editor of *The Leisure Hour*, the first English paper to publish W. B. Yeats's lyrics.

Next Sunday we dine at the Blogues and no doubt we shall meet Chesterton who is to marry one of the Blogues on June 24th to which wedding I think we are invited. . . .[1]

Todhunter told me he had spent an evening with you at George Moore's. I tried to get some details from him—but he answered me in a very surly manner, significant of God knows what. . . .

I wish I knew a Pro-Boer somewhere. Here they are all against me. . . .

24

W. B. Yeats and George Moore were collaborating in a play called Where There is Nothing. *Their disputes are recorded in W. B. Y.'s* Dramatis Personae.

43 Harrington Street, Dublin
Sunday (1901)

My dear Willie—I was at Moore's last night. Almost at once with great animation he told me Russell[2] had found a via media, or at any rate some solution of the difficulty between you and him. I hope this is so. It would really be a calamity to quarrel with Moore. He may be a mustard plaster—but no matter. I used to call certain friends of mine Hair Shirt friends.

Douglas Hyde[3] came in late and threw Moore into ecstasies with his account of his play about the T.C.D. Council and the Irish language. Moore protested strongly against it finishing with the words implying that it was a dream—and I supported him in this protest. D. Hyde gave Lady Gregory the credit of having planned the story. He also stuck up for Lady Gregory's book.

How volcanic the ground always is at Moore's. What a pity if the sullen peace of a mutual distrust should settle over the scene.

I told Moore that I thought it a mistake for you ever to collaborate with any one—because of a sympathetic fibre in your mingled personality. . . .
—Yours affectionately—J. B. YEATS

[1] See letter 208, in which Yeats recalls the wedding.
[2] AE.
[3] Dr. Douglas Hyde, leader of the Irish Language Movement.

25

3 Blenheim Road, Bedford Park, W.
Oct. 27, 1901

... I am so long in answering your letter that you must think I have not fully realised the *significance* of such an event as the success of your play in America.[1] However I do fully realise it and have thought a great deal about it. I wish your play had been separately done from a play by Browning—a success with which Browning has anything to do will always very rightly be suspected of being a *succès d'estime*, since Browning occupies that kind of position in public favour. As regards your plays I have never had the slightest doubt. They are eminently *acting* plays, and will take their place among the classics as acting plays. It is natural to an Irishman to write plays, he has an inborn love of dialogue and round him is a dialogue as lively, gallant and passionate as in the times of great Eliza....

26

86 Lower Leeson St., Dublin
Xmas Eve (1901)

O'Leary has been very seriously ill, as no doubt you know, but he seems to me to be in mind and body as well as ever he has been lately. I have seen him several times. This news from S. Africa will cheer him up, though it will make the jingoes madder than ever. I am often quite glad to be over here to escape from the gloomy jingoes—they are no longer merry.

I have had a splendid letter from Powell describing Henley and accounting from his peculiarities for that extraordinary article on L. Stevenson. I have promised to show it to Dowden.

Powell said he met you lately at lunch. What a terrible pity it is that Powell and other good men should have gone so vilely wrong over this war.

27

43 Harrington Street
March 21st, 1902

... A few days ago reading Sir Walter Scott's Journal I came on a thing that I think might interest you. Speaking of Campbell—he writes he is a

[1] *The Land of Heart's Desire.*

man of genius who yet somehow has not done what one expected of him—and he goes on to say that he is wanting in audacity, is afraid of his own reputation and above all is *a great corrector* adding that many a school-boy has been whipped into a dunce. It seems that these three defects arise from *one cause*—that which in an amicable unphilosophical frame of mind I would call oversensitiveness, too high an ideal of execution etc., in a judicial temper of mind, I would call mere indolence. It is much easier to polish and perfect work which one has already done *and in which one is already fully interested* than to go on to fresh enterprises—and speaking generally much easier to exercise the critical faculties on one's own or other people's work than to exercise the imagination. Thus the people of Dublin have found Art. They are very much occupied with imagination *but as critics*—and they would paralyse everyone else as they are paralysed themselves.

I think Magee with all his abilities is a prominent member of the farm yard—since to this trick of criticism he adds an admiration for the fait accompli which makes him turn eyes of admiration so constantly on things English.[1]

I have great hopes of Jack. He seems to have audacity and to be perfectly careless as to his reputation. His imagination is highly active—his faculties of judgment wholesomely quiescent—moreover he is in constant touch with life—inanition which might so easily overtake the poet who is a great corrector will never touch him—*Nature I loved and next to Nature Art* applies to Jack. In my mind he will some day surprise this world with serious plays; working with these puppets and his mimic theatre he is forced to study the *broad* effects. In time he will master details, and with fine sustained dialogue, etc., he is beginning the right way studying the broad effects. It is so easy to lose oneself in details. If you catch the dog you catch the fleas.

Excuse this long discourse. My mind for some time for weeks back has been full of it.

I would like to say a little now of Jack's play. I think its construction perfect or nearly so. The way in which Flaunty is the hero up till the last scene when by the most exquisite surprise ever written in a play Pine takes his place is marvellous—A piece of true poetic drama—I can never read it without a break in my voice. Flaunty to his Nancy—how *tenderly*

[1] W. K. Magee, 'John Eglinton', critic and author of *Essays on the Remnant*. He frequented George Moore's house with AE; W. B. Y. used to describe the young poets gathered round AE as 'AE's farmyard'.

they are put before us. They come out of the very heart of pity—and yet to the unreflecting it is all fun and good jolly fun. I said the play was *almost* perfect. There is a flaw—In the first scene where Flaunty rescues Pine the rescue should be done with some risk and effort on Flaunty's part. Flaunty should have appeared here as a man of mettle—a valiant hero and without any makebelieve—*and possibly Jack meant this*. In fine I would say to the young aspirants for play writing honours study the works of J. B. Yeats junior. All this might interest Jack so perhaps you will send it to him.[1]

If I get my story finished I think you will be pleased. I read the first part to Moore and Magee and their commendations have induced me to go on with it.

My portraits at the R.H.A. are a success. I have received many compliments but I have no sitters. We Yeats have such bad characters the people who live in good society and have their feet on the rock of ages and order their portraits disapprove of us—so that I am likely to starve for my sins.

28

43 Harrington St., Dublin
March 22nd, 1902

My dear Willie—You will be surprised at getting such a lot of letters from me, only I don't want you to think that I accuse you of being the least afraid about your reputation, *that is the last thing I would impute to you.* I only accuse you of being too critical. You were brought up in a critical atmosphere. Jack escaped this by being brought up in Sligo among people who never uttered an opinion about anything and thought intellect a poor sort of thing. Latin and Greek and learning never affected Jack since by the mercy of God he never paid any attention to them.

I dined last night at Rollestons. Why is T. W. R. so disappointing? He is artistic, intellectual, a born litterateur—but he has no *desires*, that is to say no imagination. When you express to him some joyous, swelling idea —he does not meet you joyfully in an attitude of hope and belief—but produces some foot rule made by the University or the Department and *made on wrong principles*. In fact he has a dourish and bureaucratic mind. In a country like Ireland when all the popular forces are in full play what he can find is only *disorder*.

---

[1] Jack B. Yeats had a puppet theatre of his own.

Walker is so pleased with my designs for the panels that he offers to buy them as well as the panels. I am not sending anything to the R.A. after all.

To-night I am going again to the Rollestons. Some lady is to be there to discourse on Archaeological Matters. This is what Rolleston likes. He and York Powell and such like would have us gather tithe of mint and anise neglecting the weightier matters of the law. The latter awake desires. Gathering tythe of mint and anise leaves the desires unawakened. Rolleston is an enemy to the poets, the more so as he comes in the guise of a friend. You cannot touch Jack at any point without awakening desires. That is why he often says such *luminous* things.[1]

Another reason why T. W. R. is so disappointing—he looks a first rate man. He is so handsome and has such a regal air and he is only a good secondrate. I like his wife. She is our relation.—Yours affectionately—J. B. YEATS

29

Harrington St.
Sunday (1902)

My dear Willie—Just a line to say I yesterday met Miss Gonne,[2] who was very urgent for you to come over and look after the rehearsals.

—These practical people are often right.

I don't think Scott meant that Campbell spoilt his verses, but that the poet himself was spoiled. Altho' I myself have known a poet to spoil his verses, and publish them spoiled.[3]

The best work is got out of oneself sometimes by resisting and sometimes by yielding to one's tendencies—as a ship beats to windward.

I have finished my story and am looking to read it to you. I shall be disappointed if you do not like it—so far no one except Susan Mitchell and Norman have heard it—and they are very enthusiastic.

George Moore heard the first part some time ago and commended it much—altho' it is not the sort of story he would naturally like.—Yrs. affectly—J. B. YEATS

[1] T. W. Rolleston, author of the anthology piece, *The Dead at Clonmacnois*, scholar, worker in Ireland, afterwards a *Times* reviewer.

[2] Maud Gonne, now Madame Gonne MacBride, the Irish nationalist heroine. She acted the title part in the first production of W. B.'s patriotic play, *Kathleen-ni-Hoolihan*.

[3] An allusion, no doubt, to W. B. Y.'s revisions.

An Irish play in George Moore's Garden

TO LILY YEATS

30

George Moore gave a Gaelic party in his garden at Ely Place, where a play in Irish was performed. The author, who acted the part of the Tinker, was Douglas Hyde, now President of Ireland, and the part of the Fairy was played by Miss Flanagan, now Mrs. de Valera.

Dublin
(*Summer*) *1902*

My dear Lily—. . . Yesterday was G. Moore's great day. *The Tinker and the Fairy*, written in Irish by Douglas Hyde was acted in his garden. There was a great crowd there. Tyrrell, F.T.C.D. was the only F.T.C.D. there. I suppose Moore's attack on Mahaffy did not hurt *his* feelings.[1] Miss . . . . was there and looked gorgeous. She was very busy talking to everyone. Rolleston came up yesterday with myself and Susan Mitchell. He liked the work I showed him, I think very much. He objects to the Summer being in a ball dress (Mrs. Pilcher's dress). He is delighted with Spring and Winter.[2]

The weather held up allright at the play. There had been a bitter, black storm of rain in the morning, but it cleared up.

The play ought to have started at 3 o'clock when the sun was shining and it was quite warm, and that was the time appointed. But the delegates (I don't know what delegates) did not arrive. Meanwhile, the sky began to blacken and we all felt anxious while Moore, in his peculiar manner, kept softly gesticulating his despair. At last, the wretches arrived and the play began, and though expecting every moment to be drenched through, we got safely to the end; though for a time all umbrellas were up, which might have been pleasant for the people trying to see. Fortunately, this happened towards the end, when the musicians and singers (out of sight behind a screen of leaves) had the performance to themselves. Douglas Hyde was tinker, the Fairy was a pretty young girl—Miss Flanagan.

[1] Moore had written an outrageous article on Dr. Mahaffy, who was hostile to the Irish language revival.

[2] These were panels, done for a restaurant which was subsequently destroyed by fire. Mrs. Pilcher was a sister of Madame Maud Gonne MacBride.

'The Celtic Twilight' and other matters

TO W. B. YEATS

31

43 Harrington St., Dublin
July 11th, 1902

My dear Willie—Yr book is an immortal book, a convincing book. Years ago L. C. Purser called it to me a wonderful book—but then on the other hand I fear Judge Madden thinks it rank nonsense.[1]

It is a book you begin anywhere and leave off when the dinner or a visitor arrives. This is well called 'Celtic Twilight' and is only intended for people who live in the twilight—

I should like to make a distinction between longing and desire—desire is the imagination of the grown man and the matured artist—longing is for little children and peasants and simple silly folk such as mothers when they think about the mighty things their children will do when they grow up, how they will have ships on the Liffey or be judges, etc.

I wish you saw my panels now—you would not recognise them. I am gradually getting them to be *more effective* so that they may catch the eye like a bill poster—tho' I fear they will never do this sufficiently—

I enclose an interesting letter of Lolly's describing two visits she paid to two well contrasted houses—The Mrs. Russell she is staying with is sister to that Lathom (some such name) who published a book of verse (vers de société) [2] and was for a short time Editor of Daily News.

—Lolly would make a good novelist—she hasn't Lily's literary knack, not being meditative enough, but she has a vigorous intellect and a certain salient talent for constructive work, had she had a decent father (i.e. a father making a decent income), she would have carved out for herself some sort of a path of her own choosing. However it is too late to repair. She has been picking up great knowledge of life and will turn it to some use.

I am very glad to hear about your work, you seem to be getting very quickly through with a lot of work.

—I hear George Moore is interested in the question of Bacon and Shakespeare—Fancy it! We shall next hear of Moore going up in a motor balloon. I hope to go and see him next Saturday.

I am very sorry to hear about your eyes being troublesome,—I suppose there is nothing for it but complete rest. It will perhaps make you turn more and more to poetry.

[1] *The Celtic Twilight* had been reprinted.   [2] R. C. Lehmann.

I see in O'Grady's paper a very well intended and well devised review of Lady Gregory's book by John Todhunter.[1] It is more or less his own subject and he writes a charming review, effacing himself completely in his delight in the book. It is always a pity Todhunter has never stood on 'the spring-board of starvation'—he has always needed that kind of discipline.

I hope you have good weather, in Lily's letter to-day she says they have had a thunderstorm.

Reading this letter and also the enclosed one from Lolly will tire out your eyes I fear.—With kind regards to Lady Gregory, Believe me, Yours affectly—J. B. YEATS

32

43 Harrington Street, Dublin
July 31st, 1902

My dear Willie—Barry O'Brien was here a few days ago and twice over asked me to write to you and beg you write to him as to whether your *Kathleen Ni Hoolihan* may be produced by the Irish Literary Society in London. He says you have been written to several times but that no answer has been received from you. Miss Walker who is sitting to me tells me Fay is in the wildest delight with your two plays just sent to him. She herself is much gratified by your choosing her to be Mrs. Angel in one of the plays.

John Quinn [2] is the nearest approach to an angel in my experience—he has bought ten of Jack's and given me several commissions. He and Jack have been going about London together. Jack is just the man to guide a newly arrived American among the mysteries of London.—Yours affectionately—J. B. YEATS

Walker is well pleased with the Panels. The Winter only is not quite what he wants, but another week will finish them all.

33

43 Harrington Street, Dublin
(1903, probably)

. . . Last night I was at Moore's—Martyn for a half an hour, talked of nothing but your morality play.[3] 'Superb, magnificent, most dramatic, far the best thing he has ever done, and the things he has got into it.'

[1] Lady Gregory's *Cuchulain*.   [2] See *Memoir*, p. 38, *passim*.   [3] *The Hour Glass*.

It was beautiful to see Moore's restlessness, the jealousy of the artist which Blake says is like the sting of the honey bee, as you remember. He questioned and questioned, and was something relieved when he heard it could be acted in thirty minutes.

Moore is like a Doctor, who remembers all his cases, but is without theory. I am just the opposite of this. He would be a great curer, but I could advance Medical science.

34

7 *Stephen's Green, Dublin*
Friday (1903)

My dear Willie—I forgot in yesterday's letter to caution you not to let anything I told you of the desire of 'the people here' [1] to capture you and the players—of course it would make me appear worse than indiscreet if I were treated with fullest confidence and I betrayed this confidence—

Father Dineen yesterday went to Dun Emer to see the Banner and the girls asked him afterwards to come home and dine. After dinner George Mitchell who sings magnificently came out and the father spent what was evidently a most pleasant evening.

If I live another six months I am quite sure everyone will see an *immense change* in my fortunes, I am quite confident—and easy in my mind— I have always said that my life was vexed by two demons or familiars —the demon of the immediate future and the demon of the ultimate future. The first is just now very importunate but the other comes much closer.

Miss Keyes of the Viceregal Lodge who is extremely attractive with all sorts of subtle charms and who is private secretary to the Lady Lieutenant and general brains carrier and tactician to her Excellency, is coming here on Sunday, then I may do a pencil sketch of her. She was greatly delighted with Colum's play, saying there was not a word too much or too few in it.

The girls are in great spirits—that place seems to me to advance very fast in general knowledge among the public. Lily's instinct and Lolly's intellect keep things straight and on the even road to success.

It is terribly wet just now, lately we have had fine weather and in

[1] 'The people here': George Wyndham, Irish Chief-Secretary, and some members of Lord Dudley's entourage, who cared for poetry.

London it has been bad. I see Davitt and family have gone to America 'till April.

George Moore says it was that brute Yeats who started the report of his marriage,[1] he told Mr. Corder so, with whom he was staying in London. Mrs. Robertson told us this in a letter to Lily.—Yours affectionately— J. B. YEATS

35

7 Stephen's Green
Monday (1904)

My dear Willie—I hear Synge is intending to reside permanently in Dublin.

I should be very much obliged if you could lend me a few pounds until Irwin pays me the £15 for O'Grady, whose portrait will be finished the day after to-morrow.

I have been painting Miss Lane [2] in competition with Orpen, his style is learned—like an old master, mine of course is modern and impressionist; however I am satisfied that mine is the better portrait. Orpen was most generous in his appreciation of my work. At least I thought I gathered this from conversation I overheard between him and [Hugh] Lane—he is of course exceedingly clever and very much in earnest. I heard him say to Miss Purser, 'Do be serious'—he has a great future.[3]

Today Russell was to go out and arrange things at Dun Emer, Lolly and Lily are to be a society by themselves, and Miss Gleeson by herself— this I think is well. I wish George [4] could be induced to become their capitalist. He would not lose a penny. I dare not suggest this to him or to them,—all the same I will if an opportunity arrives.

. . . In a little while I am sure I shall be making money, commissions will come in and I shall be able to raise my prices, etc.

The Guildhall cheered me and this painting with Orpen has cheered me. I hope to make my portrait of Miss Lane a success of the highest mark. —Yrs affectly—J. B. YEATS

[1] A report of his engagement to 'John Oliver Hobbes', the novelist.
[2] Mrs. Shine, Hugh Lane's sister.
[3] Orpen being at this time twenty-five, and J. B. Y. sixty-five.
[4] George Pollexfen.

36

An exhibition of the work of Irish artists, promoted by Hugh Lane, was held in London during this year.

> *7 Stephen's Green, Dublin*
> *Undated 1904*

. . . Who wrote that article on the Guildhall Exhibition in the Westminster sent to me by Miss Horniman.[1] There was a certain knowledge of art history and a contemptuousness for things Irish and *a desire to make his point* against us that suggested to me Sir W. Armstrong. . . .

That letter of C. Shannon which Lady Gregory so kindly and thoughtfully sent to me is the most important event in my art life. You can't think how it has *enlivened* me with new hopes. Powell used to think more of Shannon than of anybody else and I wrote to him telling him of Shannon's words; but he was dead before he got my letter. Powell's death as you may well suppose is a heavy blow to me. I feel now as if I had no friend left, he has made such a gap in my life—the last few months I wrote to him every two or three days, receiving constant replies from him. He seemed to me to be in many ways like poor [Isaac] Butt. He had the same power of evoking affection, and he threw himself altogether into friendship as Butt threw himself into politics. *Powell's learning and industry and genius were all for the benefit of his friends*—and we never gave him any thanks or acknowledgment. We reasoned very much as children do about their mother—a mother likes doing things for her children and sacrificing herself, why thank her for what carries its own reward?—Only when she is gone is she valued. For a long while after Powell's death I ceased to be able to think, and I feel now like a man recovering from some tremendous shock which has entirely altered his point of view.

I hope something may turn up enabling me to go over to see the Exhibition, and I want much to see Shannon's work.

[1] Miss A. E. F. Horniman, the lady by whose generosity the Abbey Theatre was established. Her portrait by J. B. Yeats is in the vestibule of the Theatre.

Opportunities

37

My dear Willie--. . . . For weeks and weeks I have been working strenu-ously—at the one task, to get rid of these technical defects which con-tinually keep me back.

To give you an instance of what I mean. Those good comrades the Markeovitches [*sic*] [1] tell me that they told the Lady Grosvenor [*sic*] [2] that I wished very much to paint her portrait and that she was greatly pleased and quite flattered. Well, suppose she were to give me some sittings and that I did her face pretty well, but came to grief in my usual style over her draperies, her jewels, etc.—obviously it would be disastrous.

The opportunities that I am now having or about to have entirely through Hugh Lane's activity and courage, have fired me with hope but at the same time with the greatest anxiety. For this reason I have been spending all my time and all my money, got whenever I could scrape it n wo rking from models—this has left me entirely without money.

At the same time I have now completed the student labour, and I have quite made up my mind to employ models no further at any rate than this week by which time these panels will be finished. I think that these panels will surprise people, when they are put up. My skill now is far ahead of anything you have yet seen.

I am awfully sorry to bother you like this for I know your shillings are not very abundant.

I am making a good thing of Dowden—Dowden a success, and the other T.C.D. people Traill and Mahaffy, etc. will quickly submit.

Lily and Lolly are obviously much cheered by their Guildhall success, and by Liberty giving them orders. They are in better spirits than I ever remember them in before— . . . —Yrs affectly—J. B. YEATS

That article in the *Saturday* sent to me by Miss Horniman to whom I must write in acknowledgement, is the article *I have long been waiting for.* [3]

[1] Constance Gore Booth and her husband Count Markievicz, who at this time were Dublin society people. She took part in the Rising of 1916 and was con-demned to be executed; reprieved, she was the first woman to be elected to the House of Commons, in which, however, she never sat.

[2] George Wyndham's wife.

[3] An article by D. S. MacColl on the Irish Guildhall Exhibition.

TO LILY YEATS

38

H1 *Montague Mansions, Portman Square, W.*
June 27, 1904

. . . Last night I saw the play.[1] Miss Horniman, Willie, Shannon and Ricketts, Robert [Gregory], Mrs. Emery and myself all dined in a restaurant close to the theatre. . . . I sat in the front row in the middle of the gallery, the best seat in the house. Miss Horniman went and sat in W. B. Y.'s box, where were also A. Symons and his wife. The play was splendid and most stimulating, although the last part (and best part) fell away and became puzzling because Paul had a bad cold, and so had to save his voice. After the performance W. B. Y. made a very happy and ingenious little speech. . . .

I asked Willie last night if I could see George Pollexfen. In his fussy way he said I could not. I wish Willie had Jack's tender gracious manner, and did not sometimes treat me as if I was a black beetle. However I made him laugh by telling him what you said, that the Sligo people would say George was in a lunatic asylum [2] . . .

TO W. B. YEATS

39

7 Stephen's Green, Dublin
Sept. 22nd, 1904

My dear Willie—Many thanks. I have been so busy and so distracted and overwhelmed with bother and excitement that I couldn't write till now.

Rossetti was never a painter in our sense of the word; of craftsmanship he had only the slenderest equipment, finish and tact.

Had Nettleship recognised that this was to be always his limitation and had he abandoned all effort to compete with the painter he would have become a great master in another way which whatever it is is not painting— .

[1] W. B. Y.'s five-act tragedy, *Where There is Nothing*.
[2] George Pollexfen was thought queer in Sligo owing to his practice of astrology.

Of course Blake might have been a painter; *he was really lost to us*.

Obviously a portrait painter is a craftsman—a born portrait painter as I believe myself to be (W. Osborne always said so) imprisoned in an imperfect technique—that has been my tragedy.

However if you saw O'Leary's portrait worked on since I got it back and my portrait of Miss Lane, you would see how I have benefited by my struggles with the models.

Poor York Powell was an infinite spirit prisoned in a finite mind—a winged and aspiring Celt captured and put into the cage of an Oxford Donship. I never contested his opinion with any controversial purpose but merely to set the poor prisoner free. *His technique* was these opinions— his jingoism, his materialism all stained and incrusted with Oxford cum Jew wickedness. He was not a thinker, but an artist always, and *thus* perhaps tho' incidentally the most valuable of thinkers. The Jew occupies all the high places in England. . . .—Yrs affectly—J. B. YEATS

40

In this letter J. B. Yeats contrasts his own people with his relatives-in-law, the Pollexfens.

Gurteen Dhas, Churchtown
Saturday, Dundrum, Co. Dublin (1904)

My dear Willie—It is the easiest thing in the world to arrive at a misunderstanding.

I think you have acted very well by us, and I have said so several times with considerable emphasis quite lately *and we all think so*. The other day when writing to you the hasty note from a much worried man I was thinking about my own difficulties. . . .

. . . In my family we have always all of us been in the same situation in life for many generations living naturally and have entirely occupied ourselves with mutual affections and ideas; for instance we supported Aunt Ellen and enabled her to bring up a large family of little children. Among us we gave her an income for about 30 years. There was no fuss— no one in Sligo, above all none of the Pollexfens knew of it.

Sir W. Wilde [1] never met me without asking for my Uncle and saying 'Fancy Tom Yeats [2] buried in Sligo'. Tom Yeats was buried in Sligo

---

[1] Oscar Wilde's father.　　[2] Thomas Yeats, the writer's uncle, a mathematician.

because at his father's death he gave himself up to the immediate support of near relations,—in those days women did not support themselves, and I could give you lots of other instances in our family. I would not write so freely on this subject but that you have never met any of my family—and also because you know how much I admire the Pollexfen nature tho' loathing some of their notions. I find the soil rich in fertility and even with something volcanic in it, but I do not like the crops that grow upon it—and the odd thing is that in this great business of making money none of them has made a success—that George[1] is well off is due to other people. Andrew Jameson[2] told me George knew nothing about business. They were intended for a much more interesting kind of existence.

I have inflicted on you a long letter in very small writing, for which forgive me.—Yrs affectly—J. B. YEATS

I think before very long you will hear of my making some great success—I have seen Miss Horniman and got four commissions for pencil drawings.

TO CH. FITZGERALD

41

'The glorious fight about pictures' was caused by a scheme, promoted by Hugh Lane, to buy for Dublin a number of carefully selected pictures and drawings from the Staats Forbes collection, works by Constable, Millet and Corot, and a collection of later French pictures lent by Messrs. Durand-Ruel. Dublin finally lost many of the later French pictures, owing to the Corporation's failure to accept Lane's conditions.

7 Stephen's Green
Dublin, Jany. 30th, 1905

My dear Charlie—I think C. Shannon, when he paints, keeps thinking about his painting and the style thereof, and Manet, when he painted, did so with his eye on the object, getting all his effects by not thinking—scrupulously not thinking—about his painting, and that the object of both these men was to paint well. I would say of Dean Swift that he wrote always with his eye on the object and that Pater's method was the opposite of this. This expression 'with his eye on the object' was first used by I forget whom, and I think it admirably expresses a certain kind of writer and painter.

[1] George Pollexfen   [2] Andrew Jameson, the distiller.

We are having a glorious fight over here about pictures, and so far Politics has not become mixed in it. I think it is the first time in the history of the British Isles there has been a fight about pictures, and it is funny that it should have taken place in Ireland. The Academy issued a Manifesto against these pictures, a mean, scurvy document, which expressed nothing excepting that the Academy was willing to wound and afraid to strike. They all think that if money is spent on these pictures there will be none to spend on their paintings: they don't know that pictures is one of those things where the greater the supply the greater the demand—reversing the ordinary economic law. I should feel strengthened and encouraged by a new artist settling here. Walter Osborne's death to us personally as well as to art itself has been the greatest loss we have had for years. A good artist is in spite of himself a missionary for art, and a bad artist is our worst enemy. Sir Thomas Jones ruined the portrait painter's industry here in Dublin and Osborne revived it. I wished often lately when finding myself in a minority of one at the R.H.A. that Osborne had been there. When roused he would express himself in a very trenchant way. I suppose you saw the Academy Manifesto and if so you probably saw my letter signed 'Audi Alteram Partem'. The Academicians are very angry with me because I told the secrets of the Confessional—as the words explained how the Manifesto was written by an architect (Sir T. Drew—Particularly ignorant of pictures) and representative only of the Council's opinion. They said I was 'no gentleman' etc., however sometimes one is not a gentleman because one is something more important than a gentleman. When I found that the Manifesto was doing a great deal of harm to this National movement to buy those pictures I recognised that my allegiance to good pictures was a higher obligation than my allegiance to the Council of the R.H.A. So I wrote my letter. Very much against my will I did not sign it, but this was because it was thought it would less enrage the Academy if I did not sign it. However my letter took all the force out of the Manifesto. I wrote to D. S. MacColl, sending on the Manifesto and my letter, and he has commented on them very forcibly in the Saturday, and the three papers have reproduced his remarks. So that I hope from this on the Academy is out of the Saga as an Icelandic bard would say.

I send you an Express with a letter of mine which I think you will like. I hope you will like what I say about ugliness and why it has been so often handled by artists, and what I say about the English liking for what W. Small calls 'the pretty-pretty'.

I occasionally see G. Moore—his is the most stimulating mind I ever met. It is because he always keeps his own point of view—he is always like a man tumbled in among us out of some distant planet where everything is different from what it is here. It is all, I suppose, because he never learned anything at school, Nature having made everything safe for him by presenting him with natural industry and a good intellect. By all accounts he allows himself considerable licence, but won't do work slackly or badly. His mission is a good one, though not a popular one. He attacks respectability and conventionality and successful people and things generally. I don't think his pocket suffers in this kind of campaign, but I don't think he would desist even if it did. Like Hugh Lane over the pictures, he has the disinterestedness of the born fighter.

It is the greatest pity you are not here to help us. We are all watching the rich men, Lords Ardilaun and Iveagh and the Judge, etc. We look up at them as if they were so many Mont Blancs in springtime, hoping every moment for an avalanche of sovereigns to come tumbling down about our ears.

If we could get Manet's 'Itinerant Musician' and the other Puvis de Chavannes (one is bought) and a few sensational pictures of that sort, Dublin would become a place of pilgrimage—and wouldn't our posterity brag about it! . . .—J. B. YEATS

TO W. B. YEATS

42

7 Stephen's Green
Saturday (1905)

My dear Willie—I think it would be a good thing if you would see D. S. MacColl, I am certain he would help us.

I have already written to him sending him the manifesto and also my reply, the letter signed audi alteram partem—I did not sign it because Lane thought it better not, and rightly so as I think—

D. S. MacColl lives at

13 Montpelier Terrace

Twickenham.

Probably if you wrote to him he would arrange for you to go there in the evening (probably dine) and you might talk matters over.

This ought to be made a whole world controversy, in which every one that *cared for the true* and hated *the false* should take a part.

Of course Dowden won't help. Exhibition too one-sided (our old friend cosmopolitanism); besides he likes English pictures (of course—is he not unionist) besides he keeps to his own business and knows nothing of pictures (except that he loathes French impressionism).

Interest MacColl in Lane, *who has the disinterested air of the born fighter*.

—There was a short letter yesterday from N. Hone [1] in the *Irish Times* —nothing much in it except that he blessed the pictures altogether. I suppose the manifesto roused him, *even him*.

My letter is a good one, I think, except when I give details that I personally knew, all the arguments come from Lady Gregory—in fact but for her it is doubtful whether the letter would have been written.

All Wednesday I was fuming in my own mind about the manifesto; but when I consulted E. Martyn and Dermod O'Brien, they appeared to think that as a question of policy it was better for me not to write. Next day H. Lane showed me a letter from Lady Gregory with suggestions for a reply, and I at once took the hint.

It will amuse MacColl if you tell him that Judge Madden has been denouncing the exhibition, being spirited up there to buy something.

John, the sculptor—John knows as much about painting as I know about sculpture, so that his bust being shown here in a bad light was enough to turn the scale.—Yrs very truly—J. B. YEATS

Yesterday I saw the Editor of the *Irish Times*, as he would not put in my letter till I personally vouched for its contents, he said: 'I am an Englishman to the bone', which is about all he is—

43

Wednesday, 7 Stephen's Green
(1905)

. . . In my forthcoming article I shall touch on the question of *poetic art* as a special property of English civilization, and will give my own theory as to why it suits in England rather than elsewhere.

I should have liked very much to have you down last night but the last few days I have not been very well. For the first time in my life I have to consider the moods and caprices of that thing—*my health*, damn it! it is like a bad wife, and there is no possibility of divorce or even a separation—

[1] Nathaniel Hone, Irish landscape painter (1831–1917), trained in Barbizon school, a friend of Corot.

and were I to indulge in a frisk it would only be the worse for me afterwards. In my young days a gentleman did not bother about either his
health or his finance, now we are all miserable bourgeois—like George
Moore and such like timorous souls!

TO OLIVER ELTON

44

Extract from Frederick York Powell: a Life and a Selection of his letters
and occasional writings by Oliver Elton. *In two volumes: Vol. I: Memoir*
and letters, pp. 439–445. (Oxford: Clarendon Press, 1906). The extract is
reprinted here as a letter by kind permission of the Clarendon Press.

Dublin (1905)

York Powell was human nature itself. 'Bother intellect', he would say.
This was his value: he was human nature, with the gates of knowledge
wide open. He knew all languages and literatures and all the schools of
painting, and the whole region was traversed for him by one or two
personal affections. For these last he lived; and this is the reason he so
utterly despised his own learning and intellect, a feeling carried so far that
at times he seemed to adore ignorance.

There is a kind of human nature, intractable, subtle, composite, that
would *devour* life, seeking satisfaction for its senses or its dull will-power.
But in Powell we had human nature, frank, emotional, free, seeking
happiness as a plant seeks sunshine: and often it was human nature in
flood—rarely a winter flood, but oftener a summer flood, overflowing its
banks and sparkling in the bright sunshine. And this would have been so
more, as the years went by and his enemies ceased to thwart him. He was
a Nile seeking to fertilize the adjacent desert; a river under compulsion of
the moon and the stars, insidiously, imperceptibly overflowing its banks,
asking leave to flow along this channel, that opening; for I never once
detected him trying to influence any one. He seemed too shy, too timid,
too full of reverence. Nothing less than the compulsion of the stars would
make him meddle with any man's conviction.

He was an original man because, living in virtuous England, he loved
sinners best of all; living in Oxford, he regarded learning and 'culture' not
as ends in themselves but as means of self-expansion. He thought there
were many things better than being a *savant*—for instance to be a good

carpenter or a good fisherman or a good doctor. Where every one is ambitious, his only desire was happiness, that is, happiness as he defined it, and this is not always to be found in the alcove, but always in living and dying for others. But that sentence I must recall. There is nothing Powell would more have disapproved of than people living and dying for others. It would have seemed to him mere humbug, and quite impossible for a healthy person. In this I don't say he was right, but I am sure he would have so expressed himself. Yet this was his salient characteristic, that into affection for this and that person, sometimes old friends, sometimes friends of a few days,—into the channel of such affection he poured all his energies. When asked to do a good turn for a friend, alacrity would spring up into all his limbs, and he was off like a rocket. I remember seeing this and being impressed by it as something novel, never seen before in anybody else. I believe if at the moment of death he had been asked to do a man he liked some service, he would have managed somehow to live a little longer, that he might write the letter, or sign the necessary cheque, or do for friendship's sake the preface that made the fortune of your book.

I think Powell's humility was a little peculiar in this way, that he thought nothing about his own merits as compared with the merits of other people. But he was always thinking what good times he was having, —life and friends after his own heart, and every want satisfied. He did not think it a merit, but a lucky accident that he could open out his arms and take in great armfuls of happiness. He was almost ashamed of his faculty for enjoyment. Some people never go into life at all; and Powell was to them like a sailor fresh from many voyages, who has come to see his cousin the church sexton. Those people prefer the kingdom of dullness, where they make the best terms they can with fear and dullness: with neither of these would Powell live an hour, not even when he was dying, as his letters show: he always defied death and fear. For that reason he always seemed to me a healthy man living among invalids, and his health was contagious.

You remember how he worshipped any one he was fond of, a fisherman or a little child. Indeed, this trinity possessed him, affection, happiness, and worship. If he got one, he got the other two. The fleshly or pagan school of art and literature, having to do with the senses merely, brings no happiness, however magnificently it may be decorated with all the devices of the most mournful and beautiful art; it never means happiness. The literature of the senses and the literature of despair go hand in hand, Powell's value to his friends was that he was human nature unspoiled, unsophisticated—human nature in the crystal clearness of its source, and unmuddied either by Puritanism (which teaches suspicion and treachery towards yourself and others) or by the devilishness of aristocratic vanity and insolence. He was the embodiment of innocent joyousness; innocent, because it sprang from the unselfish part, the affections and the spiritual desires, and for the same reasons a real joyousness.

And then the powerful brain of the man! this completed the charm. So much power and force, and all as gentle as the smile of a woman; the brain, and the stores of invention and knowledge and thought it brought with it. And it was not merely that it was gentle; but you felt secure at having so much power on your side: you seemed to touch Mother Earth; you felt happy and at home in so much strength, so much affection. Joy and pain mingle in our lives, at one moment we smile and next we grimace; Powell saw joy so clearly that he tore it away from *the other*.

The most important part of his equipment for joyousness was his extra-ordinary power of instantaneous mental concentration. Most of us when thinking of one thing are always thinking of something else as well. Powell gave all his energies to one subject, and that was always the passing moment. The busy bee sunk in the heart of a flower is the true symbol of his intellect.

Living in the present with such immense gusto, he with a mere gesture, as it were, drove off all the bogeys, the bogey of death as well as the more urgent bogey of tomorrow; and the saints themselves could enjoy his company because his happiness was all made up of affection and sympathy and friendship, while his noble intellect, freed from all vileness of fear, played radiantly over the philosophy appropriate to those feelings. In his company fear fled as the devil shuns holy water: you did not need to cross yourself.

A strong will would have spoiled Powell. The wild garden, blooming with every flower of every season, all growing together, would have been changed into a builder's yard, or a Manchester factory with its slums.

Of all men I ever met he was the freest from vanity, which is a form of personal hopefulness,—hope, that is, of some personal success or glory or distinction. Powell had no form of personal hopefulness, because he was never interested in himself at all, either as regards the present or the future. Himself was a horse he never backed: but he loved praise, because he thought it meant liking. He leaned towards those who liked him, as a shy boy or girl would in a world of strangers look about for friendly faces. It seems that I told him he would have made a surpassing parish priest. I could conceive him rolling along the roads, in some western parish, brim-full of piety and visions and laughter and merriment, loving the boys and the girls and the sinners of both sexes; a fervent believer of the narrowest kind, only with all his beliefs irradiated with intellect and affection: in his life no dark corner, except where loomed the English government and Protestants. And how he would have hated these last! The R.C. religion would have suited him exactly, and that seems an extraordinary thing to say. Powell's reasoning faculties were never very strong, and he could easily have put them under lock and key, and gone forth whole-heartedly to enjoy the imaginary side, the visionary side, and the human side, of the R.C. religion. The crimes he would have forgotten, or forgiven, or even (God help him) condoned.

When I say he was deficient in reasoning power, I only mean that he had no turn for logic, that baser form of reasoning which is the bane of the super-educated, or imperfectly educated person; but he was mighty in the imaginative reason of which education, so-called, so constantly robs a man. I always maintain that in conversation people should avoid argument, contenting themselves with uttering rival opinions; for then you get the imaginative reason into play, which is as the fertilizing west compared to the east wind,—the east wind, that takes colour out of the sky and fragrance out of the flower. You know how Powell would shun argument, how he would push concession to the utmost limits so as to escape it; and he was right. If he liked your doctrine he took it gratefully. If he did not like it he would make wry faces and pretend to swallow it, that was all. Argument is not the test of truth. Meditation, experience of life, hope, charity, and all the emotions—out of these the imaginative reason speaks. His dislike of argument was one of the reasons why you sought his company. Another reason was a negative one. He had no spite in his composition, no cruelty. However irritated, he did not wish to revenge himself. The reason why we would always submit to him was that we could not discover anything to beware of, no jealousy or envy, or even a competitive instinct of self-love.

I have a reminiscence from my daughter which I had forgotten. In 1897, the first day after her illness that she had left her bath chair, she and I walked along the High St., Turnham Green, and Powell met us. She remembers how he circled round us, laughing but saying nothing. The first shop we came to, he rushed in and came out with a penny mug; at the next shop he did the same and brought out a penny picture post-card; and at another shop he got a penny toy; and finally, at another shop, some flowers. These all in succession he gave to her. I think that is characteristic of Powell; it paints him to the life; he had nothing to say, no phrases, only the offering of gifts.

I often said to him that he talked telepathically. To catch sight of him and to hear his laugh was to find yourself possessed by the Powell doctrine. You did not often, considering, hear his voice; he talked, comparatively, so little. But he was the air that we all breathed. He would propound no theories. I remember him so well, when he would remove his pipe and say 'that's it', or 'that's true', or 'My God, that's true', or 'My God, that's fine'.

He always thought himself inferior to his friends, though, speaking generally, he never valued himself or others on their ethical qualities, unlike George Eliot and the typical English person for whom she writes. He never looked about for people to respect; he looked for people who would give him plenty of delight, excite his sympathy, and make themselves beloved; 'I do believe, Powell, you would not object to a murderer', said some one to him. 'No, not if he was a really good fellow', said Powell. I believe Shakespeare was like that. He, like Powell, probably regarded these moralists as cunning rascals who wanted to strangle human nature. Powell liked life and the game of life so much that he regarded any one with suspicion who wanted to reform it. Those were a poor sort of people, and like vegetarians or water-drinkers sitting down to a feast. I believe it was this love of human nature and the game of life that made him a Tory. The Tory is more appreciative of life as it is in all its plenitude. Your Radical looks at life a little sourly.

I have heard people say Powell was hostile to ideas. What nonsense! He was a child of the ideal; only his ideas all came from love of human nature. He sought everywhere the concrete, which he could handle and love, and laugh with and laugh at. He did not care for dreams of intellectual beauty. In his Imperialism he was thinking of Englishmen and Irishmen and Scotchmen lustily enjoying themselves, first of all in fighting and afterwards in colonizing.

His Imperialism was to me portentous: without pity and without chivalry. I could never understand it. Yet even here I had only to tell him of a poor Scotch dragoon out of the reserve, called away to Africa to leave a beautiful full-bosomed Irish wife with two little children and another coming. I am glad to say he came back all right. For a short time his wife nearly lost her reason, but the Scotch clan gathered about her and took care of her. She was a splendid placid woman, like a summer sea. I remember telling Powell all about her case, and how Powell looked, how serious he got, and how silent. He was like Shakespeare's Hector, who in 'his blaze of wrath' would 'subscribe to tender objects'. This was a defect in Hector's warriorship. There were many such defects in Powell's warriorship.

My brother-in-law George Pollexfen, the astrologer, called him 'a Jupiter man, honourable to the finger-tips'; which means that however jovial he was yet strict with himself. Strict with others is another matter, though this he might be wound up to, if put into careful hands, and made drunk with something like the late Boer war, and provided the victims were kept out of sight.

It seems to me that one of the foolishest ideas is people's habit of constantly looking for a *complete man*, a kind of nonsense handed down from Goethe. What we want is incomplete men. I like all qualities to be in excess, or rather that each person should be a specialist. Powell loved his friends to excess, and from this came everything. Complete, well-governed men have their value, no doubt; they make good clerks, look well after routine, &c.

Powell was lovable, because he was a portion of some kind of eternal goodness, whose existence is proclaimed by the existence of such men. Isaac Butt had the same lovableness—poor Butt—superb in his weakness as in his strength.

TO W. B. YEATS

45

Gurteen Dhas, Dundrum
Undated, probably 1906

My dear Willie—There are no domestic worries and of course there have never been any storms. . . .

If I could get rid of my money worries and if Lily and Lolly had their affairs on a securer basis, I should be perfectly happy. I do not desire any asylum for my old age except this house where I am a great deal too well treated.

Fanny Newenham when she stayed with us in London said I was spoiled and I often think [she] was right—

At present my object is to paint better than Orpen—that is the only path of salvation. I have set myself to do it. I can already beat him in power of getting a likeness, in this from the first I was better.

I think when next you see my work you will see I have made great progress.

Except Orpen no one makes a substantial income. Presently judges, etc. will find me out,—that I am cheaper than Orpen and my likenesses a little more pleasing. His faults as a portrait painter arise from the fact that tho' he can model forcibly, he cannot model subtily—he can give with great force of relief a nose or a cheek or a chin—he cannot model the *delicate* gradations, that make for finer expression—

In these finer gradations I excel, and lately I have been trying to acquire knowledge of how to give the broader and bolder effects.

—Everyone who comes in is struck by the improvement in my work—

Once a little success and money came in I should start some pictures. I am sure that a reaction will soon set in and that a demand for subject pictures will arise again among people—I have of course lots of subjects.— Yrs affectly—J. B. YEATS

46

Monday
7 Stephen's Green, (1906) Dublin

My dear Willie—Miss Tobin [1] is a princess and it was a lucky day when you brought her here and I thought of sketching her—for this sketch has so pleased her that she has commissioned to copy it and make a picture in oils from it; and when I, not very eager to do it, said my price would be £25, she said Oh, that's very little—and behold she has sent me the money. Had [Isaac] Butt ever gone to America and lived in dalliance with a fair woman who had small eyes, I should think Miss Tobin his descendant. . . .

—I am glad to tell you that that paragraph by York Powell does not refer to me. Elton is greatly amused at my mistake—for he says it refers to a most blatant philistine of an Englishman,[2] he says it is a judgment on me to have made this mistake. Lily and Lolly had already ridiculed my mistake saying it quite obviously did not refer to me. It shows that I have depths of humility in me hitherto undreamed of,—nor am I mercurial. Only a man shackled in impecuniosity is like a bird tied by a string; the bird thinks the string very long, as it sometimes is; or forgets that it is there at all and so flies up to tumble back distractedly.

Have you seen Doughty's poems? They seem to me really good and no mistake.

[1] Agnes Tobin, a Californian poetess, friend to W. B. Yeats and to Arthur Symons.
[2] A reference to a paragraph in Professor Elton's biography of York Powell.

Cleopatra—a Portrait

I have read through Miss Travers's book and am surprised that Dowden should like it. Yet she occasionally writes a good line—only she is then so pleased with it, that she must needs go on and add other lines that seem meant to explain and expand and exemplify the meaning of the first line.

Now, I think every work of art should *survive* after all the labour bestowed upon it, and *survive as a sketch*. To the last it must be something struck off at a first heat,—this is the meaning of impressionism.

I have lately been reading Shakespeare's *Cleopatra*, and it has all the pregnancy of a sketch because it is a sketch. The details are not filled in —no *conscientious* labour has been spent on it. It is all a riot and extravagance—now the essence of a sketch is that it leaves much to the imagination, and that is right for the supreme reason that your poet creates great spaces where the imagination must travel alone, raised to its highest volatility and unencumbered by the necessity to find words or reasons.

. . . Again as to ideas in Poetry. These must never be expressed, they can only be implied. I say this because of my reverence for ideas—and because as I think if expressed at all it must be done with mathematical precision, forbidding alike eloquence and poetry.

I did a sketch in water-colour of Miss Marie De Bunsen, friend of Miss Tobin, these two ladies were greatly pleased—but they are easily pleased. Miss De Bunsen has written to ask my price for a water-colour sketch and I have answered £5.

I have had £20 of the Harrington [1] portrait fund, I believe the rest will easily be got. Harrington is doing his best for me, I don't think he cares a damn about the portrait or his apotheosis as a person whose portrait is hung for ever in the Mansion House. But he does care a lot about getting me £60 . . . and that is Dublin all over. Dublin also is waiting for its dramatist that it may know itself and be proud of itself.

. . . We are all looking forward to seeing Jack and Cottie . . . Just now Lily and Lolly are preparing for a sale in London. Lolly will go over and stay at the Chestertons.—Yrs affectly—J. B. YEATS

47

In 1906 Swinburne reprinted his critical essay on William Blake with a new preface, in which he referred, without the mention of names, to the elaborate edition of Blake published in 1893 by Edwin Y. Ellis and W. B. Yeats. The

[1] Lord Mayor of Dublin (1901-1903).

passage described by J. B. Y. as being of 'a particularly insolent and contemptuous
sort' ran as follows, and is reproduced by permission of William Heineman Ltd.:
  '*While we were able to regard this Londoner born and bred [Blake] as not only*
a fellow towns-man of Milton's but a fellow countryman of Shakespeare's, it did
seem an almost insoluble problem to explain or to conjecture how so admirable
and adorable a genius could be so deeply flawed and so continually vitiated by
such unutterable and unimaginable defects. But if we regard him as a Celt rather
than an Englishman, we shall find it no longer so difficult to understand from
whence he derived his amazing capacity for such illimitable emptiness of mock
mystical babble as we find in his bad imitations of so bad a model as the Apoca-
lypse: his English capacity for occasionally superb and serious workmanship we
may rationally attribute to his English birth and breeding. Some Hibernian com-
mentator on Blake, if I rightly remember a fact so insignificant, has somewhere
said something to some such effect that I, when writing about some fitfully
audacious and fancifully delirious deliverance of the poet he claimed as a country-
man, and trying to read into it some coherent and imaginative significamce, was
innocent of any knowledge of Blake's meaning. It is possible, if the spiritual fact
of his Hibernian heredity has been or can be established, that I was: for the excel-
lent reason that, being a Celt, he now and then too probably had none worth the
labour of deciphering—or at least worth the serious attention of any student be-
longing to a race in which reason and imagination are the possibly preferable sub-
stitutes for fever and fancy. But in that case it must be gladly and gratefully
admitted that the Celtic tenuity of his sensitive and prehensile intelligence throws
into curious relief the occasional flashes of inspiration, the casual fits of insight,
which raise him to the momentary level of a deep and free thinker as well as a
true and immortal poet.' (Prefatory Note. Swinburne's William Blake, *pp. vi. to*
vii. 1906.)

7 Stephen's Green, Dublin
July 2nd, 1906

My dear Willie—Have you seen this week's *Athenaeum*? Something
is quoted from a preface by Swinburne to a book on Blake. It is a
reference to you of a particularly insolent and contemptuous sort.

It is not worth anger or any reply—only it makes me disgusted.

Byron's mantle of vulgarity has descended on Swinburne, for it is a kind
of aristocratic insolence.

Blake was often angry. Indeed he poured forth lava streams of head-
long wrath—but he never condescended to the calculated venom of insolence either the major or minor sort, and this after all like everything else
coming from Swinburne is only minor. But then Blake was a mighty poet.

More than thirty years ago I heard many stories of Swinburne—

amongst others of his reciting his ode to Mazzini himself, and often bursting into floods of tears. A capacity for nervous weeping is exactly what I should expect from his kind of lyrism. I also heard he used to say in conversation that he and Shelley were the only great poets because they alone were gentlemen. Here again he comes up to expectation—yet to be a poet it needs more than that you be an aristocratic cad even tho' you have in addition Greek and Latin, an Oxford education and a gift of language that is like the sea for strength and copiousness. Out of these you may make a lyrist, granted a gift for musical speech you can make that sort of poet *out of anything*.

To be a poet in the true and great sense of the word needs much more. It is *quite possible to be lyrical and not poetical*—to be a poet it is necessary first of all to be a man. The high vitality and vivid experience, the impulses, doings and sufferings of a Tolstoi, a Shakespeare or a Dante,—all are needed.

The other morning I woke out of my dreams, saying out loud several times over while still only half awake—

'A man can only paint the life he has lived!'

As to Swinburne, he has lived always among a circle of Toadies, and is a creature of his special clique as much as if he were a brilliant writer of the *Times* newspaper hired and sometimes cajoled to do the Editor's bidding. His roots strike nowhere, he grows in light soil. . . .

You and Ellis have done more for Blake than possibly he ever did for anyone in all his life.

His criticism that the Celtic movement puts fever and fancy in the place of reason and imagination is I am afraid a true criticism—as true as to my mind it is obvious. It is not however specially Celtic—the Irish do it because they are primitive and kept so by a church which in its Irish form at any rate exists on fever and fancy.

Landor was an aristocratic poet, yet he never wrote an insolent line—deferential towards his equals, still more deferential with his inferiors—with his superiors or those who thought themselves so, scrupulously polite and vigilant.

Lolly did well in London—but their work at Dun Emer is terribly anxious. It requires huge exertions to keep it going, yet if they had a little capital I believe they would work out something good. Their devotion is extraordinary.

My work here is *much* better—I think I shall soon have a big reputation, and . . . money.

Do let me have a line about this scrubby fellow Swinburne—people treat him as if he was a sort of Royal Duke—immune from criticism.— Yrs affectly—J. B. YEATS

[To this W. B. replied: Thank you ever so much for your letter about Swinburne. I have seen nothing of his criticism except one rather absurd sentence quoted I think by the *Sketch*. I did not get the *Athenaeum* as I did not intend to reply. The passage about him in the Blake book was by Ellis, and was entirely just and civil. I am not at all surprised at Swinburne's attitude for one practically never converts anyone of a generation older than one's own. . . . Andrew Lang was hardly civil when I sent him my first book, and was very uncivil indeed when he reviewed the Rhymers Book. Two years later he wrote a very generous article of apology. He excused himself by saying that new work was very difficult to him, and that when he first read Verlaine he thought it no better than one finds in the poets of a country newspaper.]

48

P.S. This letter is written in great *hurry of mind*.

July 5, 1906
7 Stephen's Green, Dublin

My dear Willie—What are you going to do about Mrs. Pat. Campbell? I think it is a difficult question. No doubt the ideal thing is to keep the play for the Irish theatre, and we all and you especially ought to do ideal things—it might also be the prudent thing. The theatre is a very *serious product* of the Irish National movement, we are all embarked in it—giving it your best play will give you a considerable accession of fortune and authority with such people as *John Quinn*, and besides all this, it is the dignified thing to do.

In giving it to Mrs. P. Campbell or any other famous personage, there is nothing very significant. It would simply be a piece of self-interest, which of course is a very good thing in its way, and especially in your case who being a poet suffer much from lack of pence.[1]

Only I think whatever you do it should not be done hastily, and you should not forget that you are a public man in the Irish movement—and

[1] W. B. Y. hoped to induce Mrs. Patrick Campbell to play in his *Deirdre*, first produced in December 1906.

its leader in all literary and philosophical movements and that your influence here is really more important to you than anything else, *and dearer to you*—and more important than anything else to other people as well.

How would young Kettle who has just got in for Tyrone advise you? (Oldham tells me the other side in the contest had made full preparations for celebrating a great victory.)

Don't you think there is something in my distinction between Protestant and Catholic Agnosticism and that Shakespeare's was the Catholic variety?

Catholic Agnosticism is full of self-knowledge, self-esteem, it makes people reason with themselves rather than with other people, the result of this and the fruits of this spirit are humility and sympathy, and much probing of the soul of man.

Protestant Agnosticism makes a man turn his eyes outward, to watch the doings of other people, and when it reasons it does so contentiously in hot debate with other disputants, and it does not judge a deed by the motive but by the law. There is no humility or sympathy and no willingness to forgive—because there is no searching of one's own conscience. A man who has nothing to forgive himself has nothing to forgive others.

Protestantism makes a people energetic about *external* things and also arrogant and self-complacent, you know the Belfast-man's grin.

Agnosticism means that reason is supreme. And there is the Protestant reason and the Catholic reason.

I think too; it is interesting, Shakespeare's attitude towards self-love, which according to him I think the besetting sin, alike of poets and lovers, —his Catholic self-criticism made him fight against it. (I wonder has the R C any special pronouncements on this subject), and besides, as Colum once said to me, Shakespeare knew that self-love makes a man solitary. The few glimpses we get show Shakespeare to have been very lovable and fond of his friends, and *how he couldn't have been otherwise. How else could he have written his dramas?*—Yrs affectly—J. B. YEATS

49

7 Stephen's Green
Undated (1906)

My dear Willie—I hope you will not think your parent altogether too tedious if I write again—when I say a poet must be a man, I don't mean anything that the English Philistine says—only, that all poetry is woven out of *humanity*; and for this purpose Lamb or Goldsmith is better material than the masterful Dr. Johnson tho' he also was a man. The English admiration for strong will, etc. is really part of the gospel of materialism and money making and Empire-building.

. . . Had Socrates come across Ancient Rome possibly there would have been a Socratic dialogue on strong will. Did I know a little more about Socrates and were I a witty man I would devise a dialogue.

I have just had a letter from Paget, a dear and characteristic letter. The Graphic is turning off all its artists having determined to work henceforth with Photographs. Paget is in despair, but I suppose to cheer himself up has undertaken the keep of his brother Arthur's wife and children. . . .

. . . It is a few Englishmen like Paget and York Powell and Oliver Elton that prevent the Almighty from destroying England—Paget's brothers, hitherto more prosperous than himself, are not able to help with Arthur's family, depression having hit them, and their families I suppose being numerous and of tender years.

. . . I detest the kind of man Swinburne is.—A man must lose his soul to save it—this was written for the warning of artists and poets. Had his humanity been exercised by a various life, his verse would not be so turgid and so monotonous. People who can write verse are so few that we allow ourselves too much to regard them as something wonderful—and so they don't receive the needful discipline.

I call Swinburne's insolence by that name, not merely because of its venom, but because of a certain smack of self-complacency, a sure mark of intellectual underbreeding and of an inferior kind of pride, tho' a quick passport to success with the kind of readers we are pestered with. Take any line you like of Swinburne's and it is three parts journalism—there is always a something that savours of the great newspaper. If he were only a little easier to read, he would be the most popular poet at the fashionable clubs.

Of course I don't deny his gifts or that he has written lovely things.— Yrs affectly—J. B. YEATS

50

There had been differences of opinion between W. B. Yeats and his younger sister over Miss Elizabeth Yeats's conduct of her printing press. These came to a head when W. B. Y. tried to veto the publication of a book of poems by AE on

the grounds that AE had made a bad selection. In this and the next letter J. B.
Yeats stands up for his daughter.

Friday
7 Stephen's Green, Dublin (1906)

. . . Lolly has courage and courage to the bystander, indifferent or not, always appears indiscretion and often is so but that Fortune, being a woman, admires the brave.

As regards the other matter in your letter. As you have dropped affection from the circle of your needs, have you also dropped love between man and woman? Is this the theory of the overman, if so, your demigodship is after all but a doctrinaire demi-godship.

Your words are idle—and you are far more human than you think. You would be a philosopher and are really a poet—the contrary of John Morley, who is really a philosopher and wants to be a statesman. Morley is never roused except when some pet synthesis is in jeopardy.

The men whom Nietzsche's theory fits are only great men of a sort, a sort of Yahoo great men. The struggle is how to get rid of them, they belong to the clumsy and brutal side of things. . . .

Robert called here this morning. I hope he will give a good report of things. I am awfully worried but in the highest spirits—but I fear I am wasting your time and that this is *trivial fond record* to a man who has cast away his humanity.—Yours affectionately—J. B. YEATS

I never show your letters to them at home. Women are always apt to treat every utterance as if it is something final—and I don't think anything you say at present or for some time to come *if ever* is to be treated as final. You are haunted by the Goethe idea, interpreted by Dowden, that a man can be a complete man.   It is a chimera—a man can only be a specialist.

5I

7 Stephen's Green
August 6th, 1906

. . . At present Lily only sees that they have to work very hard at a dull and slavish kind of work, and think they get very little reward for what they do, and possibly or probably after all it may end in ghastly failure, and she sees that you live very pleasantly, doing work which is your choice—getting plenty of public and private consideration. Everyone anxious to help and make smoother your path. I also have a very pleasant tho' unprofitable profession.

Did you stay too long at that English School, and have you a sort of airy contempt for women? If so cast it from you, it dishonours you as a man and a poet—and the least drop of the accursed thing within your soul would be sure to come up in your letters, in spite of their deliberate courtesy and reasonableness, and it would be detected at once. I think the Protestants were the first people who tried to keep women 'in their place', imposing servitude on them. The Middle Ages were very much afraid of them, but took no stern measures.

York Powell's attitude was medieval, he was afraid, he was medieval also in another matter, he thought Intellect a something quite secondary, and when women *worshipped* Intellect he was against them,—for he thought they deserted what for women and men alike is the true ideal which is to cherish that clairvoyant faculty which goes with personality and which has been always woman's speciality since they more often than the other sex escape *bad education*. People who lean on logic and philosophy and rational exposition end by starving the best part of their mind.

Genius is personality—I always say that had Shakespeare had a strong will he would have read for a fellowship in T.C.D. and there would have been no Shakespeare.

Poetry is written not by Intellect but by the clairvoyant faculty.

I have wandered away from my subject which is how to make the Dun Emer Press a success—for this purpose I agree with you it must be made a kind of literary principality and to bring this about peace must be patched up between you and Lolly.

I think also you should treat Russell [AE] and Magee [1] with great respect—after all a writer knows his own work, and he should be anxiously consulted, besides there is her amour propre which should count for *something* in all business. You must keep strictly to advising, otherwise you wreck everything.[2]—Yrs affectly—J. B. YEATS

I think that it came naturally from the Protestants' standpoint that they should make much of Intellect, our Religion professes to be scientific truth.

[1] 'John Eglinton', the Irish essayist.
[2] In a further letter Yeats thanked his son for 'taking in such good part what I write'.

52

My dear Willie—As you asked my opinion last night about Miss Darragh[1] I will give it you now more deliberately, not because I think my opinion of any importance, but because you asked for it.

I think in her present form she is a bad actress and the worst possible for your play. She is an actress born, an actress genius, possibly a great actress. But her present style is altogether too florid, what is called too stagy. She should not always be so intensive and so impressive—it is monotonous. There were moments when she reached extraordinary levels of passionate sincerity; let her keep these moments and let the rest be ordinary speech. She has wonderful transitions (would that the others had this gift—notably Frank Fay) in voice and gesture, and her lowest whisper must have been audible in every corner of the theatre, but in good acting as in good painting emphasis must be employed sparingly. Thrift is the great principle in style—as we all know, you especially.

Had I had last night a copy of the play I could have marked each passage as she gave it with letter indicative of what I thought and as I believe with *what others felt*—such as V.B. or V.G. for very bad or very good, etc., but she will improve, as you know we must all sow our intellectual wild oats. We begin with redundancy and end with severity. Were she and . . . . Moira acting together, they would learn from each other. Moira from her would learn not only technique but energy and imagination, and she would benefit by Moira's infallible judgment.

I think also (this is a delicate matter) she should cover up her neck more. Deirdre was not a Cleopatra. Altogether she should be gentler, more *cloistral* till the moment comes for passion and nature, that at any rate is the Irish idea of heroic womanhood.

It is unfortunate that Miss Darragh's acting 'shows up' too glaringly the faults of the others—she has too much style. They hardly any. Frank Fay's dragging deliberation in speech and movement is a growing evil.

I don't think you are right in making the R.C. Church responsible for the defects of women's acting in Dublin. It is the false ladylike that is early Victorian which is to blame.

[1] An actress from London, who played the title-part in *Deirdre* on its first performance.

. . . I think *Deirdre* far the finest play you have written and *I think Miss Darragh the best piece of luck yet come to you*—only, she must prune her luxuriance,—here is my opinion—which I don't want to press upon you. —Yrs affectly—J. B. YEATS

53

My dear Willie—I have had a long letter from Quinn, very interesting —and besides he writes to make two requests:—that I write the general introduction to Synge's plays, which I am quite ready to do provided it is done on approval (by which I chiefly mean my own approval), and the other request is *that I do a portrait of you for £30.* I need not say it would be an immense kindness and help to me if you could manage to come up sometime reasonably soon, and give me a few sittings. A week will more than suffice, as it is you know I have done a good deal. If the eyes were opened and the hands finished it would now be almost done.

By getting up early I have been working at an article on Art training. I make a distinction between the artists who bring with them what I call full minds, and those who have empty minds; the latter take naturally to Art Schools, but the others keep away from Art Schools.

Ingres seems to me head and chief of those who have empty minds— great artist tho' he was; Turner and Hogarth belong to the other category, and I should say Monet. All modern artists or almost all are studio bred. Must we wait till the working man is as much awake esthetically as he is politically, before we get again into art the full mind? . . .

Synge is in hospital; yesterday he was operated on, and on Wednesday he will be accessible to visitors, he is going on well. I saw him the day before the hospital business and he was in good spirits, wanting to see Jack about a book on Irish types he is meditating.—Yrs affectly—J. B. EATS

The portrait painter with the full mind will find interest in his sitter his chief, his sole inspiration—to make his technique equal to his thought will be his humble painter's hope. The other sort will think only of his technique. Do you think I will flutter the Dovecots of the Slade School?— What does Robert [Gregory] think?

54

I saw to-day Count Markevitch [*sic*]. N. Hone had bought one of his pictures. N. Hone thinks very little of ——, he says he has seen too many pictures, and that when he paints he looks at his painting not at what he paints: he says he has faculty but no brains and that he is a stupid man. . . .

He thought Russell greatly improved, but did not say much more.

This morning I looked up the life of Turner, and I find that he made exactly 144 appearances at the Academy School of Art—of which 98 were in the 'Plaster School', and this was the only school of Art he ever attended. He did a great deal of work copying Sir Joshua Reynolds's pictures. Reynolds employed him.

So much for Art Schools. . . .

TO RUTH HART[1]

55

Gurteen Dhas
Churchtown, Dundrum
Sept. 18th, 1907

I was never so pleased or so surprised with anything as with your delightful present of Lamb's letters. It was for me a happy thought—and for the whole household also. Lily undertook cutting the leaves, and it took her just three hours to do it, she found so much to read out.

Lately I have been reading Flaubert's letters, and the contrast with these is most entertaining. Lamb in the manner of the 18th century accepts life so contentedly, and humorously, and Flaubert is so angry with it and so fierce. Lamb I think hated reformers of all sorts. I had a lot of 18th century relations whom I remember perfectly—and to read Lamb is to be back once more in their company. Of course I am comparing the great with the little, for tho' my relations never got drunk, went to Church regularly and never broke any of the social laws, yet Lamb was the better man, and tho' in their bookless way they had wit as well as humour, they were none

---

[1] A daughter of J. B. Yeats's friend, George Hart. See *Memoir*, p. 37-38.

of them geniuses, and their religion was, that God would not condemn a person born of decent people. Other people had to *work* for their salvation.

I saw young Hone yesterday and reproached him for not turning up at the wedding. I told him all about the pretty girls and I hope and I think made him sorry.

It was by far the happiest brightest and most joyous wedding I ever was present at—your father mother and the pretty girls, all the constituents in perfect order and of the best. As to Ethel she seemed to take possession at once, as if she already held the house keys. Just a little touch of peremptoriness so delightful in one of her benign beauty. I never enjoyed myself more. I felt like a person in a dream. It was intoxicating both to Lily and myself.

The latest news here is that Lily is going to New York after Xmas to some sale there. She is in great spirits. She is making prudent arrangements—however perhaps I am a little premature, as all is not quite settled.—Yrs affectly—J. B. YEATS

TO W. B. YEATS

56

At this time W. B. Yeats was seeing his Collected Edition of 1908 (A. H. Bullen) through the press. The portrait by Mancini, an Italian artist whom Hugh Lane brought to Dublin, duly appeared in the Edition.

> *Gurteen Dhas*
> *Churchtown, Dundrum, Co. Dublin*
> *Oct. 21st, 1907*

My dear Willie—I think you would make *a serious mistake* if you put Mancini's portrait into your book, you are not a Caliban publishing a volume of decadent verse—nor are you in any movement of revolt that you should want to identify yourself in elaborate humility with the ugly and the disinherited.

Do you notice that in each of those thin drawings at the Nation (?) Mancini has put the left eye lower than the right—it has a curious ignobling effect. . . .

He is a wit rather than a serious artist. A wit painter, as Whistler is a poet painter and Sargent a prose painter.—Yrs affectly—J. B. YEATS

57

My dear Willie—I am glad to say this card is not for me, H. Lane tells me it is meant for you.

It seems two members of the R.H.A. are to be put on the committee for the modern gallery.

Sir Thos. Drew [1] wrote a venomous letter against the Lane Collection—he is also moved by a special spite against H. Lane *and you*, he is singularly ignorant of art, and his only idea of doing his duty as President of the Academy is to make himself on all occasions as obnoxious as possible, he thinks that making himself prominent he pushes the R.H.A. fortunes; in reality he ought to keep his disagreeable appearance as much out of sight as possible.

Catterson Smith [1] is a nobody who probably, removed from the vicious neighbourhood of Sir T. Drew, would try to do right *if Lane* insisted on it. Myself and Allen would be good men to propose. N. Hone of course is a good man—if he would attend. Allen is intelligent and absolutely simple and straight, and *high minded*.

Hone and Allen would be an admirable selection. —— is an opinionated crank—in art imperfectly educated.

Sir Thos. Drew must be kept out—were I selected to go with him I should refuse to serve.

You remember Sir T. Drew's famous letter. I have a copy of it here in the Studio.—Yrs affectly.—J. B. YEATS

If artists are selected, they are selected as experts and therefore ought both to be painters, and this principle ought at once to put Sir T. Drew out of court.

58

This letter was written after Yeats had been about five months in New York with his daughter Lily. (*See* Memoir, *p. 38 et seq.*)

Salmagundi Club
Fourteen West Twelfth Street, New York
May 9th, 1908

My dear Willie—A few days ago I met Olga Nethersole and a young lady, Miss Field, and they both together and separately told me of the

[1] These were members of the Royal Hibernian Society.

extraordinary admiration for your poetry that possesses the young Rostand. He knows English as well as French and translates his father's works. They said he would read out to anyone who would listen your work, and does it hours together. I think perhaps this will interest you.

I have had a good deal of success—real success—since I came here, and I have no doubt but that if I could venture a little, hire a studio for instance, I should soon be in full employment.

I have made several speeches and found myself as much to my own surprise as to any body else's, quite an orator. When I see you I will tell you all about it in my most flamboyant manner.

Lily has been in much trouble of mind—feeling she ought to be at home, yet very reluctant to leave New York where for the first time in her life she has had a personal success, and very reluctant also to go home without me. I do not know whether to stay or go. She sees that I am *making* a success (it is not altogether *made*, since I am only getting 15 dollars—£3— for each sketch) yet wants me to go back with her. I think I ought to stay, but that she ought to be with me. She would be off like a shot if I would consent to go with her—and I do not know what to do. To leave New York is to leave a huge fair where any moment I might meet with some huge bit of luck. Everybody says why not go to Newport whither all fashion is now wending. Some nights I sleep like a top dreaming of luck. Then again I can't sleep at all. Lily says she wishes she had a father who could make plans—so do I—yet how could I make plans? I am like the children of Israel who were not allowed to have plans—only their trust in Jehovah, and that he would provide manna the next morning. . . .

I am perfectly certain that some day you will come and sojourn here for a long while. Next to Ireland here is your country. Here and not else-where you will find destiny.

You are wrong in thinking that the artists here make display of technical skill. A few days ago I wrote to [name indecipherable] introducing a friend, and said the artists here are like Constable and his contemporaries, and are all *pious souls*, thinking nothing of themselves and much of nature.

I have read Swinburne's preface to Blake. In old days as I remember (Nettleship told me) Rossetti would never invite Swinburne without Whistler, who alone was able to keep him from drink. These two little men with aspiring souls—Which taught the other the self-assertiveness, the sacerdotal assumption,—up till then unknown to poets, and quite alien from Shakespeare, as it was from Shelley or Browning? Their attack upon you would be nothing without the insolent airs of infallibility. Swinburne is the poet of surely the thinnest humanity ever known —the damned homunculus, as Walt Whitman said, without sweetheart or wife or child or friend but for Watts Dunton who, kind creature, doubtless toadies him. It takes goodness to be a flatterer. His poetry at best is a sort of choric rhetoric. *The true poet is a solitary, as is man in his great moments.* Shakespeare is so even when he writes his plays.

Lolly keeps us assiduously posted up in the doings of the theatre and your movements. We hear from her every post. Lily keeps on making friends, finding them in all sorts of unexpected places. Her experience here has been a sort of University course for her. It is surprising how well she talks sometimes.

John Quinn is our great standby. With him at hand it is impossible to lose confidence. Sometimes he is low-spirited himself and then recovers courage by angry bragging. I have made immense progress. This practice with the pencil, doing small sketches, portrait sketches, necessitating the closest study is exactly the discipline I wanted. I have had some ill-luck— my best sketch just needed another half-hour, and on the day appointed for it, the lady, the subject of my sketch, lost her brother in suicide, while I lost my fees and an entrance into a most fashionable and wealthy connection. Also it was arranged for me to do a painting (£40 worth) of a lady, but the unexpected happened—the lady is indisposed, being the mother of a large and ever increasing family.

The Fords are most kind.[1] We are stopping at their hotel but charged very little for our rooms. . . .

Your name has been my great *Open Sesame*—at any rate at first. Now I think I have a little position of my own.

By the way you were wrong in thinking Fitzgerald [2] did not appreciate Jack. He told me himself that Jack's only fault was that he did not think enough of his work. His friend Luke also who is supposed to be the coming man here—an Impressionist and Revolutionist—several times lauded Jack both to me and Lily. You have a great position here—the ladies (the next epoch in America belongs to them) meet together to study your *Ideas of Good and Evil*. They go through it as if it was an Act of Parliament where every monosyllable is of importance.

If I could find out that someone had made a mistake about my birth and that I was ten years younger, how my heart would swell!

[1] See letter 59.
[2] Charles Fitzgerald, a dramatic critic in New York, son of Dr. Fitzgerald of Dublin.

J. Quinn says you are the straightest and most generous Irishman he ever met. He says you are always generous—he says this often particularly when he has been railing against Ireland.

Give my kind regards to Lady Gregory.

Lily has decided to go on 21st. I shall be rather desolate—Solitude, *but living alone* in a vast solitude like New York, is not just the form of it I like.

59

The Grand Union Hotel—the address on this letter—where Yeats first stayed in New York, was owned by Simeon Ford, a famous wit in those days, slow of speech but said to be the best after-dinner speaker in the town; he resembled the drawings of America called Uncle Sam. His hotel was one of the oldest in New York; it was sold afterwards as a site for the great New Central station. Miss Yeats writes: 'I saw a ghost the first night I slept in the hotel, a man who had hung himself in the open doorway between my room and the bath room. I asked Mr. Ford if anyone had hung himself in that room, and he said that many people came to the city, spent all their money in other hotels and then came and committed suicide in his'.

Both Mr. and Mrs. Ford established a friendship with Yeats. Yeats often saw them, after they had sold the hotel, at their country place by the sea.

Grand Union Hotel
New York, July 1st, 1908

My dear Willie—Many thanks for your letter. I get so touchy if I don't get letters. Your news about Synge is much better than any hitherto received. We thought him hopelessly ill and that everyone in Dublin knew it except Synge himself. I sent word at once to Quinn—that most intense man will be greatly relieved.[1]

Lily is a great loss to me. I had come to depend on her for everything— *She has such good memory and consequently such good judgment.* She was a wonderful success here, really it is not too much to say that the whole hotel down to the bell boys watched her comings and goings with a kind of affection. All the old ladies living in the Parlours had discussed whether or not they would go and see her off, and finally they decided that being old and some of them on crutches they could not, but *they let her know* that they had thought of it. The Chambermaids stop me in the passages

[1] Synge died early in the following year.

to ask about her and to send regards. Some of them are actually writing. They say 'Ah she had sense'. I think—in fact I know—from her letter that she is profoundly glad to be home—*the sea-sick pilgrimage* all passed and gone, and that wearisome semi-lawsuit as good as settled. She and Lolly render full tribute to your help and also they found Lady Gregory inspiring. When trouble comes (and this to them was gigantic) people find who their friends are.

For the first time in my life I am a success. I used to say I should never be successful without a position—and that therefore success was impossible. Now thanks to your name I got this position—whether I made speeches or made sketches, invisible agents as it were distributed handbills and people listened or watched with admiring attention, so that whether I sketched or made speeches I was able to concentrate all my energies.

At a dinner given lately at Delmonico's by Quinn to 23 guests, 7 of them judges of the Supreme Court, I made the chief oration, and one of the judges, the most famous of them all, a most scholarly and distinguished man, made a long and eloquent speech, the subject being After-dinner Speaking in which he said they had never equalled the men 'of the other side', *and he used me as his example*, and called my speech 'a gem of after-dinner speaking'. My speech was impromptu, or almost so, since I had only heard I was to speak at six o'clock and then at Quinn's office, and the dinner took place at 7 o'clock. I find that when I stand up to speak my mind for the moment becomes *blank*—a sheet of white paper, and that then thoughts begin to pour in on me, pouring in no doubt from the people in front of me—so that I speak with a full mind. Of course I want practice, which I shall now never get—if for instance their attention wanders from me for a moment I am done—like a ship suddenly becalmed.

Just at this moment I am watching anxiously for a letter from Mrs. Osgram. I was at her house for a couple of days and did four sketches (everyone thinks them my best) and now I am trying to induce her to sit for a painting. *If she sits for that painting my future is made.* She is a person of great authority in the social world here, and that picture will be the crowning achievement of my artistic life. She is handsome—artistically most sympathetic, and will sit well. Her children are quaint little things who quarrel together in French or English, whichever comes uppermost and (wonderful in America) well-mannered, due possibly to their having a French Irish governess and French maids. I mean the manners are due to this. You visited them.[1] The Byrnes often speak of you and of some bore that obstructed conversation and of your witty description of him. The Byrnes are surrounded by wealthy people and such people make good sitters. At any rate they pay well. Byrne himself is now in Europe. Mrs. Byrne talks freely and exceedingly intelligently. She says that in England people treated her as if she was a freak. John Bull's preëminence is slipping away so that these airs are becoming a little ridiculous—to me they always have been so—since I had been at school with so many English boys.

To have left America with Lily would have positively broken my heart. This is hardly an exaggeration, but sometimes it is a little lonely now that Lily has gone. Quinn is like a son to me. He is the crossest man I ever met and the most affectionate—affection and crossness go together with him, as with animals when they have their young with them. I seem never to be out of his thoughts. Andrew Lang says the American humourists have no reverence and for that reason Mark Twain and the rest are inferior to Dickens and Thackeray, but they have a tenderness for old age and for weakness that is a passion. The English are too brutal for this—If they have reverence (which with them is a form of self-complacency since it is all reserved for their own past history) they have also aristocratic contempt for anything and everything that is not strong enough to strike back. Andrew Lang is clever but he is too clever—that is too rapid—so that he is not 'deep'. These people write a kind of clever nonsense suitable for after-dinner speaking, which you know is my art.

I wonder, will you read all this, or ought I to get it type-written? I am just reading G. Meredith's *Amazing Marriage*. When his mind is full he writes like Shakespeare; when it is empty he slogs on all the same only with laborious artificiality. His sentences often remind me of Shakespeare, and Shakespeare's of his. For instance, when Ophelia says: 'Rich gifts wax poor when givers prove unkind'—and there are lots of sentences of that sort, all Meredithian in flavour.

If the *Player Queen* [2] is up to its title it will be a great play. I hope before I die that I may see you find yourself and find your public in play writing. You have found yourself and found your public in some of your plays, but not *quite triumphantly*. Democratic art is that sort which unites a whole audience—Is not an Oratorio democratic? and the great religious services and cathedrals and military pomp and oratory, when on the large

[1] A reference to W. B. Yeats's tour in America in the winter of 1904–5.

[2] A play begun by W. B. Y. at this time, but not finished for many years, when it was changed from tragedy into farce.

scale? I am sure that in Ancient Greece drama was democratic. You will say my recent experiences make me love a crowd. Well—a coterie of discontented artists may be something like a tea-party of old maids discussing marriage and large families—perhaps it is the narrow way that leadeth to destruction. In these thoughts I think Lady Gregory ought to agree with me—she has a democratic fibre, as she ought to have for is she not a born leader? I am certain that she must love these people that gather on the benches of the Abbey Theatre.

When Quinn heard of Synge's illness he was like a raging lunatic. He inveighed against you, Russell and myself and all Ireland. He seemed to think that no one cared whether Synge lived or died. He is like that— strong feeling enrages him into easily excited activity, and the hopelessness of activity in this and other cases turns his blood into vitriolic fury. I had a lot of trouble to quiet him. When he is like that he is not a pleasant companion and you must soothe him.

You don't say anything about my lecture. Do you not see that the industrial revival is *a certainty*. Nothing can prevent it *sooner or later*, but intellectually and spiritually everything may be easily lost *and lost for ever*. A gentleman is such simply because he has not the doctrine of getting on and the habit of it. For this reason a poor peasant and a true artist are gentlemen—but people talk as if the doctrine of getting on was greater than all the law and the prophets. In my young days people quite understood all this.

The contest is not against material things, but between those who want to get on and those who don't want to get on, having other important things to attend to. A good play might be written about all this. With kindest regards to Lady Gregory. Believe me, yours affectionately— J. B. YEATS

TO RUTH HART

60

New York
August 26th, 1908

. . . I mustn't write a long letter—long letters are a mistake, they are a bother to read and correspondents are frightened to reply, for they think, they must write at equal length. That is why your mother did not answer my last state paper of a letter. But please do *you* send me something however short, something between a letter and a postcard. I am staying here another year. I won't raise the siege here in New York at any rate till I have gone through another winter.

At present by a piece of good luck, I am in a fine studio with bedroom in the most fashionable part of New York—only till October. If I could have it all next winter I would praise all New York. Send me all the Howth news. My girls know nothing of you hill folk. I see by the papers here that Watson the poet has married 'an Irish girl of the Hill of Howth'. Watson is a poet of renown, on occasions a madman.

I send you a little pencil sketch. Sometime ago going on an expedition into the country where I had sundry commissions awaiting me, I saw the girl in the rain and sketched her surreptitiously; she looked to me so like what I remember Ethel, very pretty only not half as pretty as Ethel [1] and she had Ethel's quick decided ways, and like myself was excited by her journey.

I hope you are all well. I hope to be back next Spring and I hope a conqueror. I shan't lose any time in coming to see you. I used to be prevented coming to see you in the evenings, because of the long journey home afterwards, not that there was fatigue, but that on the way home, in the dark I used to be bludgeoned by a very disagreeable kind of highwaymen, dark spirits full of evil suggestions. I suppose it is what is called the Celtic temperament. I am always in the mornings *cheerful*, and sufficient to myself but in the evenings after Sun-down, it is different story.

Here I dine every night at a queer French restaurant where a large party gather mostly foreign, and dine without either coat or waistcoat—in a garden d'été, which is a backyard. Three good looking young Breton women who used to be servants run the place, all three with pleasing personalities, hospitable and gay.[2] Such quantities of talk, all smoking and drinking claret at 5/d a bottle. The ladies as talkative as the men, the talk sometimes, only sometimes, in English—but I am an artist, and am there to *see*.

I read the papers a great deal and try to write articles on Americans versus English. During the winter months I go every Sunday to New Rochelle and spend the day at Judge Keogh's. In summer they are away. He is well known to Sir H. Plunkett, and Jellett K.C. and Bailey K.C. A Waterford man—came over here when eighteen and is now Judge of

[1] His correspondent's sister, two portraits of whom he had painted: see *Memoir*.
[2] This was 317 W. 29 Street, where he presently went as a boarder.

the Supreme Court, and very well off—a wild Irishman of great force and ability. His wife,[1] grand-niece of the famous Emmet. The Emmets here—(I have met lots of them)—*hold a very high position*, and have not lost any of the charm and urbanity of the Irish Protestant of the 18th century—and they are all clever. Henry James whom they know very well is their cousin—by the way he is in some degree Irish. Mrs. Keogh *constantly* reminds me of your mother; amongst her numerous children she is exactly as I remember your mother. All New York could not manage Judge Keogh, but his wife has him under perfect control. That is the way with *manly* Irishmen. Like the timid race they are, the English organize themselves better, but the Irish are the manlier race. In England the husband rules his wife.

When there are no commissions and dollars are scarce, I get very homesick. All my life I have chased the chimera of success, and sometimes the chimera of art. Willie writes often (for him) and seems in high spirits over his theatre. The theatre has been his Old Man of the Sea, but he hopes soon to get back to lyric poetry, and away from it.

Jack writes that he has been doing well with his pictures, and the girls have done better this year. So it is my turn now to have a little success.

I have made some friends among the artists, that is, the good select artists whom I believe in.

Give my love to your father and mother, and Believe me.—Yours affectly—J. B. YEATS

A Dr. Solomon, who had been staying at the Jamesons, brought me some news of them. It was at their kind suggestion he called to see me.

TO W. B. YEATS

61

Grand Union Hotel
New York, Sept. 28, 1908

My dear Willie—I send you two short stories. I don't know what you will think about them. You will recognise the source whence one of them comes.

I saw at Judge Keogh's young Emmet, who had met you at Lady

[1] She was an Emmet. The Emmets of New York are of the family of Robert Emmet, the Irish patriot, who was executed in 1806.

Judge Keogh, the Emmets, etc.

Gregory's and [whom] I met at [word indecipherable]. It was pleasant to hear about you both, but although he told me he had had a great deal of talk with you he did not tell me much else. He admires Edward Martyn very much, and is an extremely attractive young man.

I am looking forward with much hope and fear to next month after a summer—well! the less said about it the better—even the heat, even the mosquitoes were minor matters, even the loneliness; however, I have come through and I am still afloat tho' with damaged rigging. Quinn like a good storm tug has stood by all the time in a sort of grim faithfulness and he means if he can to tow me into safety and—not to break the wind of the poor metaphor—I may say that the ship is rather old and was originally, though of good timber, not built according to the latest ideas of ship building.

Emmet was delighted with the theatre. I suppose, being a lawyer and a practical man, he was not able to tell much about it either. Besides I only saw him for a short time; afterwards I came into town with Judge Keogh in his auto, he to dine with Redmond, I to get my own dinner and afterwards to go to the Lyric Theatre and hear Redmond speak. The speech was a very finished performance. Bourke Cochrane also spoke, an extraordinary looking man to be an orator and a popular figure—he spoke only a little—not so honest or engaging as Redmond but more interesting, though a sinister kind of interest. I should say a good actor. He is now 'down and out' with the Tammany Party. Quinn blasphemes if his name is mentioned. He is turned out of all his jobs by Murphy and Cohalan. Quinn is now in politics and on *all* the Committees. I think he finds much satisfaction in it.

Judge Dowling sat next to me. In the *academic* sense he is the most cultivated man I have met, he and Charlie Johnston. I have for a long while been busy over an article. It has given me a lot of trouble. Sometimes writing about a subject is like a sailor on a yard single-handed furling a huge sail in a gale of wind—patience and strength and cunning, all necessary, while the sail is trying to fling him into the sea, and will do so if luck does not help as well.

I like the Keoghs very much. Mrs. Keogh is one of the nicest women I ever met. Mrs. James Byrne is nice also, but Mrs. Keogh has more character and if I may say so is less of an *eclectic*. She embodies the American tradition and breeding at its best, and mind that is something very fine. She is a proud woman, of herself and of the Emmets. Judge Keogh tells them they would have been nothing if that poor boy hadn't been hanged. Young as she is she is grand-niece of the poor boy. All the

Judge Keogh, the Emmets, etc.

Emmets pride themselves on their courage, make a vaunt of it. Keogh tells me that when surgical operations are necessary they refuse chloroform.

Lately I have been frequenting a French restaurant where the dinner is cheap and the company amusing, and among these last a marquis and marquise, with whom I have become friendly. They are quite young, he a Spaniard, great linguist and *very* musical. I dined there the other day and heard some fine music. After dinner Madame said: 'Mr. Yeats, this is my birthday: Mr. Yeats, you must kiss me'. Before I knew where I was I was kissing Madame on both cheeks—it was done with a sort of brutal violence that caused me to remember that 'baiser' is in French what we call 'kiss'. The first is a pistol shot, and the last a whisper.

The French restaurant is a mild dissipation—my French friends don't come any longer, so it has got milder, I am sorry to say. Living here thinking about articles which won't come and waiting for promised letters from promising patrons which don't come either is a little dreary.

Thanks to Quinn I did a portrait of a Miss Coates whom you met in Paris. She has that kind of cleverness which draws all its ideas from the outside, not from within. The effect is that after a time you become exhausted and depleted, since she cannot replenish you. This is a little obscure, but she was a good subject to paint, only being an American woman she would not let me have my way. However on this matter Quinn and I hold opposite opinions as he backed her up and ruined the portrait. In America liberty is not understood, either for artists or any one else. They are so mad for justice that liberty comes second best. If we had liberty who'd bother about justice. England is the only country where they understand liberty, and there consequently no one cares about justice.

As I told you, I have been an unexpected success as a speaker. I spoke again some time ago at the Salmagundi club—my theme was that, though in America they could praise and denounce, they could not criticise—to praise and denounce is ethical and puritanical—Carlyle is here the prophet. To criticise is to neither praise or denounce, but to *get nearer your subject*, and here we have Charles Lamb for teacher. One does not get very close to what one admires. It is this sort of attitude that makes Swinburne so tiresome. It is the father that admires and praises; it is the mother that loves and criticises (I do like to hear Mrs. Keogh talking about her children). Out of this criticism, out of this effort *to get nearer to things* comes realism, of which we have had enough, but also the *intimate touch* of Shakespeare and the great poets.

Will it amuse Lady Gregory to hear that young Emmet was very much surprised to find her so quiet. As there was only a minute I don't know what he meant. Can it be that clever women here have established a record for being noisy and *prancing*.

I am watching the election with much interest, though without any insight. I have no one to instruct me. Quinn has not the time, or I should say the patience.—Yours affectionately—J. B. YEATS

If I were 40 years younger I could be a great success. An old artist seeking work is like a ticket of leave man looking for a situation—either of them might run away with the spoons!

TO HARRIET JAMESON

62

Grand Union Hotel
Oct. 9, 1908

. . . The Americans, because of the fact, the disagreeable fact, that they have not the slightest respect or sympathy for Art or artists, make first-rate drawing masters. From start to finish it is constant quarrelling. In a hard nasal voice come constantly the words, 'Yes but that does not appeal to me', and this in spite of the fact that everyone except the sitter finds the likeness perfect. These are not the conditions for imaginative art—Titian and his Venetian school could not have made a living in New York—but they are ideal conditions for learning how to draw, and over here the rule which prevails in Great Britain of half the money being due after the first sitting does not apply. They don't take the portrait if they don't like it. . . . Lately I painted a girl. She is long-legged, high-shouldered, languid-eyed, lazy, luxurious, spoiled, decadent and rich. I started with my own idea and apparently hers and designed my portrait thus (sketch), the background a scarlet curtain and the dress blue, the 'waist' loose. When the portrait was nearly, if not quite, finished, some fool of a woman, a sort of parasite of hers, came in and said it did not do justice—etc. The result was that she insisted on being painted thus (sketch), and when I demurred she sweetly said, as she waved her fan, that she would not take it if I did not change it . . . my opinion never counted. . . .

TO W. B. YEATS

63

Grand Union Hotel, New York
Nov. 11th, 1908

My dear Willie—Your letter just received for which many thanks. You don't give me any clue as to which story of mine you read. There were two. I am very sorry that I sent them, but I shall now be very much obliged if you will send them back to me as soon as possible. *I want them.* Of one of the stories 'The Ghost Wife' I have no other copy.

I am very glad you told me those sayings of Mrs. Campbell. I shall be very curious to see her act. It is an everlasting wonder from the beginning of time how some women climb to such giddy pinnacles of fame, *their minds being all the time quite banal and flat.* I suppose it is one of the marvels of will power, they using their physical gifts as men use their money— what will can do is to me a constant amazement. The gods themselves fight in vain against stupidity because the gods themselves do in their turn become infected by this stupidity when it lodges in a fair woman.

It is a struggle to get on here. I have written and sent for acceptance two articles, one on conversation, the other on manners, each with reference to America, but with *modesty and adroitness.* I am also engaged on a story, which I won't send to you. . . .

I met Mrs. Isadora (Duncan) privately and just missed seeing her dance in private. She is self-contained and regulates her life according to her own ideas, being, as such women are, free to do so. She said some daring things in a rather captivating way. People are much divided about her merits, the rival parties hating each other like the Capulets and the Montagues. The young girls are full of enthusiasm for her. Those a little older puzzled and somewhat shocked, the elder ladies furious. She herself wears a bonnet with a long veil and has a most demure expression.—Yours affectionately —J. B. YEATS

64

N.Y.
Undated (1908)

. . . Just at the time when I got your letter about Mrs. P. Campbell I was meeting Isadora Duncan. It seems to me that *great personal charm only belongs to people who are self-contained or when they are so.* They only can say and do the *spontaneous* and the *unsuspected*—everything Miss Duncan says is curiously interesting; it never becomes 'chatter', such as those things you quoted from Mrs. Campbell, but which probably I should not have thought 'chatter' had I been under the influence of Mrs. Campbell's physical beauty. An American lady a few days ago described Miss Duncan as old, at least middle-aged, and 'homely' (American for ugly). I first met her in a restaurant and at once understood her to be the oddest and most unexpected person in the world. She forms her own plans and is quite indifferent to what people think or say, for that reason she is never aggressive just as she makes no effort to conciliate any one. I met her twice in private and since that I saw her (from her own box) dancing in the biggest theatre, and on the biggest stage in N. York—a figure dancing all alone on this immense stage—and there again you felt the charm of the self-contained woman. Several people said: Is it not like watching a kitten playing for itself? We watched her as if we were each of us hidden in ambush. I don't wonder that at first New York rejected her—she stood still, she lay down, she walked about, she danced, she leaped, she disappeared, and re-appeared—all in curious sympathy with a great piece of classical music, and I did not sometimes know which I most enjoyed, her or the music. America's great sculptor was in the box and led the appreciation.

Quinn says she dances like a cow &c. and has beefy limbs—he also says that tho' he paid for a very expensive seat he only stayed half an hour. Exactly! he did not stay long enough. The other day there was an enormous house who were as still as if we were in church, except that no one coughed. Genée the rival dancer whom Quinn likes so much has the other *the lesser charm*, that she is eager for appreciation and popular affection, and is indeed a delightful creature—*you wish her to succeed*, in the other case you are dominated.

TO HARRIET JAMESON

65

N. Y. (*1908*)

. . . Remember I am as much in love with the country as ever. They don't understand art and have no manners, but there runs through all ranks a goodness and kindness, and their humour is all based on this kind-ness. It is as if the stern countenances of the Pilgrim Fathers had [word indecipherable] into a grim mother, full of pity . . . pity but yet no indul-gence. When there is indulgence you get sentimentality which is just the opposite to humour—especially American humour. English humour is based in cruelty, in order that they may enjoy the consciousness of their strength and superiority. They strike bare your weakness and inadequacy, exposing you in shivering nakedness to their laughter and wits. The Americans are the kindest people I ever met, but they are the grimmest. They keep their countenances sour. The little children do it. . . . I look round the various tables and can at once 'spot' an English person by his smiling countenance and talkativeness for which he would not be dis-tinguished anywhere else. [Sketches, see facsimile.]

TO W. B. YEATS

66

Grand Union Hotel
New York, Mar. 24, 1909

My dear Willie—I enclose a little paragraph taken from 'The Sun' to show you that Percy Mackaye who is so enthusiastic about my play is a person of some position, and now let me add these remarks. I think the reason you have the popular gift is because your *talent is benign*. That is its essential quality—[word indecipherable] are *malign*; so are aristocracies and pessimists—it is the *whole* of Nietzsche—so are College Dons and *their retinue*; but so were not Shakespeare or Shelley. Had the latter lived he would have proved it. His 'passion to reform the world' which he him-self avowed made him quarrelsome, but later on, the quarrels over, he would have been wholly benign. Just think about Shakespeare and how he was at his best when most benign. Wordsworth was malign, so was Byron and so is Swinburne. These people could not get away from their self-importance. They must denounce and scold. This benign quality you get from me; I say this remembering my father's family. They all of them in every fibre of their being were 'the Good people', in a sense the fairies are not. For that reason people loved them but did not fear them, so they passed making no mark.

I am lecturing on you next Friday and have been to the Johnstons to learn something about you and I am trying to get hold of Gregg.[1] I think you would like very much the intimate knowledge Charlie Johnston shows with your work and Mrs. Johnston also, and the spirit in which they speak.

I am reading your *Ideas of Good and Evil* with growing wonder and pleasure and also your poems. You are at your best in verse. Not because verse in itself is superior to prose, but because you are more wholly yourself. Prose is fettering, verse is lightness and freedom and *coaxes* the soul out of you.

I am *painting* a life size half length of my rich and great and stout lady, and getting on, I can tell you.[2] If it finishes as well as it has begun I shall be a great man, my head striking the stars. She is daughter of an ambassador and had her husband lived he would have been Bismarck's successor. She is clever because of her quick and abundant perceptions and would have been a great barrister. My tendency over a portrait is always to become too much interested and lose my head. This time so far I have been astute.

I hope Lady Gregory is getting quite well.—Yours affectionately—
J. B. YEATS

67

Grand Union Hotel, N.Y.
April 14, 1909

I have just read two volumes of Bernard Shaw. How naturally and inevitably he rises out of Irish Evangelical life (not Belfast). The Protestant *sauve qui peut* trying for religion and finding it in socialism; also he is still the evangelical superior person.

68

Grand Union Hotel, New York
April 14, 1909

. . . I send you a paper with two things marked. One refers to the aforementioned Percy Mackaye. He is author of a play called *Mater*. It was

---

[1] Frederick Gregg, a northern Irishman, formerly belonged to W. B. Y.'s youthful circle in Dublin, and worked for the New York *Evening Sun*. In the distant past he had been considered by AE and others as Ireland's hope in poetry.
[2] See letter 68.

written specially with the idea of Ellen Terry's taking the principal part. The objection to her is that being seventy-one, she can no longer be relied on to remember her words quite accurately. It was produced here some time ago, with what results I forget. Percy Mackaye is the man who was so taken with my play (described to him) that he told me he felt sure if I submitted its scenario he could get me a *commission* to write it. He spoke of the matter to me not once but a dozen times.

I am now seriously thinking of giving a series of lectures. I find lecturing come quite easily *when I know my subject,*—this last is the rub.

. . . My life-size half-length portrait of Mrs. Phelps (daughter of a great German statesman and wife of Phelps, American Ambassador at Berlin) will be finished in next sitting. I think it is a great success, at least would be among artists. It is, however, different from other artists' work, and I have no big reputation to give it vogue. However I have done well in my own estimation and my other friends praise it. These however are all rich people and judge works of art by the reputation of the artist and the price he charges. The lady is very rich and very grand and always talks in a sort of official language. One of her most intimate friends is the sister of the Kaiser. She is about 35 years old and very stout and tall. Had she been poor she would have been very intelligent and kind-hearted and simple.

. . . I shall be very glad to get home, provided I can make it peace with honour. I do so long for my studio and my armchair—here it is *fever.* One moment I am quite happy and then the next moment very much the reverse. I have often lost a night's sleep—time goes on—this month I shall be 70. Miss Butt who attained that dignified age some months ago laughs at me and mocks me with my approaching fate.

I am glad you have inherited the Pollexfen orderliness, only don't let it freeze you as it has done George. A low vitality in his case has been a most marked trait, because of it he is in a state of constant quarrel with life and with everybody in it, since it takes him weeks to shake off a painful impression. A little more vitality and he would be the most loving and humane of men and not so orderly—he is very proud of the courage with which he can face dentists and surgeons—possibly a low vitality means a dull sensibility to physical pain. It was Mrs. Johnston who drew my attention to the importance of a high vitality. . . .

. . . I am delighted with Shannon's portrait of you. It is miles ahead of the Sargent—in conception and execution. Sargent, Kipling and Sarolea give people what they like—a vigorous, brilliant, above all a clear statement of facts. No poetry or dreams to obscure or impair the statement. Corot, Shannon, etc. gives us a statement of emotion and the facts suffer.

The winter has been extraordinarily mild, but just now it is frightfully cold.

Some time ago I saw a letter from you to Charlie Johnston. It seemed to me rather laconic and cold written to an old friend and a good friend. Mrs. Chas. Johnston told me that they both worked very hard for you before you arrived. She said Charlie and Quinn were both 'too bossy' ever to get on together—there is no doubt about their loyalty to you.[1]

Yours affectionately—J. B. YEATS

TO MISS GRIERSON

69

J. B. Yeats declared once that the English had been too prosperous and success-ful for too long. He said this had caused them to lose a real sense of love for their country, and that they would only regain that love in days of defeat and disaster. When, he said, they are flying before the hosts of the victorious —— (here he paused for a word) Irish, they will worship the sacred soil under their feet—they will kiss each blade of grass, each grain of sand, etc., etc.

Grand Union Hotel, New York
June 2, 1909

My dear Miss Grierson—I ought to have answered your letter long ago, particularly when you write under circumstances of so much anxiety, as to which, after this long time, I hardly dare to question you.

It was very kind of you to write to me and I was very glad to get your letter and flattered to find you had not forgotten me. I hardly know when I shall return. I may come back very soon and may stay on. A sort of duty and a sort of gambling excitement keep me here. In Dublin nothing happens except an occasional insolvency—here *anything* may happen. At

[1] Charles Johnston, son of an Orange M.P., was at the High School, Dublin, with W. B. Yeats, who influenced him considerably. He became a leader of the Dublin Theosophists, married the niece of Madame Blavatsky, and entered the Indian Civil Service. His later life was lived in New York. In another letter J. B. Yeats says that Johnston has described his son as 'the most self-centred man I ever knew, but not in the least selfish'.

present I am making ventures into pastel drawing, charging a little more for my work, it takes long but is more attractive. I have only just begun it. The difficulty is to get sittings. People will sit once and with great enthusiasm but a second sitting is a burden not to be borne. They are like that about everything, yet not always, I have met most patient sitters and the *finest friends*, so long-suffering and so tenacious. The more I see of the Americans, the more I admire them—what you hear in Ireland and in England is all lies. I believe myself they are far ahead of all nations, and will in time produce the greatest poetry and the greatest art. At present, young and old, they have all the naïveté and attractiveness of young University students, that is, when those students are swept by some great wave of enthusiasm —loyalty or patriotism—or better still for some idea.

The American gentleman to my mind, is far ahead of the English or Irish gentleman, a truer dignity and unselfishness, and such an alert mind and will. I heard yesterday of a German schoolmarm who said the American man lacked dignity. Of course the poor slave missed the heavy foot of her German taskmaster placed upon her neck. A servile race like a strong máster. It is always easier to obey *if you dare not disobey*. German women are to their lords like so many black beetles.

Lately I have been staying for some days in a long settled part of the country, three hours' express train journey up the Hudson, and this had all the repose and charm of English scenery, only the repose was deeper and the houses, big and little, more homelike. In England one has to shut one's eyes to so much. The summer is now beginning. In the old country we dread the winter, here it is the summer, with its heat, its mosquitoes, and its aridness. . . . and to me personally there is the dread of people being away and of no commissions. That would mean starvation. Last summer was dreadful.

In art they do very well here but will do much better. Everybody is too eager for real art or poetry, too much sense of responsibility . . . art only comes when there is *abandon*, and a world of dreaming and waiting and passionate meditation. It is only when *time hangs heavy on our hands* that we turn to art and demand the right thing from artists and dramatists and poets and painters. Here they are too busy with the material conditions of happiness, as yet they have not addressed themselves directly to happiness. And happiness . . . what is it? I say it is neither virtue nor pleasure nor this thing or that, but simply *growth*. We are happy when we are growing. It is this primal law of all nature and the universe, and literature and art are the cosmic movements working in the conscious mind. I said this a few days ago at a literary club and it was hailed with shouts of welcome, lots of people coming round to introduce themselves and shake hands. Anybody coming to America soon realises that hitherto his education has been provincial.

I see a very illmannered and impudent and lying attack has been made on my son's management of the Abbey Theatre. It is so *patently* lying and spiteful, that I think it will entirely fail of its object. I rather hope my son has taken no notice of it. It is written by a great friend of ours, but she is a woman, which means that some men are behind it—she herself, left to herself, is incapable of spite. The article appeared in *Sinn Fein*.

I showed the article to an editor here and he said that an article of that kind, so low in tone, could not appear in the yellowest journal here, 'there would be such an outcry.' Did you see the article? I could send you a copy. Please give my kind regards to your Mother and to your sister.—Yours very truly—J. B. YEATS

FROM W. B. YEATS

70

Oct. 10, 1909

Coole Park, Gort
Co. Galway

My Dear Father—There is an unfinished letter to you on Lady Gregory's typewriter—I was dictating it, but she went to Dublin a week ago to start rehearsing her new play and to fight down a quarrel between two of our players, a lovers' quarrel. Each one said that he or she would leave the company if the other did not stop his or her insults during rehearsals. It is always the way with the members of the company—when they are out, they are very much out. I have intended to write for a long while, though I think it is you who owe me a letter, but I have been in a dream trying to get my new play finished for Mrs. Campbell on Nov. 1st.[1] I have now abolished all my work for four months. I started quite afresh and am as a result in the highest spirits, a scheme before it is carried out always seems so delightful. . . .

I think you may have thought I was not interested in your letter, because I did not reply to some criticism in it. The criticism interested me very greatly. It is just the sort of letter I delight in getting from you. How

[1] *The Player Queen*. It was not finished for many years.

are the pastels of the girl whose sisters are married to French noblemen? I do not remember any pastels of yours. I agree with what you wrote about Russell.[1] I think he has set his ideal in so vague and remote a heaven that he takes the thoughts of his followers off the technique of life, or leaves only their poorer thoughts for it. No one has ever come to anything under his influence. The poets he gathers begin with a little fire but grow worse and worse. I am still reading Balzac. I have only four or five of the forty volumes left to read. How he hates a vague man,—there is a certain poet in one of his books, Canalis by name, who is Russell, without Russell's honest heart.

I shall go to Dublin in a few days and get to London in November when I shall give some lectures for the money's sake. I will then return to Dublin and take charge of the theatre, as this is its time of crisis. All depends on our getting the capital.

I met an American woman in London who said to me: 'Your father, we think, is the best talker in New York.'

I have found your two stories—they were among papers of Lady Gregory's. I must have lent them to her and asked her to read them. I send them to you. The one without a name is much the best, I think.—Yours affectionately   W. B. YEATS

TO OLIVER ELTON

71

317 W. 29, N.Y.
Nov. 11, 1909

There are no critics in America and the critical mind is non-existent. At first it was a constant disappointment that if I asked what sort of a person Mrs. B was, or Mr. B, I could get by way of reply nothing but enthusiastic appreciation. They are in that primitive state in which people think that to criticise is to condemn. How Chas. Lamb would have puzzled them.

The fact is, we are in the midst of a vast creative impulse—a wave which started years ago and has not yet exhausted itself on any shore.

[1] J. B. Y. had written that 'Dowden and George Russell [AE] are at once mystics and materialists. . . . [AE] would cure all the ills of Ireland by setting up a priesthood and a church and be as anxious for the material prosperity of his devotees as other churches are, and for the same reason. Liberation has no value for him except as a mystical doctrine.'

Hence this restlessness.—Of course they are too Puritan, so that their ideals are towards practical life, and what pertains to practical life, on didactic poetry.

TO W. B. YEATS

72

317 West 29th St., New York City
March 5th, 1910

My dear Willie—I did not have any manuscript for my lecture only notes, it is easier for me to talk than to write. My theme was as I have told you the antagonism between will and human nature. Will represents abstract ideas. The will power is like the police in a city, and sometimes as you know, there are cities like Berlin where everything is in the hands of the police, and then again there are other places like villages in the west of Ireland where one is only aware of the concrete facts of human nature; in the ways, humours, voices and looks of the people; or as in London in the time of Queen Elizabeth—which probably was very like what New York would be if there were no police here, only on a very minute scale. In those days a man went out into the street, if a gentleman, with his hand on the hilt of his sword and the meanest messenger did not go abroad without his staff and his buckler; and as to what happened among the boys and girls—therein probably the priests had to toil continually. Human nature without will, things become like Sodom and Gomorrah— it becomes decadent and abominable. On the other hand too much will, too much strenuousness, too much efficiency, and there is no chance for the poor fine arts or for literature. Yet will must be the servant of humanity, not humanity the servant of will. Wordsworth to my mind was a sort of servile poet enforcing always will power. Browning who was only interested in conduct, much the same, and Shelley suffered also, wasting himself in conflict with the servitude to which Wordsworth complacently yielded. In England character always means a man in whom the will power is predominant, it is in fact the bureaucratic mind, and is as interesting as Berlin governed by its police. Such men are valuable for administering empires, provided they are directed and controlled by people who touch life at many points as do young Irishmen at the present moment, since though without the modern Englishman's will power they have the ancient Elizabethan Englishman's abundance and variety of human nature and therefore their initiative and charm—as the natives could tell you. Had Shakespeare possessed a strong will or *an admiration* for it he would have gone over like Browning and Wordsworth to the side of the authorities and the preceptors instead of remaining as he did among aristocratic 'publicans and sinners'. As you know he often speaks of doom and punishment but always as if he was a sinner whose feelings were with his fellow sinners. A schoolmaster might know his schoolboys very well, yet he could not know them or write about them as it would be done by one of themselves. He could not get *inside the skin*, as Synge does in his plays. My complaint is that all literature has gone over to the side of the schoolmaster and that it used to be carried on by the boys themselves. Also I complain that it requires very little human nature to carry on modern English civilization but a great deal of will power, very little intellect also. I myself, for instance, have enough intellect and more than enough to carry on a mercantile business; but my complicated human feelings for and with people and for happiness would probably very soon trip up my feeble will power. It is the men of will who rule the modern England; she breeds dull men as we in Ireland breed bright men. In Ireland we still pursue more or less the simple life and Irish human nature is still a bird uncaged. Personality to my mind is human nature when undergoing a passion for self-expression. This whether a *dry personality* like Rockefeller or a *full-blooded* one like Roosevelt—it is character in movement to declare itself.

The value of Protestantism is that it enforced will power by the powers of superstition. It did not need much intelligence to learn by rote the ten commandments and understand them, but it needed a great deal of will power to do them. The Catholic religion cares very little about morality but enforces religion by the power of superstition, and you are saved by having a poetical mind; unfortunately with the intellect and the will power left out. Protestantism produces poetry which is mainly oratorical and didactic or hysterically rebellious. Catholicism produces poets in abundance, but being without intellectual strength, they have no desire to think or write. Shakespeare and Milton, we must remember, began their lives under Catholic tuition and influences and then 'got' free thought and arrived too early to suffer from the deadening effects of Protestantism.

The English have become great through Protestantism; that is if we are content to call great what to me is mere bigness. If only we could get rid of the gospel of getting on and the deluded people who preach it and we could bring the right teachers to the peasants in the west of Ireland, the musicians and the *free thinkers and the artists*, and could touch those lips with the wand of the enchanter. If at the same time we could by some miracle free them from the fear of starvation and give them the kind of large and comfortable ease which every Englishman possessed when there were only about 5,000,000 in all England, population being then kept down by plague and pestilence and by the fact that then immigration was as impossible as armed invasion. . . .

England being merry because death was so busy. As to my philosophy I gathered it in from all sources chiefly in a way from York Powell, but never would have found it had I not been an Irishman, the son of an Irish Evangelical father. . . .

When I say I learned it from York Powell, I am quite aware that he would have *rejected all my doctrines*, but that is because I am a better Powellite than he ever was. Powell had an *inductive* mind—my mind is deductive. He could not draw conclusions. I can. An ejaculation, an animosity, an affection from him would set me thinking—that's why I always found him so profitable. I was the priest to interpret the Pythian utterances.

Of course the early Englishman used not his will power but *his personality to enchant his followers*. Will power makes the disciplinarian and the martinet. The leader is a man full of the witchery of a man who is all flexible with human nature—hot one moment, cold the next. Napoleon was like that—he did not bear the least resemblance to the modern English *machine*. We follow such men because they are so visibly enjoying themselves. Napoleon was always an *improvisatore. We follow happiness wherever we see it*, even to our own destruction, following it we seem, because of our sympathy, to possess it. We follow duty because we are *taught* to do so. I always think a great orator convinces us not by force of reasoning, but because he *is visibly enjoying the beliefs which he wants us to accept*. This is my recollection of Isaac Butt. The cause he was fighting for enshrined itself in him—to follow him seemed health which is another name for happiness.

At last spring has come, and it is welcome. I used to be miserable with intervals of happiness, now I am happy with intervals of misery, because I am doing better *and have more funds*, and all because I left the Hotel and came to these apartments.—Yours affectionately—J. B. YEATS

73

Grand Union Hotel
New York [1910]

... Do you remember staying with a Mrs. Worthington at her country house down the Hudson, somewhere? She is a very great friend of John Quinn's and is helping me; she is a person of some social importance. She also met you in London when you introduced her to Symons. On hearing of his illness she at once in a sort of tempest of feeling (you know the American woman) wrote to you asking about him. She has several times referred to this letter and to-day she asked me to ask you if you ever received it. She is a very nice woman, *really valued* by Quinn, and *valuable to me*, so perhaps you could write to her. She is a sort of Duchess over here. Socially clever and a friend to all the distinguished people—she is an intimate friend of the musician Elgar. Altogether perhaps you will think it well not to leave her letter unanswered. ...

A few days ago I met a Miss Hornbrick who seems to have known very intimately the Symons's. She tells me Mrs. Symons idolized her husband; she added that she was very ambitious for him, also that Symons had altered from the days of the Temple—that there was too much of the Duchess of Sutherland in his conversation, she thought. I asked was this due to the ambitious wife. To an artist an ambitious wife would be a curse—as regards everything, art or career. Ambition sets up external standards; by ambition the rebel angels fell and so do the artists.

I have just sent an article on American women to *Harper's Weekly*. I am lecturing on Art in relation to life at the Barnard Club on February 2nd.

If I had a studio and peace of mind for a few weeks I would start a great career here as a portrait painter, but alas, it is impossible—no money.

I find Mrs. Charles Johnston one of the most interesting women in New York—I am tempted to think she is the most interesting. She is so wise and also noble-minded and sincere.

I am dining to-day with Harrington Mann and his wife and another English artist named Gray, a friend of George Moore and Dermond O'Brien and John's &c. He says Moore is an enthusiastic admirer of yours—how lately he has seen Moore I don't know.

I am afraid you don't like my letters when I urge you as I have always done to use your popular gifts. You will, some day when I am dead and gone.[1]

Weather is summer-like.—Yours affectionately—J. B. YEATS

74

317 W. 29th Street, New York
March 8, 1910

My dear Willie—I think my last letter will show that we are quite of the same mind and that your splendid sentence 'character is the ash of personality' has my full assent. When I read it out to a friend here, he said: 'Ash is soft and character is hard', then he reflected and added half to himself, 'but *lava* is hard'. English educational methods are producing *character*, when as I have often pointed out they should seek to produce *personality*. I will send you my article on Englishmen compared with Americans. I have not sent it because the Editor cut out such a lot that I considered the article did not represent me any longer. What was cut I have now embodied in a new article which I mean to send them. Gladstone's personality never sank down into *Ashes*, though he had been a good deal injured by their methods at Eton and elsewhere—was always getting himself *into line* with his dull followers. In one of my lectures I pointed out that he would have been a much finer man had he been brought up like Sheridan, and Beaconsfield would not have had occasion to say he had not a redeeming vice, for his personal potentialities were of the finest. Napoleon or Nelson were [word indecipherable] even in their own trade unless roused by some *primal passion*. Both these men improvised. Napoleon's hatred for England would endure for months, long enough for him to make all his preparations.

I am going to read Browning's 'Strafford' and afterwards Strafford's life and find whether he did not alter the facts to suit a poet of the abstract will.—Yours affectionately—J. B. YEATS

75

317 West 29th, N.Y.
April 7th, 1910

My dear Willie—A really great friend of mine is going to London and Paris and Dublin. He leaves this May 28th—Fred King is Literary and

[1] Not a bad prophecy, as W. B. Yeats ended by writing ballads, which he hoped would be sung in public houses.

F. King

Dramatic Editor of the *Literary Digest* (he is also a friend of Chas. and Mrs. Johnston)—he has been to me extraordinarily kind. He has a most attractive and receptive nature, collects rare editions. . . . I would ask you to show him any kindness you can. *I am sure you will like him.* I think he is the most unselfish man I have ever met and the most natural (I have often said this). He has the same pleasure in doing anyone else a service that other people have in looking after their own interests. He wanted me to visit with him his home in New England *at his cost.* As you know an American always likes to pay his guest's expenses. I am very fond of him, yet I don't believe he expects me to be fond of him. You can see he is a person whom it is a pleasure to do a good turn to—it is so easy to please him. His brother is a distinguished musician. Lily knows him well and will recognise this sketch. (Sketch.) He and his friends think her a person of the most surpassing wit and charm. His friends are innumerable. At heart he is very timid because very modest, even though sometimes he has a little of the warlike New England manner as when he says 'What t t t t t' in what I tell him is Ulster accent. Only an Ulster man and a New Englander can say 'what' as if it ended in a multitude of t's. He likes to think he is from Devonshire. Next to Quinn and Mrs. Ford he has done most for me. It was he that got up my 100 dollar lecture besides commissions for portraits.

I am now busy with two lectures, one for an Irish Club which will pay me 25 dollars, the other for the Church of the Ascension, 5th Avenue, for which I will get nothing, but it means fame, and my subject is 'The human side of the Catholic Church by an ultra-Protestant'. The title is, you will see, a *stroke of genius*—to be delivered May 1st. I am of course very anxious.

I have also to write an article on the Women's Suffrage for the *Harper's Weekly*. It will be my fourth article for them. My portrait of John O'Leary is now exhibiting at 'The Independent Artist', a sort of rival body just launched in antagonism to the Academy here.

King goes away on a six weeks' holiday—he is greatly pleased. I wish you *would introduce him to some of your distinguished literary friends*. He is a genuine literary man, though perhaps he will always remain a sort of novice, yet with the graces of the novice who is also modest. All American literary men are novices.—Yours affectionately—J. B. YEATS

Sincerity

TO OLIVER ELTON
76

317 W. 29 St.
Sept. 23, 1910

Poets love sincerity, not because of high morality, as Browning the pros[a]ist would put it, but because they love freedom; freedom is the condition of their existence. Poets also are solitary (however sociable) and for that reason are the friends of true marriage, while their hatred of insincerity makes them hostile to false marriage. Marriage is to the solitary who is behind every man, and most of all behind the poet, a hermitage and a well-fenced solitude. What America needs to rescue it from its unrest and its delirious collectivism is *poets and solitaries*, men who turn aside and live to themselves and enjoy the luxury of their own feelings and thoughts.—Poets here are orators—have to be so, since the public is their paymaster and ready to pay them handsomely if only they will desert their caves of solitary personal feeling and come out and work for their generous and affectionate masters.

TO W. B. YEATS
77

New York
Novr. 29, 1910

. . . Augustus John's portrait of Quinn is wonderfully fine. I admire it very much. Only Quinn is a much better-looking man. If I had my old studio here in New York I'd paint him and beat them all. I am a far more sensitive painter than any of them. I say that after seeing (last week) my portrait of John O'Leary hung among the best portraits here in New York in an Exhibition called 'The Independents' . . .

TO RUTH HART
78

New York
Decr. 15th, 1910

Altho' my brain is all frozen up with cold and botheration, I must write and wish you and your father and mother and all of you, a happy Xmas and a glad New Year.

Home Thoughts—Friendly New York

I saw Charles Fitzgerald the other night, and until one o'clock I kept questioning him, putting him through what the Police here call the third degree, so as to get all the news. He was in the best of spirits, and full of the most joyous recollections of Dublin. How people do love Dublin! It has a kind of Parisian gaiety, and good heart, bad luck to all the croakers who talk against it; 'here's better health to you girls', as a man I used to know said when his pretty wife and her sister both fainted because of something or other—he sitting on at the table slowly sipping a glass of port, and never budging from it. There is no news. I have sworn a deep oath that I will not spend another Xmas in New York—a powerful home-returning instinct possesses me. It has always been there, and at Xmas it gets terrible —and *now worse than ever*. I do *so long to see you all at Howth*—tho' now you are scattered, so that I shall have to go looking for you, finding you in several houses. I would like a visit of a few days' duration at Woodside, that I might have some long talks with your mother. I fancy I could amuse her with things about New York. She and I have one thing in common, we are interested in people, like Wm. Shakespeare. There are people who are only interested in *things*; and these people always give themselves airs and say 'they don't like gossip', but Shakespeare, your mother and I like to talk about people. I fancy in Elizabethan times they talked nothing but gossip when they assembled in the Coffee houses— there was nothing else to talk about when there were no papers or maga-zines or suffragettes, or novels. To be sure they used to listen to long sermons but that was after Shakespeare's time. The sermons drove out the players and the playwrights, and England has got duller and duller ever since—and the people who could not stand the sermons migrated to Dublin. You know what is called the Irish brogue is simply English of the 16th century. Shakespeare now would have to get some peasants from Kerry to read to him his own plays, our reading of them would only affront 'gentle Shakespeare'.

Charles Fitzgerald talked a lot about 'Ethel Babbington' (how strange the name sounded!) but had not seen Hilda which he much regretted. He praised you and Nora a lot, and spoke of your mother's persistent youth. I think Charles' good spirits were in some degree due to his delight at finding himself again in New York—for this is the friendliest place in the world. Everybody so young, not a croaker in all New York, except here and there an unhappy Englishman who only gets laughed at for his pains, unless he turns very crusty, when he is dropped out of notice and out of memory—after a bit however he generally recovers and shows himself a very decent fellow, considering. Charles is a good talker—because he is so frank, never concealing his thought—and then he has the open ingenuous and *wide* mind of the American which nothing startles and nothing frightens. Elsewhere people are so anxious and timid, and from deadly fear, so distrustful of each other. Here the idea still exists, handed down from Early Settler days, of mutual helpfulness. They have a weak sense of law and of property, and are not enthusiastic over their civic duties but they easily become your friend—a real friend with an open hand. And *there is no class*. You have to come to America to find out the blessedness of those words.

Ever my love to your father and mother and believe me.—Yours affectly —J. B. YEATS

TO W. B. YEATS

79

317 West 29th Street, New York
Feb. 4, 1911

My dear Willie—Many thanks for the £5 and for sending it in a form easily cashed.

Last night about 1 o'clock I was at Quinn's apartment with John Sloan, and Quinn suddenly said 'Mr. Yeats, do me a portrait of yourself of such and such a size, and you can charge me what you like and there's Sloan for witness'. So I am now once more a contented and tranquil spirit, and *very sorry indeed* that I wrote to you as I did a few days ago . . .

I find writing for the Editors here a good discipline—I really have learned to trust their judgment. I think also *young America* is doing very well in art. Sloan paints New York and etches it—above all its war of the poor against the rich—and tho' a Socialist he keeps his pictures pure art. Their writing both in books and papers seems to me to be often very immature—nothing thought out—either the words or the ideas. Everybody is in too great a hurry; as they themselves say; they are engagingly frank in acknowledging their faults, and are good children. Some words of yours about the result of the Black Death in England *destroying the traditions* of [word indecipherable] &c. are exactly applicable to this country. As the people learn English and forget their Italian or German or Norwegian or Irish, *with the language goes everything that kept imagination alive*. The old people have the language and all it contains, but not the children who are taught in the N. York schools, and who do not understand even their parents' tongue.

To-day I am going to a Matinée of *The Scarecrow*. Unfortunately the last matinée—has not been a success, tho' greatly praised and admired by the judicious. Its author Percy Mackaye gave me tickets. Percy Mackaye has a wife and three children and lives in the country on his literary and dramatic work, and this play at the start promised well, people seemed to like it and the critics were sympathetic and Mackaye dined here one evening in good spirits. All the Mackayes are very clever— one of his brothers when only 4 years old could beat his own father 'playing at chess'—the cleverness as of freaks—and so affectionate and sympathetic. He is always wanting me to go and stay with him at Concord, 8 hours from New York, he paying all travelling expenses, modo Americano. Last summer a family wanted me to go with them to Lake Michigan for the summer—a long journey costing £10, but it would have been impossible to do any work there. In common gratitude and courtesy I should have had to keep myself at their beck and call all day, and I have no time to waste.

Do you notice the fight here to get Sheehan into the Senate—the majority is for him but a minority can manage to keep up an exhausting fight. Of course they blacken Sheehan's character. Quinn says he is a perfectly honourable man, and that the fight against him is merely because he is Irish and Catholic, only they dare not say so.—Yours affectionately— J. B. YEATS

80

317 West 29th Street, New York
Feb. 11th, 1911

. . . Have you met Ezra Pound? Carlton Glidden, an artist of talent who has a lot to learn, but who is a very nice fellow indeed, told me to-day that Ezra Pound was at his studio a few days ago and talked a lot about you, quoting quantities of your verse, which he had by heart, placing you very high, and as the best poet for the last century and more. I tell you this as he is going in a few days to Europe to stay in Paris, &c. Quinn met him and liked him very much. The Americans, young literary men, whom I know found him surly, supercilious and grumpy. I liked him myself very much, that is, I liked his look and air, and the few things he said, for tho' I was a good while in his company he said very little. As I have just heard this I thought I would let you know in case you met him in transit through London. . . .[1]

I have no news, and shall not have any till my lecture on Monday night has become a thing of the past. It is very important. I will read your *Green Helmet* after my lecture. Heaven knows what will happen. I shall feel relieved when it is all over. I am like a woman approaching her confinement.

It is very cold, but winter is moderating a little. When the lecture is over I may go for one or two days to stay with a young barrister and his wife who live outside New York, and when there, give a reading of one of Synge's plays. I like these people very much, there are some books and the house is quiet and delightfully warm and cosy, with two little children on whom the whole house are in busy attendance, while I watch them—a mere onlooker—at the same time I am interested, as if after a time I could get really fond and human over these children. About other people's children I am, I suppose, inhuman, yet properly encouraged and left to myself, as I am in this case, I become gradually human. At any rate it adds to my pleasure in the house that they are there, tho' I am glad other people have to take care of them. The mother is a good mother, and the father is extraordinarily fond of them, and yet they never bore you with them. After all is said there are no people so nice and *so tactful* as the Americans.

81

317 West 29th Street, New York
April 5th, 1911

My dear Willie—You can conceive the delighted surprise with which I read the paragraph in to-day's paper, announcing your getting a pension of £150 a year—this will strike off all your shackles. I hope you will soon find time to write to me and tell me something about your plans &c.[2]

I am lecturing this week at Philadelphia, 25 dollars and all expenses and a luncheon paid for. I mean to take as my subject that Ireland is now an example to the world (at least as it is among the peasants in the West) in that it is more occupied with the question *how to live* than it is with the question *how to make a living*. Herein it is mediaeval with all its energy thrown into contemplation and desire of truth and beauty. Some weeks ago I lectured on this theme, and I said 'Give an Irish peasant the sweet

[1] W. B. Y. and Ezra Pound were already friends at this time.

[2] Through the good offices of Edmund Gosse and others W. B. had been placed on the Civil List by the Asquith Government.

accomplishment of verse, and he is a poet fully endowed; give it to an educated American, and he still remains a man of prose. He has not the poet's learning which the peasant has.'

To be a man of Intellect in America means to have opinions—and live in that kind of medium—these opinions being entertained not for the sake of intellectual happiness, but for the sake of moral progress and action. The Americans are the most idealistic people in the world and the least poetical. Opinions such as theirs mean logic, oratory and didacticism, and all the *restlessness* which is fatal to poetry, and to poetical learning.

The distinction between materialism and ideality is a false distinction. It is a new form of the old error, the distinction between the senses and the spirit—sense and spirit cannot be separated, and we *must not* speak of one in terms which insults the other. The Irish peasant is the least idealistic person in the world and the most poetical—only the harvest runs to waste, for they do not know how to gather it and stow it, and now we have Plunkett and Russell digging it all up, so that their taskmasters may not be affronted by a kind of life which yields no revenue, either to the Catholic Church or the English capitalist.

As to the Irish population and its decline—I do not regret it. There are far too many people in the world—congestion is a curse—all we want is enough people to share expenses—in schools, literature and government, *and keep up the supply of great men.* When England was really great her population was only what Ireland's is now.

When I say the Irish peasant is not idealistic I mean in the American and modern sense of the word. You cannot be poetical and not idealistic— *by selection we keep poetry alive*; and idealism is selection—but if the purpose be *to 'uplift'* ourselves and our neighbours the selection is not the same, as when we seek only visions of beauty and peace and hope and consolation. Being uplifted is the American recreation—with this kind of exercise they make their blood quite thin and colourless. It is sensual to have many children—therefore the American mother goes on her way with her one chick—and all her 'ologies'—and no one cares 'tuppence' about her—and Mrs. Keogh sits among her children and step-children ruling her kingdom —and guests cannot come often enough to see her and to talk to her. An opinion from her on any question is worth listening to because of her rich experience, and because of her sense of responsibility. She has a *deeper* knowledge of life than her own husband or than any supreme court judge.[1]

[1] The reference is to the wife of Judge Keogh, who lived at New Rochelle, in West Chester County. Yeats used to motor there with Quinn.

Enjoyment seems to me—if it be enjoyment at all—*to begin* in the senses—that is, in the concrete—and then crown itself in the affection and in the spirit; the richer the concrete the richer afterwards the abstract. These Americans are making huge efforts to get away from the concrete and live in the abstract. This is their plan for living the higher life, and nothing comes of it except a delirious activity—the poor spirit has such fragility and tenacity that it is blown hither and thither like the lovers in Dante's Hell, and these uplifting breezes are by no means gentle zephyrs. . . .—I remain, Yours affectionately—J. B. YEATS

TO OLIVER ELTON

82

New York
April 9, 1911

A few days ago I lectured at Philadelphia to an immense crowd of grim-faced men and women, and had the courage to tell them that Puritanism was a mistake; for it only permits us to admire people, whereas the real thing is to love people. We admire people in spite of their faults—at best an effort, and never quite successful; we love people because of their faults. Shakespeare unlike Browning never admires his heroes; he loves them in affectionate detachment, Hamlet for instance.—The American recreation is in being uplifted; uplifting thins the blood and feeds it upon oratory. The real thing is to understand, and love that you may understand; that enriches the blood and feeds it upon poetry. . . . When people really understand they don't admire, and they can't quarrel. An affectionate mother never admires her children, she knows them too well, and she knows them because she loves them.

TO LILY YEATS

83

P.   *June 27, 1911*
. . . Charlie Johnston said the other day that he thought Willie the most self-centred person he had ever met, but that he was not at all self-seeking. There is something between Charlie and Willie—I don't know what. I should not say 'between' for I think Charlie has only the friendliest feelings towards Willie. . . .

TO W. B. YEATS

84

317 West 29th Street, New York
July 11, 1911

My dear Willie—I enclose a note just received from Miss Sloan. Miss Sloan is sister of the John Sloan here who with his wife has helped me *so materially in New York*. They have worked for me as if I was a brother— or a father—really *worked*—all the trouble and risk of getting up a lecture for me, and they poor themselves, and at the time very hard up. This Miss Sloan by her painting (which is very good and very artistic) and teaching keeps her father and sister, getting some help from her brother John Sloan, and last Xmas I stayed at her house for a week, she lives close to Philadelphia. They are on both sides Irish people—and they are socialist— Miss Sloan is high church, believing in the usual things. I enclose her letter to me—the letter of introduction to you I have sent to Miss Stafford —who I suppose will present it in course of time. I shall also suggest to Miss Sloan to call on you in London.

While I am writing to you in this easy way I am quite aware that in all probability you are not in London at all, and shall tell them so. It is a long time since I heard from you.—Yours affectionately—J. B. YEATS

FROM W. B. YEATS

85

18 Woburn Buildings
Euston Road, London, N.W.
July 17, 1911

My dear Father—I have just come from lunching with Mrs. Asquith. Her house in Downing Street is an interesting old house, full of uninteresting copies of famous pictures. I was next Mrs. Asquith, who asked me a lot of questions about Lady Gregory. She said to me 'I am told that she is quite simple and yet always such a great personage'. I didn't think Mrs. Asquith herself had much capacity, but she was interested in everything. I had also some talk with Sir Edward Grey. Every afternoon I go to Hugh Lane's, he has a wonderful old house in Chelsea, full of course, of pictures.

Lady Gregory is staying there, and we do there our theatre business. We are planning a second company to take the place of the first when it is away.

You tell me in your last letter that you are introducing to me two ladies who want to study the theatre in Ireland, but you don't tell me who they are, probably I shall be in New York before they are in Ireland.[1] Neither have I received *Blossoming Bough* with your portrait of the author. I wonder will I write to the author when I do get it? I think a man who tried to commit suicide 'because some girls had proved unworthy of his esteem' must have delightful capacity for abstract affection. It is like dying on a barricade for humanity.

Send me anything that you write. I want very much to see your essay on the American woman. I am sorry to hear what you tell me about Edwin Ellis. I have heard nothing about him for years. Some twelve years ago, I went to see him in Paris. . . . Sometimes, when one has not seen a person for years, one goes back to them and realises that there is some burden there which one can never take up again, though it did not seem too heavy once. . . .—Your son—W. B. YEATS

TO W. B. YEATS

86

317 West 29th Street, New York
August 30, 1911

My dear Willie—I send you a paper in which some priest makes an attack on the theatre, evidently a priest—when you come here I hope they *do attack you*. It would make your fortune—all your poets and writers and actors and actresses would become famous. People would rally to you. People that never heard of you before would gather round you. It would be a fine fight for a fine principle.

I am writing an article on Sloan for a Socialist paper. I contend that every great painter or great poet practises both the art and the *fine art*. The fine artist has only beauty for his object—but besides being artistic he is also a serious practical man, who in spite of himself will say something outside his fine art. So you have Dante with his fury of civic passion aiming at a practical end. It is as if a painter made his pictures into political

[1] J. B. Yeats had written on June 19 about two ladies unnamed, who wished to study the theatre 'in England, Ireland and the Continent'.

cartoons, or Socialist cartoons, while at the same time, as in Hogarth's picture of [word indecipherable] he remained a great artist. Eloquence is an *art*, not a *fine art*. O'Connell recognised this when he said the test of a speech was the verdict of the jury. A poet terribly in earnest for his cause would win verdicts by his art of speaking, and drop for the moment his fine art of poetry. Milton does this often by his outbursts of puritanism and theology. A poet scolding (a spectacle sometimes seen of gods and men) drops his fine art, since he aims at a strictly practical purpose to give pain and to have a victim.

A practical purpose runs through all Hogarth's pictures—but his artistic sense forces him to paint his harlots of a tender grace and his men however wicked still human, as if he would persuade Justice to break her sword. I think a novel with a purpose is perhaps the right model, only it generally happens that in such novels the purpose is made to do duty for everything else.

The trouble with all these modern poets and painters is that they are TRIFLERS. *They have never been forced into any close relation with life*—they spend their days in decorated houses. Fancy Sargent forced into a close relation with life like Millet, like Michael Angelo, with his fine natural gift! or Whistler!—Yours affectionately J. B. YEATS

The talk of your coming here is exciting people a good deal.

TO OLIVER ELTON

87

New York, 7th Sept. 1911

England and America have produced only two serious painters; Hogarth and Sloan—(Not including Blake who was more poet than painter) and not including landscape painters.

TO LILY YEATS

88

317 W. 29th Street, New York
P.   *Sept. 11, 1911*

. . . Yesterday I was at Brooklyn, dining with people called Ingersoll, who have a baby 3 months old. The Van Ingens brought me. We dined on the top of the roof where they have built themselves a wooden structure. [Sketch] Being high up we could look all round and see over the roofs of the neighbouring houses. Dinner was at 1.30, and it over we removed the table and substituted a swing sofa and sat talking of innumerable things. A young girl, Miss Hackett of Kilkenny, was there. She earns her living in settlement work and is much happier here than in old Kilkenny where she says 'there is nothing to do'. As I am sure is the case. People may abuse America but these people like it—of that there is no mistake. The young lady's father is the principal doctor in Kilkenny, so I suppose she has a good home. Her brother, a very brilliant journalist, has now abandoned the newspaper to write things after his own heart and is now busy on an article for the *Forum* on W. B. Yeats. . . .[1]

89

N.Y., Dec. 21, 1911

. . . Here is a story about Roosevelt. Dining the other day with Lady Gregory were he and Quinn and Dooley—and R. was speaking about the rough riders and describing how the best soldiers he knew were Irishmen, and he named several, and Dooley said, 'Colonel, I have a name for your book'. 'What is it, Peter', said Roosevelt. 'Alone in Cuba.' The President laughed consumedly and said he would tell that to Mrs. Roosevelt. I suppose Mrs. Roosevelt chaffs him continuously about his egotistical belief that he does everything himself.

TO RUTH HART

90

317 West 29, N. York
July 3rd, 1912

My dear Ruth—*If you can* forgive my not answering your Xmas letter till now—I have been so busy with *things*, articles, sketches, etc.—that I have been a recluse from the world, and from my friends, but I have just sold an article (for £20) and besides, all last night, I dreamed about you all, especially about your mother, and I had two little dreams about Vaughan. I often dream of you and your mother. I *do a great deal in*

[1] Francis Hackett, afterwards author of *Henry VIII*, etc.

dreaming—especially since I came to New York. Every night when I go to bed to sleep I wonder what will happen to me before I wake. The fact is, in N.Y. one is excited, and besides one eats very little meat; living on bread and claret and fruit, a body can raise an immense crop of dreams. And one has to live without eating meat, for the climate here is so beastly, (either too hot or too cold), and the streets are so horrible that exercise is impossible—for that reason one avoids meat.

Last Xmas just after your letter arrived, when I had a bad attack of homesickness, a very nice girl from Dublin, Miss Clare Marsh, came to seek her fortune as a portrait painter and stayed for a while here in this house—and she was so good to me and so like a daughter that when she left me for Dublin I was broken-hearted and could do no work for a good while. I longed so much for you all. Miss Marsh is a Dublin artist, and probably some of your friends know her. She is worth knowing—besides being a good painter. Homesickness took her back to Ireland. Everyone in the house loved her, some being really in love with her. Had she remained she would have got on in her profession, but she was afraid her mother would die before she got back.

I don't know when I shall return—but I notice that latterly, American people are beginning to irritate me, and if this happens, why—I shall begin to irritate them—and so *incompatibility* will set up, and I will come home. Dinner is here every evening at 6–30. There are a lot of tables and we dine in the open air. In this Hotel a few weeks ago congenial people came to my table, and the conversation was pleasant and intelligent—now it is all changed. A picture dealer and his affected wife and a little Jew, and such like, dominate the conversation and I sit at my end of the table, crammed up with the sulky egotism of the unappreciated, saying nothing, for if I do, either the little Jew in shrill American slang contradicts me, or else they all turn their backs on me. He is only about 23—has a voice that almost breaks the drum of your ear, by its pressing shrillness, and incessant noise—the picture dealer has a voice like a megaphone. Probably if I was quite normal—that is to say, not as such, I should merely smile at these people in a superior way, instead of letting them disgust me.

I was awfully glad to see the Jamesons.[1] I had one charming walk in the park with Mrs. Jameson. I had always seen her amid the pomp and grandeur of Sutton house, so it was quite pleasant to meet her out of her goddess-ship in N. York. One seldom meets any one in an intimate and confidential way, for the simple reason that the intimate life does not

[1] The Andrew Jamesons, his Howth friends.

exist—no one has any cherished or secret longings, everyone living in public; that is why there is no literature and no real conversation—people live as well as talk *rhetoric*. What would I give for a talk with your mother, at the chimney corner in your drawing room—In America people talk either to say or to listen to *memorable* things—but there is no atmosphere. When artists who are congenial to each other meet, they don't say memorable things, neither do husband and wife when they love each other. I would like to hear your mother laugh, and her hurrying precipitous voice and I want to enjoy her quaint humour of *detachment*. Do you know what I mean or are you too close to her to observe these things?

One thing I value very much, are my three landladies. Breton young women. It is I think because of their unfailing courtesy and social tact. One is Cook, Marie—she is the brains. Next is Josephine. She is the 'chucker out', and keeps order and looks after the bills. All are good looking with black eyes and black hair. The youngest is a beauty, Celestine. All work terribly hard. Celestine says, 'I do not think I will have rest, till I am *died*'—her English is imperfect, but her manners are exquisite—she looks a Sylph among these fat German American women—and her voice sounds so courteous and musical among these nasal voices——and yet, you must not think I do not admire and really adore this American character, which is now growing up, even while it is so easy to laugh at and even sometimes hate. A sort of European old-maidishness gets between me and them. Depend upon it it is a mistake sometimes to have been too well brought up, it prevents you realising that in America everything hitherto respected including your politeness and reticence is *quite out of date*. Every day of my life, I meet with some fresh surprise. People will do and say anything, and except a few things like the multiplication table, nothing is sacred.

I hope your father is quite well. I am sure he misses Vaughan. Why does he live so far away? How are Ethel, and her babies, and everybody else. I love you all. When shall I see you?—Yrs affectly—J. B. YEATS

I got Miss Marsh when coming from Ireland to bring me Lamb's letters. I get a great deal of consoling philosophy out of them. They at any rate have atmosphere, like your mother's talk, and your house and your garden.

Art Doctrine

TO W. B. YEATS

91

317 West 29, N.Y.
July 9, 1912

My dear Willie—Who was the little cuss that sent to *T. P.*'s that account of your school-days? Among other things that you would not do Euclid. Why! you have the Euclid mind, like most artists and poets. It is the deductive mind.

Did you ever happen to meet a lady novelist, May Sinclair? I have just read a book by her *The Creators*, in which is a poet superficially drawn from you I think. It is a good novel—some of the characters, especially the women very well imagined.

I am trying to write an article which will have for subject that art for art's sake is a good principle, but not the principle now so long in vogue—technique for technique's sake. Swinburne, whether he writes prose or verse is very largely the latter. Underneath his shining, many-coloured coat of technique beats a heart in which were some engaging feelings but mainly a craftsman's delight in the practice of his own craft. This delight is a very real thing, and interesting especially as being something mediaeval and monkish, but not enough to make a poet. I want to preach to artists a new doctrine which I will call the doctrine *of the environment* as more important than all. A man of genius is not only divine. There is also the child's heart within the man's, *and the child's heart is all for the environment.* This doctrine needs especially to be preached in America. In old times we all belonged to large families—12 or 13 to each family and could not get away from the environment—in spite of education and my best efforts to belong to 'higher things'. Reality, minute and particular and flushed with life, pressed in upon everybody and does now upon peasants. The artistic effort went along side by side with the effort to live and a fine artist meant a fine personality. Swinburne was a starved personality—nothing came from him but miracles, beautiful flowers of technique. Sargent gives us only fine painting if he attempts to leave portraiture—if any of them attempt to leave portraiture how immeasurably they fall behind, not only the great serious painters of Italy and Belgium but also behind such painters as Hogarth. Sargent's paintings in Boston are nothing; Mrs. Chas. Johnston showed some photos of sacred pictures (all life size) done by a modern painter in Russia which are magnificent.

A Fortune Teller

The countryman of Tolstoi could not fail to be a real man before he was artist. Art is going to have a new heaven and a new earth. All art is *reaction from life* but never, when it is vital and great, *an escape*. There is of course beautiful art which is an escape but it is languid amid all its beauty, Rossetti's for instance. In M. Angelo's time it was not possible to escape for life was there *every minute* as real as the toothache and as terrible and impressive as the judgment day. Everybody here is busy *escaping* from life—not into art like Rossetti's, for that they have not the necessary cultivation nor the leisure—so they escape, if I may so put it, in automobiles, and all personalities are so slight that personal sorrows have little effect.

Rachel weeping for her children could not have escaped but she might have *reacted* towards *visions* that would have enormously increased her grief and yet converted it into beauty—beauty that would wring her heart and hasten her death and yet be beauty *and life*.

Two Fortune-tellers, nay three, whom I have come across predict for me the most tremendous success though they say that I am not yet out of the 'period of distress'. I am to let nothing stop me but to go forward and meet my chances which are all good, promising both material success and recognition—'tremendous' is the adjective used. The first of these, as long ago as last December told me of your journey across the sea 'to meet your enemies whom you would overthrow'. She did not know my name —a very clever little old woman, simple and gentle with the brightest eyes I ever saw. We sat in a darkened room and she never even looked at me and yet she told me my whole history—she said I should have been a mathematician, and when I laughed incredulously she said it could have happened, but that my education was neglected till I was ten years old. It was my father's dream that I should have been a mathematician, because of some fancied resemblance to my uncle Thos. Yeats who was as he himself told never beaten in honours examination in T.C.D. At school I never learned anything except Latin and Greek and Euclid, in all of which I was 'top boy'. Sir W. Wilde [1] often spoke to me of Thos. Yeats and of his being 'buried in Sligo'. 'Fancy it,' he would say, 'Tom Yeats gave up everything to support some delicate sisters and a delicate brother, and an old aunt, and so took to a practical life. The Yeats's were the cleverest and most spirited minded people I ever met.' Matt Yeats had little of the cleverness and for that reason was rather a joke among them, but he had the spirituality which his most material-minded wife did her

[1] Father of Oscar Wilde.

best to crush. I fancy one of my ancestors named Voisin was a French Huguenot.

This is a long and I suppose illegible letter.—Yours affectionately—J. B. YEATS

TO LILY YEATS

92

317 W. 29 Street, New York
Aug. 28, 1912

. . . Last Sunday (from Saturday to Monday) I spent with a Mr. and Mrs. Benson and their children, almost the most serene time of my American life. He is the Socialist candidate for Congress, a writer and a clear thinker—wife and children delightful—all bound together in affection and sympathy—and lives in a house close by the Hudson which we see through a screen of trees. I am looking forward eagerly to the next Sunday which I am to spend with them. [Sketch.] From this sketch you can see how nicely the house is situated, but you have no idea of the peace that reigns, the wife good and very sympathetic, and the children controlled so that they are not a nuisance to themselves and others. All the other children I have met in America are restless with 'unsatisfied longings', nasally whining all day long, unless they are saying impudent things to their parents.

TO W. B. YEATS

93

317, West 29, N.Y.
Sept. 20, 1912

My dear Willie—Your cheque was a tremendous surprise. I got it as I sat down in a melancholy mood to dinner and it cheered *considerable*. Pat Quinlan an enthusiastic Irishman after dinner ordered for himself me and another Irishman, 3 liqueurs, unprecedented in my knowledge of Pat, but I whispered in his ears: No, I am flush, I will pay for them and I did, unprecedented in Pat's knowledge of me. So I celebrated your gift in a way more Irish than nice. I am ashamed to say that the £10 is welcome. Ever since Xmas I have done two things, neither having any immediate profit.

Pat Quinlan

I have read a whole lot (for me) and I have worked a tremendous lot on a portrait of myself for which Quinn is to pay 'any sum I like to name', and my purpose in this effort is not really Quinn's money but something else more legitimate. I am to paint a portrait of a friend of Miss Caroline Morgan's in her apartment in a few weeks as soon as she returns from Europe, and Miss Morgan is niece of Pierpoint Morgan and besides very rich herself and has one of the gentlest and most attractive personalities I ever met. She is not unladylike in the English way, having no insolence, and she is ladylike in the English way being a model of all the graces of delicate reserve, and of a delicate expansion like the alternation of night and day. It was this so charmed M. Angelo in his friendship with Vittoria Colonna. If I make this portrait a success what may not happen? Last Xmas I saw a sketch of her which she had *twice* reproduced—the second time on a large scale.

I am glad you like the old poet James Nicoll Johnston, what you say will please him and I will send it on. I fear you have not written to him— James Nicoll Johnston, Buffalo, N.Y. State, will always find him.

To return to Pat Quinlan.[1] He is a good friend to the Irish literary movement. He got all his friends to enquire over and over again at the public libraries for Synge's books, thereby helping considerably towards making his books highest in the weekly list of 'books most in demand'. He also wrote vigorously defending your pension. He is a friend of Charlie Johnston's, cabin boy, professional athlete (he is 6 ft. tall), miner, lecturer, socialist, born in Limerick, in his way 'a brilliant creature' as C. Johnston called him, strangely read in out of the way Irish histories and a good speaker and very witty in a harum-scarum way, without egotism or vanity, and really modest, and with his mind always open. Every one likes him. You cannot offend him, or stop him, or do anything else but like him even when he bores you by his self-made lack of any sense of proportion in intellectual values. I tell him he has the characteristic Irish fault of too much destructive criticism, and that what we want is constructive criticism, and he is taking it in. I think he has influence and he tells me he is always telling his friends this about the destructive criticism. He likes, *genuinely* likes helping Irishmen, particularly those in the literary

---

[1] Pat Quinlan, a well-known Labour agitator, concerned in some of the not infrequent troubles in Paterson, N.J. He went to Russia after the Revolution and returned sadly disillusioned. He was present at the riotous first performance of Synge's *Playboy* in New York and expressed the utmost scorn of the noisy objectors to it.

movement, and every one likes 'Pat'. I think he is quite without fear, he looks quite young and yet knows England and Scotland as well as Ireland and America for he has been everywhere. It is a pleasure to watch him, he is so tall and well made and so naturally courteous and refined—a true gentleman. He is a friend of Kerrigans and of some of the other actors. You will probably come across him some time so I tell you this. I think he has some kind of a good destiny. His only hatred is for the Irish priests —all other men he holds in charity. [Sketch.]

I am very busy on an article, and I *think* its subject is happiness, which has several branches, but the only branch worth considering is intellectual happiness and this can only be found by the man being thrown back on his own resources. The child with a lot of toys can't find it, nor the American who is equally busy over toys, in his case automobiles, Vaudeville shows, trips to Europe, &c. *Being thrown back on ourselves is the artistic doctrine of sincerity.* Poets generally have had lonely childhoods and this, reckoned a sadness, was their chance and out of it they draw their happiness. There is a wonderful letter of M. Angelo given in Symonds' life (311 page, read it) in which he says a man can only preserve his sincerity by meditating on the thought of death, 'Albeit death by her nature destroys all things'. The thought of death 'holds us together in the bond of our own nature'.

How ignoble beside this doctrine of sincerity, as much pagan as christian, is the Puritan doctrine denouncing human nature as vile. Of course there may have been in old age some taint of the *craven fear* of punishment which is the essence of the Puritan creed *but I think* that to the last M. Angelo bowed his head to the *rightness and majesty* of God, and never to his mere power.

I have good news from Dundrum. Lolly is now completely recovered . . . and Lily is marvellously so. I always know how she is by her letters, which are always very clever, not poetical and poetically humorous like Lily's, but trenchant, hitting the nail on the head every time. Years ago when she belonged to a little Literary Society of girls in London, she gave promise of being able to write novels.

With kind regards to Lady Gregory.—I remain, Yours affectionately— J. B. YEATS

TO LILY YEATS

94

Eric Bell, the subject of this letter, was a young Englishman to whom Yeats was greatly attached. Most of Bell's literary work was writing articles and im-

Death of Eric Bell

pressions of people, places and nature. His father was an artist and his mother wrote many books on art (before marriage) under the name N. D'Anvers, afterwards as Mrs. Arthur Bell. His sister, Mrs. Frazer Carroll, writes to me: 'I well remember Eric talking much about Mr. Yeats, especially during his last illness. Mr. Yeats made 2 very clever pencil sketches of my brother, which were much prized. . . . My brother had a roving spirit and love of change, and when his cousin and godmother offered him hospitality in the home she had made in America, he decided to go, and if ill-health had not overtaken him, he could have settled there. . , . . He was only 27 when he died. Mr. Yeats's description of him is very true to life. All that he says of him is true. He was affectionate and most lovable, and entertaining, but I feel I cannot better Mr. Yeats's portrait. . . .'

New York
Oct. 7, 1912

My dear Lily—I have just heard that Eric Bell is dying—King told me at the Vagabonds. I shall now hate the Vagabonds worse than ever and I shall shun it. Bell was my great comfort. He told me everything and showed me all he wrote sitting by me at meals. When I returned from Buffalo last Xmas and found him gone to England it was a great blow. There has been no one to take his place—except Clare Marsh who for the short time she remained was my greatest pleasure. A couple of weeks ago I had a long letter from Bell dictated to his sister and from it I inferred that he was but slightly ill and only from heat prostration as he said. I never guessed the truth. The day you went away was a black day—you never guessed how black, but at least I should soon see you again or hoped to do so. To those who took the trouble to like him Bell was the most attractive of men, such charm and so cultivated and so witty and gay and of such promise *and of course he would have got better* (it was tuberculosis), *had he consented to follow rules.* He admired Willie immensely. When he spent an evening here he never took his eyes off him. He was very tall, blue eyes and auburn hair—very handsome and well made. People used to hate him (out of envy and jealousy); he never hated any one, I think because of his sense of the ridiculous—and he was so well bred—a highbred amiability that never deserted him, even when others were provoked by his manifest superiority—I often tried to get him to say malicious things about people, but all his attempts ended in pleasant laughter. I am sure Molière was like that—*he knew how to laugh*, the witty art. They all talk about literature and ideas and art, but it is only talk. Bell understood and had the happiest phrases. I am writing now to distract my thoughts.

Socialism

It is the first real blow since I came here—the first *really* black day. I shan't be able to mention his name even for a long time. He was unfortunate from the first. He had a damned schoolmaster—head of one of those great public schools, now a Dean. The old dog he was called. Even his affectionate home was against him, as they brought him up so tenderly that when this schoolmaster insulted him (it was a course of petty tyrannies, one long insult), he could not harden himself against it all. His father is an artist living at Richmond and was with me at the Slade where I knew him a little, his mother a writer, his brother an Oxford don. After all death is perhaps an incident in a life that is infinite.

It is very hot, too hot to sleep under bedclothes. I do hate this climate and N. York, and all its noise! noisy trains, noisy tongues, noisy streets. I wish I could wander once more under those trees at Churchtown, along that lane going towards the mountains. . . .

95

317 West 29th Street
October 10, 1912

. . . A young fellow dined here the other day whom I have known a long time, his wife also. He has charge of 100 young girls to see that they do their work in some newspaper or printing office. He is amiable and kind, very dutiful—She tells me that all these girls will, every one of them, cheat and lie and do anything. I am sure this is true. Socialism and such movements have taught one lesson successfully, that all employers are robbers and murderers, and this of course releases all employees from every kind of obligation. The Socialists applaud this kind of thing. *The employees don't really know anything of socialist doctrine, it's quite beyond them, but it is easy and pleasant to believe that employers are rogues and that you may therefore cheat as much as is prudent.* This kind of thing runs all through life. Young women and wives have got hold of the doctrine. Mrs. . . . said to me that she had a perfect right to do anything provided she did not injure herself. Of course there is only one cure for this—the establishment of Socialism—a state of things in which the produce of labour will be divided among the workers. *One worker won't idle, because the other workers would be down on him*, all and each working for the common good. Meantime, it is very unpleasant. The Roman Catholic Church is fighting socialism tooth and nail.

TO SUSAN MITCHELL

96

New York
Oct. 21, 1912

Innumerable are my thanks for your letter telling what I *want to know*.

I have been reading Goethe and thinking of you all the time. I mean reading his life and conversation. Get out of the idea, he commands, and get to particulars, for in particulars is the life of art. Every now and then I turn to your few poems and like them better and better—it is because you have such a poignant way of dropping suddenly into some personal 'particular'. It is what I call your naïveté—and because of it you have something which I find neither in AE or in W. B. Y. I think it might be called a *quality of intensity*. If you would write more and *use your own life more*, we should have not only more poetry, but it would be stronger and more intimate. Goethe said *all his* poems were 'occasional'—in each 'an experience seeking to *strengthen* itself' (not to uplift itself, mind; uplifting was not in Goethe's line, for *there* we have the idea which he said you must get 'out of'). I am now trying to write on personality. *Personality is neither right or wrong*—for it is divine—it transcends intellect and morality, and while it keeps to being pure personality we love it for it is *one with our very selves, and with the all pervasive Divine*—at least this I believe and contend. Of course, if personality entangle itself with the practical world, we may treat it as the Scythians did strangers cast away on their inhospitable shores, and it has lost its instincts, for it has left its own country. Sentimental poetry deals with practical things: Longfellow's Blacksmith etc., and American poetry generally, which is either sentimental or didactic. *Real Poetry is Pure Personality*; a little child learning to talk, unburthened with ideas of right or wrong, and without intellect, and often a woman when she is in love or when she has little children—here is Pure Personality, at sight of which, Intellect and the Moral Sense both feel themselves to be *supernumerary*. While they remain pure personality, the child or the woman may do anything they want, and yet remain *adorable*. Poetry is divine because it is the voice of the personality—this poor captive caged behind the bars. I see my own meaning quite plainly. I wonder can you or anybody else?

Some day through science, we shall throw down the bars and the captive will be set free, and the omnipresent be all triumphant.

Arthur Symons, Lady Gregory and W. B. Y.

I have also been reading about Lincoln, he also had a great personality, supreme over his intellect and his moral sense. Intellect and the moral sense are only journeymen—well suited for ordinary work. A great occasion requires a personality.

Nowadays we worship intellect and character, that is the moralized will, and poor personality is thrown into the cellar; she is quite out of favour. Even the women despise her, and want to be like the men, all intellect and the resolute will. I write all this to you, because you more than anybody else have taught me the value of the personality. You are all personality. Your strong intellect and deeply felt moral attributes in their place, kept *subsidiary*:

The world must learn to work less and reason less and feel more—and every man must get back into his environment and saturate himself with it—and we shall find poets and real men. Environment is the nursery of personality.—Yrs affectly—J. B. YEATS

TO LILY YEATS

97

In the summer of 1896 W. B. Yeats took Arthur Symons, who was then his closest literary friend, on a tour in Ireland. While they were being entertained at Edward Martyn's castle in Galway, Lady Gregory called, and invited them to lunch at Coole. Symons returned to London alone, and Lady Gregory then asked W. B. Yeats to stay for a few days. Thus commenced their famous collaboration, which—to judge from the anecdote in the following letter—was as much deplored by Symons as it was by Miss Maud Gonne, and several of the poet's Irish friends.

New York
Octr. 22nd, 1912

. . . is a wonderful woman. Talked of Wells, Arthur Symons and Conrad. Conrad though he writes such magnificent English talks it brokenly, getting away constantly and more familiarly to French. It seems that 'Arthur' hates Lady Gregory and moans at the mention of her. 'Well, Arthur, it was your fault'. 'Yes, I know it was I who brought him to Coole, and as soon as her terrible eye fell upon him I knew she would keep him, and he is now lost to lyrical poetry'. Probably Arthur Symons hates this theatre business like AE who thinks the theatre only a peep show. On the whole I am very glad that Lady Gregory 'got' Willie.

151

The Personal in Poetry

Arthur Symons never speaks of her except as the 'Strega' which is the Italian for witch. I don't regret her witchcraft, though it is not easy personally to like her. They are all so prejudiced that they think her plays are put into shape by 'Willie' ('they' include Miss Tobin) which of course is nonsense. I for one won't turn against Lady Gregory. She is perfectly disinterested. She shows this disinterestedness. That is one of the reasons why she is so infernally haughty to lesser mortals—or whom she thinks lesser mortals.

TO SUSAN MITCHELL

98

New York
Oct. 22, 1912

. . . I said that in your work is *intensity*, and said you got your intensity through a certain personal intensity habitual with you. But I ought to have said that the intensity by the time it reaches its expression is no longer *personal*, entering into the world of art, the personal ego is dropped away —for I think personal art is bad art, at any rate second rate.[1]

I like Turner's pictures better than the impressionists' works because while in *them* I become curious about the painters, in Turner's pictures I become so transported to the scenes painted that I *forget to ask who painted them*.

I think also that a painter or a poet should be all on fire with his motive whether it be an impression or an emotion, and *then work with cold logic and resolute purpose*, till he has created his work of art—the work of art completed, all the fire will be *in it* for ever—all the fire with which he first started and then apparently forgot; and it is so in the achievements of practical life. . . .

FROM W. B. YEATS

99

18 Woburn Buildings
Upper Woburn Place, London

November 21st, 1912

My dear Father—I have a great project, would you like to write your autobiography? My plan is to go to a publisher and to arrange that you

[1] Yeats's mind was on this subject, because his son had at this time commenced to make poetry out of the events of his own (W. B. Y.'s) life, to write 'occasional' poetry for the first time.

152

should be paid chapter by chapter on the receipt of the MS. at the rate of £1 per 1,000 words up to say £50. This £50 to be a first charge on the book. I shall try and arrange so that you will keep the serial rights. You will probably get very decent terms for some of the chapters in America. You could go as you please, quick or slow, and say what you pleased. I suggest—but this is only to start your imagination working—that in your first chapter or chapters you describe old relations and your childhood. You have often told us most interesting things, pictures of old Ireland that should not be lost. Then, you could describe your school life and then weave a chapter round Sandymount. Isaac Butt would come into this. Later on, your memories of Potter and Nettleship and Wilson would have real historical importance. When you came to the later period, you could use once more what you have already written about York Powell, then, if you liked, you could talk about Synge and about America. I will get the publisher to illustrate the book. There are your own pictures to choose from, the portrait of Isaac Butt, of course, and pictures in the Tate Gallery by Potter and at Aberdeen by Wilson, and Mrs. Nettleship has still those early designs of Nettleship's and would probably be glad to have them published and him praised. You might do a wonderful book. You could say anything about anything, for after all, you yourself would be the theme, there would be no need to be afraid of egotism, for as Oscar Wilde said, that is charming in a book because we can close it whenever we like, and open it again when the mood comes. I think you might really do a wonderful book, and I think a profitable one. It would tell people about these things that are not old enough to be in the histories or new enough to be in the reader's mind, and these things are always the things that are least known. If you agree, the book can be done, for even if the publisher lacked faith, I know I could get the money. The point is, can you write it for £1 a thousand words in the first instance? You wouldn't have to hurry, and I think that in the long run, it might produce a very considerable sum for you. I would do all the bargaining and make the publisher collect the pictures for illustrations. Probably, a good deal that you have written recently would fit in somewhere. The first chapter or two might be difficult, but after that, I know by experience of my own books that your thought would go on branching and blossoming in all directions; in the end, it might grow to longer than 50,000 words, but I do not say it might not be shorter. The great thing is to do it in some form, long or short. An ordinary 6/- book is expected to be about 60,000 words, but if the pictures turn out well, though no longer, it might be a guinea book and very profitable indeed, for there would be nothing to pay for copyrights of pictures. If it were much less than 60,000 words, one could still—with the pictures to help—charge 6/-. Let me know as soon as you can and I will arrange the whole thing at once.—Yours—W. B. YEATS

TO W. B. YEATS

100

Jan. 29, 1913
317 W. 29 St.

... A man with a personality may talk about many things, but in things which touch his personality, he will prefer to be silent. Lincoln had this kind of silence, and Goethe when greatly moved became silent and wrote verses. Intellect and the moral sense can always explain themselves—they have words at command. Personality has too much to say for mortal speech. It can only exclaim—'Here I am, look at me, and not with your corporeal eyes but with your spiritual eyes—with my imagery and my rhythm, and the loud music of my harp, I will rouse you from mortal sleep.'

Have you seen Susan Mitchell's little volume? She is poet through and through and with intensity—a beautiful intensity that only half unveils itself—she has naïveté and is full of *'particulars'* and she has the impersonality of true personality—she gives herself to what she touches. Keats said 'When I see a sparrow outside the window, I am that sparrow pecking.' I hope all this may interest you, fitting in with your thoughts and not jarring them.

It might be said of Haydon, the painter, Keats's friend, that he had character but little personality. He was proud of his strength of character and scorned Keats's want of it. This I know will harmonize with your ideas.

I hear the players are very successful at Chicago.—Yours affectionately —J. B. YEATS

Personality in final analysis is love—only it is very difficult to put that into language intelligible to an unbelieving generation.

P.S. Yet a few more words—this modern development of intellect and the moral nature has left us a *loveless* people. We may admire or respect each other—we cannot *love*. No woman ever loved her husband for his intellect or his admirable principles—or friend his friend—*love is the in-*

stinctive movement of personality. Napoleon, dreaming among his soldiers, learning their names by heart that he might address them individually (Josephine tells us she could not get him to retire to bed—he would stay up so long getting these names by heart) and Lincoln thinking about his country, or Goethe about humanity.

In all these men was a tenderness akin to that of a mother watching her child and yearning over him. *In the strange self-love of the hero when he is abandoned by his followers* it is there also—the same movement. Forced back upon himself he must still love. Also the dearth of personality makes men all alike, all so obvious, so that we are no longer interested in each other, except of course, in argument or in drilling each other. There is no mystery in life, and nothing for sympathy to interpret. All this is exactly true of America and its women.

IOI

The Abbey Theatre Company was on tour in America with Lady Gregory.

317 West 29, N.Y.
Feb. 25th, 1913

My dear Willie—*The Countess Kathleen* is a beautiful dream in spectacle and is now a beautiful performance. The first time I saw it I thought it would *become* a beautiful performance—it is now *arrived*. It would be an *amazingly* beautiful performance if the poet did his part as well as the Countess does her part, but he is too boisterous, too school-boyish. However there is no remedy. There is no one else in the company to take his place—it needs a scholarly actor. I think the play should have a prologue—it would help the illusion and give the necessary atmosphere. All at once we are expected without any warning to enter the world of miracle and hobgoblin, and it is too much. Do you agree with me? I make the suggestion because I think it is exactly the kind of thing you could write. You have all the qualities for it—the fancy, the wit and the persuasiveness, and then is it not according to Shakespearian method?

Monck[1] with his elocutionary voice could recite the lines with apt intonation. I think indeed the play should end with the Countess dying a

[1] Nugent Monck of the Norwich players, who worked for a while at the Abbey Theatre.

lost soul, and then the angel's speech be given as an epilogue to comfort us all.

New York critics are absurd people. In the *Sun* one of them in a long article spoke of Monck as *the* success—Monck with his unsympathetic English voice—but no American can resist an English voice, for it is to him the top of fashion.

America admires England because of the materialist fibre in its heart. In England they behold materialism triumphant crowned and sovereign— glorious in ancient memories and in great aristocracies well-knit and colossal without an idea anywhere to disturb the contours.

Quinn for all his material success and his associates is entirely spiritual, for that reason he is now happy, and for that reason his deepest prejudice is hatred of the Englishman.

I hope you are improving in health. Eat fruit with every meal and salad when you can get it. Here we have it every day, and don't eat eggs. Americans tell me they always get ill in England because of the food. I am never well in any city, because of constant colds which always attack my digestion.—Yours affectionately—J. B. YEATS

102

March 8, 1913
P.   317 West 29, N. York

My dear Willie—The more I think about *The Countess Kathleen* the more I am convinced that it's destined to a great popular success—some-how, I don't think the right people are coming to the theatre. New York people are educated and alive, as we know, but are *not alive to poetry*. The American intellect is without intensity—they are far too busy, busy, that is, in an airy theoretic way. Noyes will suit them—abstract ideas all afloat in a maze of rhetoric—are their choice. So much for the intellectual classes. The common people like puns and indecency—I mean in New York.

The American system of education in their high-class schools is de-structive of mental concentration—nothing is thoroughly taught. In my day we learned nothing except Latin and Greek, but learned that in a very minute way, undergoing all sorts of moral and physical tortures, the lessons made as difficult as possible. We read Horace for the grammar, and it was always grammar.

Strenuousness

Do you notice how busy people always like ugliness. It has for them the actuality of a stench. It takes prolonged effort, and prolonged leisure to begin to enjoy beauty. The modern doctrine of strenuousness so popular with democracies is fatal to Beauty, and as to these Socialists—and I am a Socialist—they drag down the esthetic sense and trample on it. To them artists and poets are egoists—the word gentleman is hateful to them. Yet a society of *poor* gentlemen upon whose hands time lies heavy is absolutely necessary to art and literature. Being gentlemen they know how to idle with dignity, and because of their poverty there is no distraction to prevent their brooding on life and truth. Thinking of life they become poets; thinking of truth, scientific students. Yet it is all idleness because every man follows his own bent, and because of this leisure every feeling is explored and every thought followed up to the utmost, and everything finished with accurate precision. A strenuous modern, particularly your socialist, will go into a garden and find nothing so agreeable as the pungent smells of the dung-heap. It is for maudlin egotists who have nothing else to do to listen to the birds and smell the roses—and as to the lady regnant, she too is busy and practical, and asks only that her garden like her dress be of the right sort, however rich she be. Leisure is not on the market.

In England there is a society of poor gentlemen—the scholars and some of the literati; that is why, to quote a letter from Elton, 'depraved England can still write'.

I began this letter in order to suggest that you read Stendhal's *Red and White* (you can get it in English). It has enlarged my imagination: it is a tragedy. You read it in a sort of high seriousness in which is no pain.

Lady Gregory tells me that you are better and that your figure is in fine condition.—Yours affectionately—J. B. YEATS

103

March 16, 1913
317 West 29, N. York

My dear Willie—I don't know whether my letters seem to you full of half knowledge and crude judgments and therefore rather *boring*—nevertheless I am writing again.

Last night I saw *The Rising of the Moon* and found it perfect as regards the play and the acting. It is a play I cannot see too often. Afterwards came the *Playboy*, always to me a fresh wonder, and yet always spoiled by Donovan's acting. Donovan is a good actor, extremely intelligent. You always know in a general sense what he means, and he is always consistent with himself, and he is full of variety—too much so since it spoils the smoothness of the performance. In other words he is here and there too emphatic. The defect of his acting is that he has a vulgar conception of the part. The play-boy, that poor fragment of humanity, all poetry and dream in his squalor, becomes in his hands nothing better than a counter-jumper, ugly and impudent, his fine speeches without conviction—*at least generally so*, for I do admit that sometimes he rises, or seems to rise 'to the occasion'. The same actor spoils your *Countess Kathleen*; as to that play, I have not the slightest doubt of its ultimate triumph. I fancy he [Donovan] is very popular with the American public, so that if he fails they think it the fault of the play.

Sarah Algood, when she is good, and that is nearly always, is superb, and so is Sinclair. Kerrigan also has a fine naturalness and Morgan who does the sheriff in *Blanco Posnet* has an attractive quality. Sinclair is all invention and subtlety and intensity; when called upon to display sympathy, he is out of it, that not being part of his natural or acquired 'make-up'. The ... is by nature a vixen. ... Spite is to Ireland what selfishness is to England: the first is barbarism—the other civilization, *such as it is*. Spite is an entirely disinterested desire to destroy success wherever you see it. Selfishness likes success for therein it sees some opportunity for itself.

Quinn has bought a whole heap of pictures at the International Exhibition. He is wildly happy over the exhibition. All the Americans think it overtops creation, and it is extraordinarily interesting, but I think artists who have lived and studied abroad, in France and England, are not so much astonished and impressed. Matisse to my mind is an artistic humbug, though probably an honest man. If Edwin Ellis were a young man he would be one of these people. These people claim to be self-centred; it is just what they are not. All the time they are looking for disciples—hence their desire to say and do the extraordinary. Of course they hit blows in the current modes of art, it is an easy task, and this victory counts with their friends and it is the thing that counts for everything else, and we who know are obliged to listen in silence—wisdom has no chance with clever folly. The exhibition is interesting to me because of some fine things at once new and fine. 'The world is saved by the extraordinary' said Goethe, and here it is in fine form and *some of these Quinn has bought.* His judgment is really sound, if at times it goes wrong. One must do extraordinary things, *yet long for the sober and the conformable.* With this impulse and this discipline comes spontaneity—a river flowing between its well-kept banks.—Yours affectionately—J. B. YEATS

P.S. Lady Gregory seems in fine humour. I think she is happier than last time—more at rest—that is my impression. I don't think she is as much mobbed. [Here is added a sketch of Quinn bringing the Irish American orator, Bourke Cochrane, behind the scenes to see the players.]

104

April 1, 1913
317 West 29

My dear Willie—I hear that the American edition of Moore's last books announces them as stating that W. B. Yeats is a 'Literary Fop'. What he did say of course is that he thought you were a fop, and thereby avoiding you 'lost two years of your wonderful company' though for the matter of that he did not use the word fop. We used to say Now Barabbas was a publisher—henceforth we shall say 'Now Ananias and Sapphira were American publishers'. Not that it matters, except that it is amusing to conjecture that in the announcement is the hand of some Irish miscreant and possibly of a priest. I see that in Dublin there is much spitting of venom. Lily keeps me in touch.

I have at last finished my article—it is 5200 words long and I think lucid and interesting, and *suggestive.* I have also submitted to *Harper's Weekly* an article on Lord Wolseley, which is lovely. I have spent the last year chiefly in reading books got from the Carnegie Libraries. God bless old Carnegie. Did you ever come across a book called *William Allingham, a Diary?* My advice is to get it—it is both entertaining and instructive. Allingham's brother was a *very* distinguished classical scholar in T.C.D., and he tried to teach me to write Latin verse, but he came too late. I could not get myself interested—it was impossible for me.[1]

I hope to spend to-morrow with Charlie Johnston and his wife and will read to them my article. I find them always helpful and appreciative, and

---

[1] Thomas Allingham. He wrote imitations of his brother's poems and published them with the poet's initials in the county newspaper at Ballyshannon, where the brothers came from.

for some reasons I can't divine rather incensed against Russell—Mrs. Johnston at any rate. Charlie never speaks against anyone, whereas Russell regards Mrs. Johnston as his friend and dislikes Charlie. I find both of them at times trying, but at heart sound and loyal.—Yours affectionately—J. B. YEATS

105

317 West 29, N. York
April 6, 1913

P.S. (If this is illegible have it typewritten. Quinn does that with my letters.)

. . . I see that Edward Dowden is dead; among his own family and small circle of friends it will be an event of very great importance. Weak health caused him early to withdraw from this world and this was increased by his mystical doctrines, and so his writing was without actuality, or rather monotonous. A sharp and incessant concussion is necessary to release the fire in the flint. In these days in Ireland he'd have written poetry.

About the Professorship? He in his generous way was anxious for you not to take it *unless you could make some arrangement* by which you could be saved from having to lecture on early English and such dryasdust matters—all unliterary, and to which he seemed to say his own best faculties were sacrificed.[1] He was convinced that such things should be the employment of some specialists. Of your qualifications for a real professorship he spoke glowingly. Mahaffy's statement that Dowden did not work very hard in his professorship was one of those things that endear Mahaffy to all his friends and contemporaries.

I have just been reading *Timon of Athens*—not a novel idea in it —everything drawn from ancient common everyday wisdom. These myriad-minded Americans are always looking for new ideas, and yet you could not be poetical about a bran new street or castle or church or even garden, neither about a new idea. What is new is detestable to *poetry*. When we do like anything new it is when we recognise the old with a new gloss, as the dawn of a new day, or a young girl who is like her mother or her grandmother or her ancient mother Eve, or like to one's own sweetheart in some prenatal existence. I have just finished an article

[1] There had been a suggestion that W. B. Y. should succeed Dowden in the chair of English Literature at Trinity College.

in which I maintain that art embodies not this or that feeling, but the whole totality—sensations, feeling, intuitions, everything—and that when everything within us is expressed there is peace and what is called beauty—this totality is personality. Now a most powerful and complex part of the personality is *affection* and affection *springs straight out of the memory*. For that reason what is new whether in the world of ideas or of fact cannot be subject for poetry, tho' you can be as rhetorical about it as you please—rhetoric expresses other peoples feelings, poetry one's own.

Another reason made Dowden a recluse from art as well as from the world; he was with his present wife extraordinarily happy. They have a canary here who used to sing incessantly and unlike all other canaries his note was low and sweet. Now he has a wife whom he occasionally beats and he no longer sings—the nightingale sings with its breast against a thorn. Personality is born out of pain. It is the fire shut up in the flint.

FROM LILY YEATS

106

Dundrum, Co. Dublin
June 18th, 1913

My dear Papa—I did not get a moment the week I was in London. Will try now to send you a fine long letter.

I stayed with Pixie in London, got there the night before the sale, went up to Londonderry House, which is in Park Lane and like a well-worn museum, early on Tuesday morning expecting to find the hampers of work waiting there for me; no—nothing had come and the show opened at 2.30. I put in a fearful time, the work being found the next day in the last hours of the sale, hidden away behind some furniture in Londonderry House itself. The footman may have thought them to be full of rifles for Belfast, not wanted until July 12th. Anyway, there I was, no work, my two helpers, Kathleen Ball and Lady Alix made fools of.

From ten o'clock until two o'clock Tuesday I stood in the big hall of Londonderry House calling up railway offices on the telephone and waiting hours while they made inquiries. I get such little practice with the telephone that it is anything but easy to me. I saw all the life of the house go through the hall. 'Orse was ordered from the stables for her Ladyship, then came her Ladyship, who is no longer young and far from slim, in a looped-up habit, riding-boots, loose at the ankle, white sailor-hat and veil. Out she went, her mounting superintended by the two head men, in plain clothes, and a footman in powder and knee breeches. At 11.30 I was still standing, telephone in hand, looking at a life-size picture of Joseph and Potiphar's wife. The butler had just, through the telephone, put a little something on a horse called 'Loud Laughter'. Her Ladyship had just come in from her ride when, without any warning, the hall filled with a group in the plainest of mourning. 'Caught napping', said a footman, and there was Queen Alexandra, and her sister the Empress of Russia, Princess Victoria and their attendants. A surprise visit. The servants stiffened and fell in place, and up the great staircase they went. The Queen has a pathetic kind of grace, but without dignity because her wig, fair as a child's, is so very wiggy, her lips so very red. The Empress looks a little old devil. Short features, thick lips and black wig, but very much alive. They were up in the ball-room, where the sale was, for about an hour. The servants in the hall at once fell to pieces again, the head man sending an underling out to see 'oo drove 'er. See if it's Jack—Jack it was, so out he went to talk to Jack, then two royal footmen came into the hall and talked horses to the footmen. At last, word was passed down the stairs by the servants on the landing, like a bucket of water at a fire, to say 'on the move'. The servants stiffened, then came the word 'right-o', down came the royal party, Lady Londonderry still in the riding-habit and loose ankle-boots, dropping low curtsies . . .

Next afternoon the hampers were found, in the house all the time.

Lady Lyttelton took a lot of trouble and brought round all her broadsides, prints, books, etc., but by that time the work was found. She brought her friends to the stall, saying 'You must see these things done by this wonderful family; they can't live for ever, so you must buy now.' She thinks great things of Jack [Yeats].

All the worry about the work gave me a headache for the first time in my life.

Pixie is as delightful as ever and has a big-roomed flat near Victoria Station with black walls and orange curtains. She is now an ardent and pious Roman Catholic, which has added to her happiness but taken from her friends. She now has the dullest of friends, selected entirely because they are R.C., converts most of them, half educated people, who want to see both eyes in a profile drawing. She goes to confession every Saturday—except the week I was there—she couldn't think of any sins, so my influence must have been very holy. I heard the other day of a priest who said that confessing nuns was like being eaten alive by ducks.—Your affectionate daughter—(signed) LILY YEATS

[A note added later by Lily Yeats.] Queen Alexandra was quite kittenish, she bought a baby's bonnet and put it on her head over her toque, bought many other little things and hung them on to the buttons of her coat till she was festooned like a Xmas tree. As the royal party moved towards the top of the staircase going away, a lady-in-waiting hurried forward and plucked Her Majesty. (signed) L. Y.

TO W. B. YEATS

107

317 West 29th St., New York
July 2nd, 1913

. . . Poetry is the reaction from the imperfect to the perfect—to a perfect grief as in Synge's *Riders to the Sea* or to a perfect joy as in your earlier poetry—the accompanying melody whether of prose or verse the effort to keep the heart soft and wakeful, portraiture in art or poetry the effort to keep the pain alive and intensify it, since out of the heart of the pain comes the solace, as a monk scourges himself to bring an ecstasy. Some time ago I saw a young mother with a sick infant in her arms. I need not go into the circumstances, but I know that I put the question to her and that I was haunted by what I saw and heard for days and days. Why did I put these questions and why did I try constantly to recall and keep alive the incident? I regretted that I could not take my canvas and paint a portrait of her and her child. She was soft spoken, Irish and young and very pretty, from Donnybrook, and all her children had died in infancy. She was *ashamed* of her sick child and *tried to hide it from me*. She was not many years over and her father and mother dead since she left Ireland— her face full of goodness. I would fain scourge myself spiritually, and it pained me that the image should fade. The mediaeval artists lived among such sights and sounds and had nothing to console them but their art and their religion, unless like Raphael they averted their eyes. . . .

FROM W. B. YEATS

108

Coole Park, Gort, Co. Galway
Burren, Co. Clare
[1913] July 17

. . . We have come down to a desolate, windy spot on the coast of Clare, where Robert Gregory is sketching, and his wife getting health. There is a wood in a hollow of the hills where one can get in out of the wind, and feel very much as if one had pulled a blanket over one's head to keep the night air out. I don't know if one ever delights in trees and in the sea with equal intensity, and I am of the tree party.

I am working every day on the *Player Queen*, but will not for a long time yet get at the verse writing. It is still all scenario. I think it is my most stirring thing. There will be a certain number of lyrics put into the mouth of one of the characters as in *Deirdre*.

I went to Paris for a few days before I came here, and met Sarah Purser at Maud Gonne's. She was characteristic as ever, as like herself as a John drawing. Maud Gonne had a cage full of canaries and the birds were all singing. Sarah Purser began lunch by saying 'What a noise! I'd like to have my lunch in the kitchen!' . . .

I think the only Galway news is that I dined with Edward Martyn the other day and that he told me he has left the Sinn Fein organization, retired from politics altogether. He did not say, but I suspect the collecting of shares for a proposed Sinn Fein daily paper had something to do with it. Some time ago, ardent Sinn Feiners were called upon to refuse to pay Income Tax. He, poor man, and one other being the only members of the party who paid any. He is busy writing as ever, is very amiable when one sees him, but never goes to see anybody so far as I can make out. Moore is his only friend, and as he thinks Moore is damned, he has no responsibility about him.

I wrote to George [Pollexfen] and suggested myself as a visitor while Lady Gregory is here, but George has Alfred [Pollexfen] staying with him. I laugh every time I think of it. The Rosses Point house is the draughtiest I was ever in, and at Merville, Alfred used to have a little cloth flap over his keyhole to keep out the draught. George doesn't mind, as he often explained to me while I was suffering, as he is never in the house except at night, and then he walks between supper and bedtime. I am better here and am working well, and have done a new lyric and a good one. . . . I have read all your lectures and like them immensely, and so you know does Lady Gregory. She has put me out of the job of writing her epitaph, and put you into it.—Your son—W. B. Yeats

TO RUTH HART

109

New York
Novr. 22nd, 1913

. . . I know of nothing but what is pleasant about the people at Howth; for one thing that Miss Violet Jameson is to marry, or rather that she is now married to a doctor. She is a nice and a pretty girl and accomplished, and I am sure she will be happy. 'The best men I have ever known were either doctors or priests', I remember hearing John O'Leary say, and he as a Fenian hated priests, as a class. I myself think doctors and clergymen the nicest. My greatest friend was a Bishop, a high Church bishop, who did not in the least mind that I did not think with him.[1]

I am constantly being asked by my friends and implored by my daughters to come home—but I dread Dublin for very good reasons. Why do birds migrate? looking for food—that is why I am here—here I can get work enough to support myself, and at home, it is always impending insolvency. Just lately I have had some luck. I have done a large half length portrait of a pretty actress for a wealthy theatrical company Lubler and Co.; and it is hung in the entrance hall of one of their theatres and very expensively framed. I have been living mostly by writing, and compared to painting portraits I hate writing.

I was so hurried that the portrait is very unfinished as regards everything except the face, but Leibler calls it a 'beautiful picture', notwithstanding that I tell them it is no good at all. As you know I am always miserably despondent over my own work, so that I often curse the day that I was born, at any rate the day that I became a painter of portraits.

A famous American portrait painter—their best and supposed by his admirers to be far superior to Sargent—has been painting all summer in the West of Ireland. He went to Dublin and spent a week there and as far as I can make out spent most of his time looking at my portraits—at the Abbey Theatre and at the Modern Gallery—and the very day I received

[1] John Dowden.

my commission to paint the actress, I met an artist who had just received a letter from Robert Henri (the famous painter) in which he said that I was the most modest portrait painter he had ever met, for that to his astonishment he found my portraits to be the best in Dublin and *'ten times better than Orpen's'*. You can fancy how this cheered me and set me on my way rejoicing. I have met him once since his return and he renewed in conversation all he had said by letter and he is now so pleased with this last portrait that I hear he has announced his intention of writing to Leibler and Co his high opinion of it. I am in my 75th year and feel that life is just beginning; 45 years ago a lady cunning about the future told me that I would not win success till I was very old and that then it would be *universal* success; what she meant by universal success, I could not guess, but now I know—since I sometimes sketch in pencil sometimes paint, sometimes lecture, and sometimes write articles, and sometimes am well paid and sometimes am badly paid—every kind of experience.[1]

Every year I promise myself to return next year—but really now I am getting anxious. I am here six years—and I don't want to end my days here without seeing my old friends again and the sod of Ireland.

When I return what a meeting it will be—and yet as you know only too well what gaps! I was overjoyed to see the Jamesons, and greatly flattered and pleased at their interest in me, and remembrance of me.

I am afraid no one among my friends outside my own family takes much interest in America, so that I shall not be allowed to tell my traveller's tales, and yet I would have much to tell if only some one would listen. I see strange people and hear strange doctrines on all sides of me; what with us would be startling and revolutionary, is here quite commonplace.

Canon Hannay[2] and his wife are here now, about his play *General O'Regan* produced with very great success, and they are delighted with everything, especially the climate and its almost perpetual sunshine. I said wait till you taste the winter, and yet it is still summer. We have just had several days, the temperature at 72. To-morrow or next day it will snow and the streets blocked with it, piled on each side of the street, and a piercing wind—hardly any one ever carries an umbrella, since if it rains or snows the wind makes umbrellas impossible. Indeed I have seen the gutters at side of street filled with umbrellas broken to pieces by the wind. In Summer the heat is so great that the horses die in numbers. . . . Last

---

[1] The lady was Mrs. Edwin Ellis.
[2] 'G. A. Birmingham', the novelist.

Summer a friend of mine in a short walk saw thirty horses lying dead killed by the sun. There is also great lawlessness. I know quantities of people who have witnessed murders, and lots who have been held up and robbed, but New York fascinates people. French German Italian English and Irish go home, but invariably they return, and tho' I have tried my best I cannot find out what the charm is. I think part of it is that it is so easy to make friends; at a restaurant in a tram car you can quite easily pick up a friend who will become everything to you—

English people when they first come here are very unhappy. They find themselves so much disliked—then they find that sociability and an easy affability are duties, and New York's fascination falls upon them too. I have myself helped several of them through these trying stages of initiation.

Give my love to your mother and to Ethel. I am glad Vaughan is a father. I heard also of your other sister's marriage and her two children. I bless them all. I am always hoping to hear of your marriage.—Yours affectly—J. B. YEATS

TO OLIVER ELTON

110

9th Decr. 1913

I have just read a volume of O. Henry's stories. Kipling is all tinsel and vulgarity and both elaborated. O. Henry is all tinsel and no elaboration, delicious tinsel and of course no vulgarity. The delicious creature carries no burden, no patriotism nor imperialism nor morality—and the youth (he was no more) died of drink. Editors would pay him what he asked for tories not yet written—they would count on his genius and his honesty— if we can call honesty what was no doubt something much finer. Here is a personal touch—he was so overwhelmed with shyness and timidity that once going to see off a friend going by steamer and finding him surrounded by friends he escaped and hid himself. He writes in such queer English and yet it is so delicious that I think of learning it and forgetting all about Addison and Swift and W. B. Y. and Oliver Elton and all the other masters of style. There is only one drawback. There is a fry of lesser men who imitate him, writing with industriousness and seriousness what he threw off in the gaiety of irresponsibility. Many of my friends have met him, no one seems to have known the elusive creature. Ordi-.

nary poets start with a rhyme singing or seductive. Philosophic poets with an idea, O. Henry with an adventure which sprang out of his inventing mind dressed in all its properties. . . .

TO W. B. YEATS

III

317 West 29th Street, New York
Decr. 11th, 1913

My dear Willie—Of course I don't know the circumstances, but as regards Dowden's book of poems I would ask you, indeed beg of you, to remember that he not only was a very old friend, but the best of friends. . . . He took the keenest interest in your success—he wrote to me at length about your succeeding him in the professorship,[1] his anxiety being that if you took it you should be relieved of the work in connection with Anglo-Saxon and such philological worries, and so be free to devote yourself to Literature pure and simple. I have no doubt that you will do nothing illogical, but it is better to be illogical than INHUMAN. To be sure a Frenchman will never be illogical. It is their pride in business and in everything; and it is a poor kind of pride, and belongs to a people who aim at instructing the world and succeed in being rhetorical and eloquent and always charmingly lucid—yet they might do better—if their poetry was greater.

As I have said I don't know the circumstances. Only I ask you to follow Goethe rather than the French—and avoid giving pain. I know of old that from the time of your boyhood you have been liable at times, only at times, to a touch of the propaganda fiend—you get it from your father. I like poetical rhetoric very much—yours and the French—and the Shakespearian rhetoric. But best of all I like the music, when the bird of poesy sings to itself alone in the heart of the wood, persuading and coaxing and commanding and admonishing its own soul, and thinking nothing of others. The Frenchman is most charming when he is thinking about others, and so he works and lives and writes in the bondage of logic. Victor Hugo gloried in the servitude—and was splendidly ostentatious about it, it delighted his countrymen, and amazed other people, its naïveté was astonishing—the naïveté of logic not the naïveté of the feelings. There is much sentimentality which is the naïveté of the feelings, in Goethe for instance.

[1] Of English Literature at Trinity College, Dublin.

I have looked through Dowden's books of poems and like them very much indeed and *am grateful* for them—for this history of his friendship with the present wife. And from a propagandist point of view I would say that they will do good to husbands and wives, who because of Dowden will read them and love each other more happily.

In the conjugal relation there is the bourgeois point of view, which is comfortable and affectionate and sentimental, and the workman's point of view which is romantic and poetical, and the aristocratic which is cynical and carnal and atheistical—Dowden's poetry is as regards these things bourgeois.

You may be surprised at my description of the workman's marriage being a thing poetical and romantic. But I am convinced of it; my models in Dublin used to talk a lot about it. I once got Synge interested, and it was my hope that he was meditating a play on the subject.

Don't trouble to answer this letter, which is merely a word to the wise. At any rate don't act on the spur of the moment, and in this matter avoid giving pain even to your Dublin enemies, which is after all a poor kind of fun—tho' I admit it is tempting.—Yours affectionately—J. B. YEATS

112

317 West 29th Street, New York
Decr. 25, 1913

My dear Willie—Again I am writing, yet I think my theory that the beautiful is the lovable made sensible (we have five senses and to all or each is the appeal of the beautiful) was worth stating and sending to you. This never relaxing pursuit of the lovable is that wherewith all nature is travailing, and it is the 'pathos' of all existence, and it is because poetry embodies this desire and feeds it that poetry is now what Religion once was— the Queen of Sciences. Another important matter to which I have drawn your illustrious attention is that poetry and art deal with what cannot be expressed in action or in thoughts, being as inarticulate as the cry of a woman in childbirth—and this is a hard saying for Americans, who reading literature made for the million have acquired the habit of refusing to believe what cannot be made as clear and convincing as a sum in arithmetic, besides which they have another habit of testing everything by its obvious utility and its application to the problems of difficult life. In England you have a Literary aristocracy who stood together and by each other, keeping to their own standards which are not those of the million. Here the Multitude is Lord—and in its way it is a noble well instructed lord, and like the Kaiser in Germany, a minor poet. I always think the Salvation Army a splendid instance of what a democracy can and cannot do. It is absolutely efficient, and its ends those of the most beneficent utility. *But its religion is bosh*—while being so articulate that a child can understand it. The Catholic Church built up by individual men, aristocrats by their singularity and their intellectual culture, preaches doctrines whose mystery no one can unravel, and these the million—the impatient million—were not allowed to touch—and yet it was sufficient since the ignorant can enjoy what he cannot explain, as all men enjoyed the rainbow thousands of years before Newton explained it.

Protestantism made people practical and prosperous because it was an easily understood morality, enforced by lucid logic, and the menace of Hell, and because it excluded all religion which is poetry, for poetry weakens the practical will. The Democrat is proud of his reasoning power and rightly so, *and yet it is all he has got*—when he attempts poetry he only succeeds in being didactic and eloquent, and eloquent of what? Duty and morality and upliftment—matters which, however valuable, are not poetry —one cannot be eloquent of beauty—one can only pull away the curtain, and the less said about the vision the better. It would be 'a getting in the way'.

If these ideas can be incorporated in your lectures 'changed no doubt in the process' I shall be glad, only in your lectures don't make any allusion to me. My individuality must not 'get in the way'—*nothing should intervene between a lecturer and his audience* and there never can be any question of egotism between you and me.—Yours affectionately—J. B. YEATS

113

317 West 29th Street, New York
January 6, 1914

My dear Willie—I am afraid you must sometimes think me very conceited—the fact is not only am I an old man in a hurry, but all my life I have fancied myself just on the verge of discovering the primum mobile. Of course Beauty is much more than the lovable made visible, but besides being wondrous and magnetic and astonishing it, when the whole banner is unflung, is also lovable. In Wordsworth's 'Hartleap Well' is this verse no doubt by you well remembered:

> 'Upon his side the Hart was lying stretched
> His nostril touched a spring beneath a hill,
> *And with the last deep groan his breath had fetched*
> *The waters of the spring were trembling still.'*

In these last two lines is beauty made lovable.

I have just read *Father Ralph*[1] and am indeed delighted with it—particularly towards the conclusion. All through there is intensity and yet what delicacy and what restraint! I wish he had told us a little more of Hilda the mother—I mean before the Bishop and the priests took entire possession of her, about this part of her life he talks only in generalities and apparently has no facts to go on, or does not wish to reveal them.

—— have not paid me for the portrait—the last news is that it was stolen from the theatre—I hope it was not for the sake of the frame.

I have not heard from home for some days, I generally hear every mail.

I hope you admire Jack's illustrations to Hannay's book. I like them better and better and am never tired of looking at them. They are a great help to the book. Hannay who is a generous kind of man is, I think, quite aware of it—he spoke to me of them with enthusiasm.—Yours affectionately—J. B. YEATS

TO OLIVER ELTON

114

Jan. 15, 1914   N.Y.

They gave him [O. Henry] in New York the greatest funeral ever seen in these parts. Everyone went—all the politicians of every colour and shade, and all the writers—the paltriest little newspaper scribbler as well as the professors and grave writers. All hearts swelling with sorrow and joy —and his body was found in the morgue. Like the ancient heroes, he disappeared when he died; afterwards, his body was found, and they did what they could. The funeral service was held at 'the little church round the corner', the famous church where the weddings are celebrated. Thus was it ordered by the kind gods.

---

[1] An Irish novel by a priest, who afterwards left the Church.

A Talk on University Education

TO LILY YEATS

115

N.Y.
March 10, 1914

Yesterday I went to the Metropolitan Museum. You remember how few pictures it had and nearly all small pictures of the Barbizon School. Now there is an interminable series of rooms filled with pictures—how things do advance here. When next in London the first place I shall visit will be the National Gallery and I shall find no doubt some new pictures, but of course no new rooms opened. It is this constant rapidity of progress and change in every direction that makes New York such a wonder.

I met a learned young German the other day. I wish you had heard how he scoffed at American University education, to the laughing but tearful embarrassment of his American wife, but what are tears to a strong-hearted Teuton. He also said that T.C.D. is producing now about 75 per cent of the books that are published. Dr. Bellinger at whose apartment I met him told how lately he arrived at a dinner when the guests were all philosophers (i.e. men of science) and that hardly anyone spoke a word. At last Dr. B.'s neighbour was moved to say that he wished he was at home where all his specimens were drying, his subject being the sex of mushrooms. This made the young German roar. He said it was just like America where everybody is a specialist, knowing nothing but the facts of his special subject, while incapable of general reasoning and knowledge and so incapable of conversation. Dr. Bellinger is also a German and married to a clever New England woman. How these Germans did chortle! and did not I enjoy the compliment about Dublin. We all came together in harmony when we talked of England and the English. Yet we said nothing unfair, and the ladies forgot their discomfiture about the Universities of U.S.A.

TO W. B. YEATS

116

317 West 29th Street, New York
March 16, 1914

My dear Willie—I am more glad than I can tell you that peace is made with Quinn.

Quinn—Isaac Butt—G. Moore

Quinn is a man of genius—not a touch of the commonplace or any other kind of prose in his whole composition, and yet an eminent lawyer —who also sticks to his work. I remember a story of Butt. A friend of mine found him in a country hotel quite happy for days reading Milton, when every one thought he was preparing for a big case, a cause célèbre, which at the time was the talk of the country, and there sat Butt alone in his inn reading Paradise Lost.

As regards the other matter—I was chiefly concerned in your writing a good poem—and how can any one write a poem of hatred about Moore whom one may indeed despise but not hate. You are quite right in thinking I am not a politician, nor do I attach much importance to politics at any time. To think much of them is rather a woman's way than a man's way—women are essentially politicians, in everything they do, in private and in public—as wives, mothers, society leaders; always are they spinning that kind of web; they are brought up to it.[1]—Yours affectionately— J. B. YEATS

117

New York
March 16, 1914

. . . I send on two letters, which I sent after you weeks ago, but which are just returned from the dead letter office. Also another letter just received which I fancy is in Katherine Tynan Hinkson's handwriting. I don't send on a letter from myself as the news is all now stale news. I have been much indisposed for weeks. They called it influenza—an insultingly inadequate word. I prefer to call it the black death, for it was certainly death in life. The Mad[elles] Petitpas would say to me 'Mistare Yeats you look so tired'— no wonder I looked tired, whether asleep or awake I was always present at some witches' sabbath, and being hailed round the circle by invisible devils, who chased me with broomsticks and shovels and red hot pincers. My one desire was to lie down—anywhere—on the carpet and when out in the streets to lie down among the melting snow. If I lay down on the bed I went to sleep to be worse tormented. I would go to bed a little after eight and sleep for twelve hours if you can call it sleep—all the outer symptoms of constant headache and sore throat and sore bones and shivering being nothing to the hell of despair within my mind. I worried

---

[1] W. B. Yeats had been offended by passages in Moore's *Hail and Farewell*. He wrote two 'poems of hatred' upon Moore.

angrily about the people at home and about you, and was furious if I did not get a letter by every mail or even if there was no mail. When not worrying I amused myself by composing in sad earnest obituary notices such as would appear in the newspapers announcing my death, and worst of all I was fully persuaded that this condition was to be permanent. I was to be always like this—it was natural and inevitable at my age. I lost all power of enjoyment, fancy a state of mind in which the prettiest girl was to me the same as the ugliest. One day soothed and comforted by the heat of the room I as nearly as possible fell asleep *in the Dentist's chair*. Surely a thing unprecedented. I ceased to smoke and hated the sight of food—both meant exertion—suddenly the hellhounds were called off, and I felt quite well, and as it were turned round and laughed at myself, occasionally I have relapses which only last a few hours. It amuses me to write this description and perhaps it will amuse you to read it. . . .

. . . I saw a few days ago for just a minute a man named Kavanagh. He had been four months on the other side seeing a great deal of George Moore—and once he went with George Moore to Ireland for four weeks, they being together all the time as I understood—he told me that Moore said he had now left Ireland for good because no one there sympathised with him, except Gogarty. I asked Kavanagh if he had seen Russell, and he replied No, and rather implied that he had avoided seeing him, for said he Russell has grown so egotistical. Does all this mean that the friendship between Russell and Magee and Moore is now dissolved? I have always thought Moore was not worth powder and shot. It is all ending in no one wanting him, and perhaps at last he will find himself without an audience which according to my distinction is a calamity beyond redemption for the prose writer. You remember *how it overwhelmed poor Wilde*—and killed him. . . .

TO LILY YEATS

118

New York
March 24, 1914

. . . On Sunday I was all day at Quinn's. Willie was there. He looked very bright and in the best of spirits but said he felt tired. He had had a cold. I noticed in him a subtle change, a something assured, a quiet importance. Importance is too strong a word, but I think he is in funds and this not from his lectures [1] (that money is to pay a debt of £500), but from some other source. I wonder is Bullen [2] paying up and are his books beginning to make money for him. It would·be for me a proud moment when I see a Yeats with money, and I am quite sure it won't spoil him. We don't spoil *that way*. He mentioned that he has to hurry home for Ezra Pound's marriage. He is to marry Mrs. Shakespear's daughter. She is beautiful and well off and has the most charming manners.... Both are clever, and I fancy Ezra is a nice fellow. As Willie remarks, when rich and fashionable people bring up a daughter to be intellectual, naturally she will turn away from the 'curled darlings' of her own class and fall in love with intellect which is mostly to wed with poverty as well. I hope it will turn out that Ezra Pound is not an *uncomfortable* man of genius.... It was pleasant to see Willie and Quinn like brothers together. They seemed to have the same thoughts and the same interests. What one said was echoed by the other. The time spent by Willie at the art school was, as it turns out, well spent. Quinn's collection of pictures gave him great delight....

I hear the professor of literature at Trinity College is a Plymouth brother—fancy such an outrage. I'd like to hear him lecture on Walt Whitman. [3]

119

March 27, 1914

... A couple of days ago Mrs. Fleming by cards predicted great good fortune to come suddenly and it has come. Yesterday morning in about three hours I wrote for Knoedler and Co., the great picture dealers, an introduction for their catalogue to the Whistler exhibition, and they were so pleased that they said they would give me 35 dollars and when I received my cheque it was for 50 dollars and when I spoke of this they said 'yes because it is really so good'. The afternoon of the same day Willie offered to pay my debt to Petitpas and take me home with him next Thursday. Mrs. Fleming had told me that I would be offered a gift of my passage home. When Knoedler made his proposition to me it was a complete surprise. I had taken Mrs. Fleming to see the pictures by Orpen and in her presence

[1] This was W. B. Yeats's third visit to the United States, where he had first lectured in the winter of 1903–4.

[2] Bullen is A. H. Bullen, the distinguished Elizabethan scholar and publisher.

[3] Professor Wilbraham Trench, who succeeded Dowden in the Chair of English Literature at Dublin University.

the offer was made, and, absolutely, I was just going to refuse it when she 'butted in' as they say in America and insisted on my doing it.

Last night Willie and Quinn came after dinner and if I am to judge by the amount of talk and laughter and the length of time the party kept together (I was at the other end of the table) they enjoyed themselves—Afterwards it broke up and they all went dancing—Willie the most diligent of all and Quinn and Mrs. Fleming remained together for a quiet half hour. Quinn very silent and I think deeply interested. She is lately married to a husband younger than herself who is very much in love as I think any man would be. She has been everywhere, knows French like English, she tells fortunes by a method learned from the Chinese. Mistral, the French poet just dead, told her his whole history. She brought up and educated her youngest brother and made him one of the most successful doctors in Philadelphia. She also helped to keep her mother and is flowing over with gaiety and with kindness, an opulent sort of creature with a hundred irons in the fire and all of them hot. She does not know what it is to think ill of anyone. She is never sick or sorry or fatigued and goes to all the plays. She organises all the fashionable schools. With her sweet temper, her kind heart and her soft and resourceful ways she spreads order where there is chaos and helps all the lame ducks, whether they be institutions or only girls and mothers of girls—the last named being just now in America the most bewildered and care-distraught of all, as you may well believe.

Willie wanted me to go home for a season and then return. But I said 'No, when I come home it will be for good'. Meantime I want to stay till the end of the Fall. There are several things I want to see through, for one thing my own portrait. If I could before I go make a little money, so as to return with my pockets full or at least not empty. It is this want of money that spoils my health and happiness. That sale of *Harper's Weekly* is the source of all my troubles. It used to be my constant standby, and a lamp burning steadily in the darkness.

There was a man here last night who knew my brother in Rio. He said, 'He was my broker, and one year alone I did with him 300000 dollars of work.' He intimated that the brokerage on a sum like that must have been something considerable. He said that Willie looked like his uncle, as I have often thought he did. He said he was the 'life of the town'. I met this man some months ago. He looks an upright sort of man, respectable and well dressed, but like most business men everywhere rather a dull talker. Although he saw so much of my brother and evidently admired him, he could tell me nothing of him but wanted to talk of his investments and their business dealings, all of which would have been Greek to me—in fact he did tell me at length, but I did not understand. He did not seem to know my brother's family—probably your uncle found him dull, however profitable. . . . Quinn is working desperately hard against England over the Panama bill. I heard Mrs. Fleming tell him he won't get his wish, and I am sure his wish is in this Panama business, in which I fancy he will be beat. The President and the Colleges are against him.

TO W. B. YEATS

120

317 West 29th Street, New York
April 20, 1914

My dear Willie—here is a definition for you—humour is when the humorist with a crowd at his back attacks an individual, a poor delinquent who from wild courage or because of some inherent depravity dares to separate himself from the others and be the exceptional— wit, where the same individual rushes sword in hand on the humorist and all his backers and scatters them howling with rage, all of them wounded and some of them mortally. Shakespeare at will can be either wit or humorist. In the cruelty of the humorist there is much good nature. The consciousness of numbers gives them such a feeling of security [that] when the wit attacks them with a cruelty in which is no good nature their good nature also vanishes and we have the debauchery of the French revolution. As a rule the wit is a gentleman with a gentleman's education and we admire his skill with the rapier—as regards courage of course the honours are all with him—and his cruelty does not insult our intellects as theirs does.

I have just read Ferrero's life of Savonarola—extraordinarily interesting, he knows all about theology, but also everything about art—he associated as much with artists and poets and philosophers as with friars. The honour and glory sought by the poet always consist in the art he employs rather than in the subject treated by him, and rightly he deprecates a poet treating of religion. Whistler pointed out that Switzerland had produced no landscape painters, for the reason that mountain scenery was a subject too vast. Landscape painters come, said Whistler, from countries where the scenery is mild and tame. A woman kneeling in earnest prayer, according to

Savonarola, is the best expression of religious emotion. Do you not think that in Milton's Paradise there is no religious emotion?

There is a fine letter of M. Angelo's in which he expresses his humbleness as artist: praise irritated him. 'It is true they praise me so much that had I Paradise in my bosom less of praise would suffice. I perceive that you suppose me to be just what God wishes that I were. I am a poor man and of little merit, who plod along in the art which God gave me, to lengthen out my life as far as possible.' This humility is for the art, the orator is lifted up by the feeling that he is expressing great thoughts—that is thoughts that dominate because they are those of his audience, humility does not become him and would be insincerity. I quote this thinking of your speech at the Poetry Society's lunch.[1]

Poetry is the last refuge and asylum for the individual of whom oratory is the enemy.

I wish you would write and tell me of your health and if you have completely recovered. I am particularly well—that load of care rolled off my back has done wonders as you will easily imagine.

Summer is now here, tho' the trees are still leafless.

The heat to-day a little moderated by April showers.—Yrs affectionately —J. B. YEATS

121

317 West 29th Street, New York
May 10, 1914

My dear Willie—I have just read 'An Essay on Cubes' in the *English Review* of April. It is very interesting. It seems to me that the writer upholds M. Arnold's theory that poetry is criticism of life—a bad heresy I think—but he is alive, tho' his liveliness is rather malicious and not benign like Goethe's.

You, long ago, said Poetry is creation; that is, that it has its source in vision and in vision only. This writer has vision, but it is only half seen, he goes outside it and away from it to break heads among the critics. If he has the power of vision as I think he has why not leave these critics to settle their own disputes and be a law unto himself? A poem such as yours, 'The Two Kings', is worth volumes of criticism. If the rose puzzled its mind over the question how it grew, it would not have been the miracle it is.

---

[1] A speech by W. B. Yeats in New York.

Poetry and Paradises—Fielding

Poetry concerns itself with the creation of Paradises. I use the word in the plural for there are as many paradises as there are individual men—nay —as many as there are separate feelings. For 'the weeping mother of the middle ages' (Michelet's phrase) there was the Madonna and child painted by all the best artists and placed everywhere, in every church and in every house for her longing eyes. There is also the paradise for the happy—the bride, the lovers, the victors in games &c., there is also a paradise for the sympathetic—a twilight paradise where the light is not too strong for weak eyes.

Whether [James] Stephens is a poet or a prose writer turns upon whether or not he is enough self-centred to do his thinking and his feeling all by himself. If he cannot do his best without having some one to assail or cajole or persuade then he is of the prose writers—and only incidentally a poet. The true poet is all the time a visionary and whether with friends or not, as much alone as a man on his death bed. . . .

I see that Stephens denounces Fielding as not much better than an after-dinner speaker. What nonsense! he says the profoundest things—and besides he was a man attended by visions. He says some things about G. Meredith with which I quite agree. Some time ago, long before I saw this article, I used to say that Meredith had the cruelty of the sedentary man, as George Eliot had that of the old maid and I compared him with the kindly and the FEARLESS Fielding—people don't realize and don't remember that Christ was a man *tempted in all things*. Of how few men could this be said? Certainly not of Meredith or of George Eliot and yet it would be true of Fielding. Once lecturing in Dublin I proposed that the word invitation should be substituted for temptation since we really came on earth to be tempted, and that in most cases it was our business not to resist but to yield to it and take the consequences, even tho' it required the courage of a hero. St. Francis was a man of pleasure, who had gone the round of the passions. This was the history of all the great saints. It is only the great sinner who can do the two things of hating the sin and loving the sinner— the other sort only *hate the sinner*. They do not hate the sin of which they know nothing except that it looks ROSILY—even tho' like George Meredith they have a conviction interpenetrated with logical knowledge that its looks deceive.

Last Saturday I spent the afternoon and evening at a beautiful place on the Hudson belonging to an immensely wealthy lawyer and Jew named Untermeyer. I was a guest together with the Poetry Society going and returning on a special train—first of all we had Chopin rendered, it seemed even to my musically deaf ears very beautifully. After that came the poets, all sorts and ages and both sexes—we applauded vigorously with true American heartiness, criticising not at all. The house seemed to me beautiful and full of wonderful pictures and statuary which I longed to look at, preferring them to everything else, so that to me it was a Tantalus Feast.

Quinn has settled the Leibler dispute by buying Miss O'Neill's portrait for 150 dollars, they paying me 25 dollars for the sketch.[1] Quinn is the true Deus ex Machina—so I am now financially quite comfortable—which is a great deal—even if my conscience is not at all comfortable. I dreamed last night that I had a visit from your grandfather who asked me how long I expected him to support me. I thought I was staying at Merville. I awoke miserable, and remained so for a long time, even tho' wide-awake—as Homer says 'the divine dream still shed about me'.

Just now you would like N. York—the weather is so delicious, and as yet no mosquitoes, so that I am not afraid to keep my window open night and day.

What are you doing? I hope you are writing Poetry. One of the poets at the Untermeyer's said something about you and your school to which I replied by showing him that he entirely misunderstood you—he said you put things afar off to enjoy them. I replied that that was true of American poetry, but that you drew as close as possible to your subject and were actuated by love and not by admiration—he was silenced. Afterwards he was among those who read a poem—a *comic-pathetic thing about some distressful and dismal miner*—and then I knew the source of his error. A young lady with me at the time who writes (and writes well) all the poetical criticism in *Review of Reviews*, told me that you were the only poet of any account, and that of course she agreed with me. She is a Mrs. Foster[2] and extraordinarily pretty and clever—and tho' her husband is old and an invalid the most malicious tongue has nothing to say. It was she who got me my invitation. She says that since she was a child she has been interested in white magic and wants very much to know something of black magic. She comes from very poor people in the Adirondacks—her husband educated her and she married him. [Sketch.] Then he lost his money and became an invalid and has only enough to support himself in an hospital. I met her first here, everyone likes her. It is so rare to find so much really strong intellect with kindness and affection. A year ago she was dispatched to study slum conditions in England, Ireland and Scotland. She has dignity

[1] Maire O' Neill, the Abbey Theatre actress.
[2] See Memoir. She became one of Y.'s best friends.

and sense, something remains to her from the spartan days when she had to work all day in her own poor home.

I was very glad to hear from Lily that you are completely recovered.— Yrs affectionately—J. B. YEATS

TO LILY YEATS

122

N.Y.

May 11, 1914

Did I tell you of my visit to the Untermeyers? He is a Jew lawyer, immensely wealthy—made it all i'self and well there it is. A beautiful house, not so very big but with beautiful pictures and statues all good. There was such a crowd of people—it took three coaches on a special train to carry us down—that I had no chance of examining any of the works of art, but I could see that they were good. We had lovely music—Chopin—after the music poets and poetesses (of the latter one a lovely girl) read their pieces. Their poetry was not my kind, so I am no judge. On arriving at the station a long line of autos awaited us but I soon decided to walk and others fired by my example yet reluctantly (a few only, you know how they hate walking) also walked. That walk was the best part of the day for it was beautiful and most of it through the demesne, trees only coming into leaf but lots of shrubs in flower—in this topsy turvy country flowers come first—to me nearly every tree and bush a novelty—a few birds, robins etc. The mistress of the house not Jew—being the daughter of a Lutheran Minister—received every one with a well-bred graciousness. . . .

At the supper I found myself with pleasant people who turned out to be musicians and friends of Paderewski. You will regret to hear we did not talk music, although we talked a good deal. Three tall butlers in immaculate black waited upon us. I counted three but there may have been a dozen. . . .

After the music and the poetry I spent all my time walking in the grounds and mostly by myself. At last I met a girl with kind sympathetic and very intelligent eyes, not at all good looking and the most ungraceful walker possible—too eager to walk well or to have control of her limbs. What was my surprise when she told me she was a professional dancer and my still greater surprise when she told me that in Paris she had received the highest medal for dancing. I found that she knew Willie's poems and had commenced acting the fairy in the *Land of Heart's Desire* which you know is chiefly dancing. She was very intelligent without any affectation. She made my acquaintance and began at once on Willie's poetry. After a while I discovered she thought I was Willie and that she was talking to the great poet himself.

. . . One thing I very soon guessed. There is no chance of the Unter-meyers giving me a commission. Ah! if only I had the right profile! If you had a father like this sketch [illustration] you would have been like this other sketch and you would be buying embroideries instead of making them.

123

317 W. 29
May 27, 1914

. . . The outside public are no longer admitted to luncheon, so I and my contemporary lunch together, no one else. He is 84 and eats like a young man of 24 [Sketch]. He is deaf as a post but will have conversation, so I shout and shout and he says, Eh, Sir, Eh, Sir, etc. and he is a painter, oldest but one of the American Academy. To me his paintings are a joke, but they sell, and everybody here likes them, and I *say I do*. He is very diligent. The day is not long enough for him. . . . 50 years ago he discovered that the bible was not divine and that priests are impostors. He cackles over his discovery and thinks we are most horribly shocked. and that we expect lightning to strike him. He did not marry till he was 69 and then married a red-haired woman with a grown up family. . . .

. . . He is an innocent kindly man who has never felt temptation to do anything wrong, nothing can make him cross, but he is persistent as the devil. The Petitpas laugh and say 'he is the limit'—'hee as the leemat'. His memory goes so far back that he often tells me interesting things, but he is always busy looking for fakes and frauds. You would think there was not a genuine picture in the world. All the Corots, Titians etc. are spurious— when he talks of these matters he bores me. He is a little man. He once made a lot of money . . . among the Mormons. He painted life and the portraits of seven of Brigham Young's wives. He has also painted Black Princes—and has met everybody but as I say he stopped thinking 50 years ago. Of course he has never heard of Chesterton and thinks Oscar Wilde a mountebank whom the Americans found out almost at once. He is quite willing to listen but nothing you or anybody else can say can make the smallest impression on him.

I suppose he is an instance of New England conceit, and that is what they all were 50 years ago. . . .

TO W. B. YEATS

124

317 West 29th Street, New York
May 31, 1914

My dear Willie—I wish very much you would look into a book which I have just read.

Life of Lady Hester Lucy Stanhope
by
Frank Hamel.   (Cassell & Company.)

I am certain you would be greatly interested, and find in Lady Hester a woman after your own imagination. Besides she had become a believer in Oriental philosophy and none other, and on one occasion at any rate successfully prophesied, as Kinglake relates.

She had the wild Pitt blood and was haughty and domineering, but never ceased to be lovable and witty, compelling love as well as fear. She had the high romantic genius, attempted mad things and *carried them through.* In practical matters she had the passion for detail that besets the poet with his verses, both having their origin in intensity of feeling. She said she would as soon live with pack horses as with women, yet she was woman all through and *full of softness (perhaps in this hatred of her own sex— especially a woman).* She loved in the Oriental way, adopting all their ideas, holding European science in scorn; she maintained that she had only to look at your forehead to know your fate. (There is a grotesque Lady Hester conjured up by several writers—but don't heed it.) She lived for some years with her Uncle the great Pitt, presiding at head of his household, and had many flirtations, very much loved and admired as well as feared. 'I never oppose her,' said her uncle, 'for it would be useless, since she would cheat the very devil,' he also said that he wished she was a man for then he would make her commander-in-chief of the army against Napoleon—her disinterestedness was extraordinary. She lived in the East thirty years, she quarrelled with all the neighbouring chiefs, but they dared not attack, because of the devotion of the bedouins among whom she lived, and *she loved danger*. She lived for some years with a young man named Bruce, who was 14 years her junior, finally she sent him away, saying she would not injure a young man by being an old woman hanging about his neck. She was then 34 years old; he was of good family and heir to £20,000 a year. She also refused to marry the Marquis of Sligo, because of his youth, parting from Bruce changed her whole character. Most of what we know about her comes from Dr. Mervyn, who lived with her off and on for several years as her physician—a faithful chronicler and honest friend, as well as a good writer. Knowing she was going to die she sent the Doctor away a month before it happened, and he *dared not refuse to go*. She was 60 years of age, and very poor with only black servants (whom she would slap in the face if they displeased her, yet they loved her). To the last with all her poverty she kept up great state. Her beliefs were astrology and magic—Christianity she despised as much as Nietzsche or York Powell.

Robert Henri told Miss Squire that I am a better portrait painter than Sargent or Watts '*because* of a *fuller humanity*'—there! are not the Americans an intelligent people?—and Jack writes to Lily (who forwards his letter) to say that beside a good portrait by me those done by others look like the work of mere hacks.

The weather is delicious—not too warm. There is sometimes a delightful monotony in the N. York summer—day copying day.—Yours affectionately—J. B. YEATS

125

317 West 29th Street, New York
June 2, 1914

My dear Willie—I have just read your 'Wise Man' and am quite content which I was never before. The Wise Man might have lectured or held forth or been otherwise edifying in the true rhetorical way, but no, he speaks out of the inner mind of the solitary soul. It satisfies all my tests of true poetry, and the sign is that I am haunted by single lines, plucked here and there by infallible instinct—there is no critic like the memory.[1]

What strange people the English are! I have just read a powerful review

[1] The reference is to W. B. Yeats's rewritten morality play, *The Hour Glass*.

of the Parnell love letters in one of the great English papers. All through Parnell is spoken of as the English gentleman for some curious reason interested in Ireland—and this is so strange in a man of English birth and education, &c. The fact that Parnell was a personality (tho' of quite a limited sort) is enough to prove that he could not be modern English. Their characteristic product is the highly educated and highly efficient mediocrity, such as were Gladstone and Peel. As to his haughty treatment of his Irish party, it is not half as bad as the treatment accorded by Wm. Pitt to Lords Castlereagh and Liverpool—as to which see the life of Lady Hester Stanhope, page 43, as described by Wm. Napier, where an interview is given by him to these august personages—you really must read that book.—Yours affectionately—J. B. YEATS

126

June 22, 1914

. . . It seems to me that the modern movement is towards a creating of art out of some *single* emotion—which of course is an impossibility. Art achieves its triumphs great and small by involving the universality of the feelings—love by itself is lust, that is primitive animalism, and anger what is it but homicide? Art lifts us out of the sphere of mere bestiality, art is a musician and touches every chord in the human harp—in other words a single feeling becomes a mood, and the artist is a man with a natural tendency to thus convert every single feeling into a mood—he is a moody man. Browning was not a great poet because he tended away from the true mood of the whole man into the false mood of the idea; certainly he did not linger in the bestial sphere, yet reading him I am not a free man, he shackles me all the time with logic and philosophy and opinion—he binds me to the ground with thorns not of the flesh.

I have again been reading Homer—under his spell I follow this and that desire in untrammelled flight. He talks constantly of the winds as separate personalities. The South wind and the East wind working together and yet each separately like two dogs chasing a hare. My emotions aroused by him are like these winds, only there are thousands of them all working together and yet separately in a riot of enjoyment, and the poor hare they chase is precisely that single emotion that dared to start up and lead its single existence—like a cry of quarrelling from some distempered servant that at dead of night rouses the whole household, even to the head of the household in his tasselled nightcap. Meantime do not forget the poor servant is a dependent born in the family. She will soon return to her senses and her duty—soothed and obedient—flattered even by the clamour she has caused, and glad to be forgiven. The 'uplift' lies here.

TO LILY YEATS

127

N.Y.
July 29, 1914

I am greatly amused hearing of Moore's book.[1] Ely Place has long been a cave of Adullam (*vide* the Holy Scriptures). G. Moore is the head Adullamite with AE and Magee and the rest to inspire him. They even once inspired Susan Mitchell who is not naturally an Adullamite, even in Dublin, where the race abounds. Willie does not care about success half as much as any of them, but he gets it and they don't—hence the trouble. . . .

I was at the theatre last night very comfortably seated in the box with Ingersoll and his wife and the two Van Ingens and King. Lady Gregory sat just behind us for a few minutes. She had a 'touch me not' air, so I did not venture on any introduction, except of a man who was chairman the night before at the meeting when I read *The Playboy*. . . . The plays were uproariously applauded—some voices shouting dissent. John Devoy[2] started up among the stalls, and during Murray's play when one brother chokes the other shouted out, 'Son of a b-tch, that's not Irish'. The old fool . . .

128

P.
Aug. 7, 1914

. . . I found a message from Quinn to come and spend the day with Sir Roger Casement. I groaned and started off. After lunch we went by automobile to Sheepshead Bay to Mrs. Smith . . . Sir Roger over here [Sketch of Casement] to promote the cause of the Nationalist volunteers—in great trouble over war. All his sympathies with Germany partly because he really likes Germany but chiefly because he hates England. . . . Quinn is in high tension about him and has him stopping with him. He talks all the time against England and is about sick with grief over 'poor Kaiser'. I liked

---

[1] *Hail and Farewell.*   [2] The Clan-na-Gael leader.

him very much. He is well educated and talks agreeably even though so much on the one subject. He is delighted with America and is a good critic at the same time—is a little like Hugh Lane if you can conceive Hugh Lane hare-brained about Ireland against England. . . . Sir Roger is astonished at the people here, their gaiety, their freedom, their good looks but above all their cleanliness, but he backed me up in saying that they kept their rooms too dark. . . .

TO W. B. YEATS

129

August 18, 1914
317 W. 29. N.Y.

My dear Willie—There is one thing never to be forgotten. *That the poet is the antithesis of the man of action.* Even though the hero is always a poet. When Achilles 'sulked' in his tent it was because the poet had driven out into exile the hero—the man of action. When Byron to satisfy his vanity or to put himself right with his contemporaries turned hero, it was because the man of action prompted and reinforced by ignoble or it may be noble motives (it is difficult to credit him with anything noble) had driven out the poet (to his own and the world's loss).

It would be a fine poetical invention to write a description of Achilles when he was 'sulking'. The beloved Patroclus with affection without a thought of self, caressing his master and listening to his complaints—the story-tellers drawing near to relate the achievements of other heroes, yet flattering him in their professional way—and when he thought of Briseis the musicians would have their chance and show their skill. Suddenly Patroclus is killed, and Hector insolently assumes his arms which had been Achilles's arms. Then the primitive man awakes—now the primitive man is either hero or poet according as he has or has not his enemy in sight and has or has not weapons to his hand. A poet indeed is a hero behind the bars, imprisoned either by circumstances too strong for him or by his own thoughts. At first Achilles was imprisoned by his own thoughts—his desire for revenge on Agamemnon and on the Greeks, who on his absenting himself from the fight would be conquered—also he would escape Fate and live long though it be ingloriously—his pride took this ignoble form —and he became *his own prisoner.* Then grief mastered him. A *single feeling,* and as is the wont with a single feeling it turned him again into a man of action. Yet in a rich and abundant nature a single feeling in time takes to itself other feelings, and the poet of many feelings resumes the sovereign power, and the man of action departs however reluctantly. The politic leader of the Grecian hosts took the chance which offered and Achilles was never again the poet. Achilles imprisoned by his own thoughts is as modern as Hamlet. At the last he is the primitive man—acting too quickly for the single feeling to become the multitudinous.

Is not the European situation curious and amazingly unexpected— civilization as Lowell said getting a lift in a powder cart. Because of that big rogue threatening their existence, the other rogues, Russia and England are making friends with as they think them the Mammon of Unrighteousness, and all the nationalities including the Jews and the Irish are invited to share the feast of victory.

It would have pained Dowden as regards Ireland, and it does no doubt pain Lyster, not that Lyster cares for anything outside his library. Dowden's mind moved very slowly, in fact was apparently without any of the impulses of progress and change—full of vitality in his way, which was that of a lichen clinging to its rock.

I have a graphic picture of things from Lily. On Sunday I spent the day with Quinn and Sir Roger Casement. The latter strong pro-German. He has not really a word to say for Germany except that she is against England—but I say yes!, but she is also against France—Germany victorious and everywhere authority will tighten the reins.—France victorious and once more in the lead! it means sympathy taking the place of cold repression—it means also ideas and the defeat of the dollar. It is curious that Dowden though caring little for money himself, was always on the side of the dollar—he came, as I wrote to him long ago, out of a rich man's house, and he never got over it. Aristocratic wealth is an accident to be apologised for, but middle-class wealth the result of honourable toil and it is difficult to escape from its religion.—Yours affectionately—J. B. YEATS

130

August 30, 1914
317 W. 29. N. York

Nowadays, especially in America (who leads the world) people live so much on the surface that everywhere is an intoxicating levity. Even marriage aims at being a love passage to terminate as soon as the impulse has spent itself. Marriage used to be a setting out together of a man and woman resolved though they wait twenty years for it to find the jewel of conjugal friendship. When Dr. Salmon's[1] . . . wife died, he said to John Dowden 'When a young man's wife dies it is not much—is nothing to what it is with an old man'. Yet Dowden, who knew them well, said he never knew them to talk to each other but once, and then it was about [household matters]. They had found the jewel and could not tell you where it was hidden; nor could any happily married couple. With people who live on the surface marriage is a failure, a grotesque absurdity, and many here are now saying so—already is it come to that.

Did the contemporaries of Shakespeare live on the surface? No! for the surface though well provided with tragedies and comedies that differed little from tragedies was poorly furnished with what modern life is so rich in. With all their uproariousness and treacheries and adulteries and profanities, they lived austerely, each man of them a lonely man, his nighest neighbour some threatening form of death or disease or sin, his interest not so much life itself as *what it meant*, life itself a wretched, miserable, however dreadful, spectacle. The active resolute spirit might enjoy himself as in a football scrimmage. But the others—the thinker, the artist, the man aloof who watches and sees the whole of it, and yet must because of his sensitiveness or other unfitness keep outside of it—What solace was there for him? He could not, as does the American, *admire* life—though he occasionally by good chance may have admired some of it, he recoiled from most of it. If he was to live he must escape from the surface of life, and he found his asylum in his dreams; here was his workshop where he mended life. Here also if he was a philosopher and scholar, his oracle and cave of prophecy. In modern life are no dreams, nothing but an overpowering and shining actuality and its logical processes. The dream workshop is deserted and no one visits the oracles—all are out in the crowded streets. There is another thing to be noted about Elizabethan ays. Getting a living was then a comparatively easy thing; they had not that absorption to interrupt their dreams, and here again let me add, that a people who do not dream never attain to inner sincerity, for only in his dreams is a man really himself. Only for his dreams is a man responsible—his actions are what he must do. Actions are a bastard race to which a man has not given his full paternity.

[1] A Provost of Trinity College, Dublin, and a famous mathematician. He wrote the book against Papal infallibility which Gladstone considered unanswerable.

Michelangelo

People in these democratic days have learned to exult in each other and to *admire* life—yet to admire is not to love—rather does *admiration cast out love*. The recluse M. Angelo with his doctrine of the fall so vivid in his mind and Italian wickedness and its denunciation by Savonarola could not have admired life. Yet his art in which is nothing grandiose or that expresses admiration is full of his love and tremendous tenderness for the humanity that had fallen. M. Angelo bowed down by love and pity was sustained by his dreams of the resurrection and of Divine justice and of Paradise. Verily if we would restore its intensity to poetry and art we must rediscover the doctrine of the Fall (and may begin with the war and the Kaiser and his legions). When you express your admiration for the great Queen it is only to accentuate the pity of her old age—as M. Angelo pondering on the fall of man would remember his nobleness. The artist who admires is a poor artist—we know that from the portrait painters.

Do you remember the statue of General Sherman which is at the entrance to the Central Park, by St. Gaudens—a fine sculptor, the finest in America. Here you have art characteristic of a race living on the surface. The general and his horse vividly rendered by a man of intense observation—the Victory, just a young American girl exaggerated after the manner of Gibson, a long-legged, long-armed, bright creature, the product of the American mind in high tension—observing and admiring —the wings are a mere excrescence, quite incongruous, unless indeed one fancied them to be the latest invention of the Paris milliner, to which we have not yet become accustomed. Now we know that for the medieval artist, the Victory would have been everything—General Sherman and his horse subsidiary. How Michel Angelo would have revelled in giving her the strong shoulders to support heavy full-fledged wings, an athlete, a woman and an immortal. How Michel Angelo *loved* life is visible in his moulding and carving of the human body which palpitates with a too sentient life. The Greek sculptor had not this pity, except in the Elgin marbles, and then it was not so much pity as delight in power and force.— Yours affectionately—J. B. YEATS

P.S. A certain Irishman, Capt. Freeman, formerly of the British Army, is in high glee foreseeing the downfall of the British Empire. He spent 18 years in the Balkans and professes to know everything. For 12 years he was foreign correspondent for the English *Standard*. He says the Ulster men are coming round to be of the same opinion. Of course I detest *all* Empires, *German* or English. [Sketch.]

131

My dear Willie—People do not understand the importance, the significance of exact portraiture in art. In every picture, in every poem, there must be somewhere an exact portraiture—otherwise there is no work of art.

Two summers ago, one day at mid-noon, when the strong sun had killed all the breezes, I was taking my daily walk without which I have no health, keeping on the west side as close to the Hudson as possible, the water being refreshing to look at, and it being a place where gathered few people (in hot weather to see other people as hot as oneself always adds to my distress), when quite suddenly I came on an open space with little gardens and all crowded with children. As these were all quite happy and careless of the heat and as I was curious to see what brought them, naturally I stopped and mingled among them. I looked about for an elder person whom I might question. Close to me stood a young woman, and when she answered my questions I knew by her voice that she was Irish, and to my surprise I found she was from Donnybrook. She was also very pretty, with a gentle sad-eyed expression, such as one seldom finds in New York. I then noticed that she held a baby in her arms, and that when I glanced toward it *she tried to conceal it from me with her hand*. It was asleep, but wasted and scrofulous and very sick, its arms and legs so thin that the hands and feet looked large ; in its wasted neck there were lumps. I could not resist questioning her and found that she had had two other children who died in infancy and that her father and mother in Ireland were dead and that she did not expect to go there again, and that her husband was a healthy man, etc. etc. She spoke with resignation as if to the will of God, or Fate—I did not know which. She spoke of the child's sickness as being due to teething, as if she wished to think it temporary. As a contrast all around were swarms of healthy children, obstreperous and noisy. She looked at them as if she did not see them.

I came away, and for days and weeks almost to this hour I am haunted and oppressed by the feeling of grief, of poignant depression which suddenly assailed me as I talked to that poor young woman. Had I been an active-minded philanthropist or a suffragette indignant with a man-managed world, I'd have got busy and never rested till I eased my heart by doing something to help. As to myself I felt as helpless as would have been a mediaeval artist—even though I was not prepared to say that such suffering was punishment inflicted by a just God—and being as helpless as one of these my mental process was probably the same as theirs. Why did I look at her so constantly, not being able to take away my eyes, and why did I ask so many questions, such as perhaps would have been resented by a woman less gentle and good? (perhaps also being Irish she thought she owed respect to one so much older), and why did I, after I left her hoping in a cowardly way never to see her again, make every effort of memory to recall every detail of what I said and of what she told me? The answer is that every feeling and especially it might seem the painful feeling, tries to keep itself alive, and not only that but to *increase in strength*. This is the law of human nature and is what I have called the spirit of growth—in other words, I would have given worlds to have painted a careful study of her and her sick infant and carried it away with me to keep my sorrow alive. *Here we have art as portraiture,* a kind of art great in its way; there is also the conflict of feelings—the ghastly repulsive sickness of the infant, the real charm of the mother's face and form, her mother pride all abashed, her hopelessness and yet her effort to be hopeful that it was only teething. This hopefulness, itself a conscious lie, said perhaps out of a social instinct to ease the situation as she talked to me, and then her manifest love as she looked down at the child asleep, *blissfully sleeping*. Of course such portraiture is incomplete art—so the artists and poets of old invented the Madonna with the divine infant. But in this case and in these times there is no Madonna with the divine infant, and the artist, having made his portrait, must pass by on his way, unless indeed he pays a visit to the Philanthropists—and in this particular case they could do nothing. The artist would be excused if he threw a little touch of rhetoric into his portraiture, such as the crowd loves—though if philanthropists were cultivated as well as rich, they would only offend and bring his truthfulness into doubt, convicting him of vulgarity and commonness.

At any rate have I not made it obvious that all art begins in portraiture? That is, a *realistic* thing identified with *realistic* feeling, after which and because of which comes the Edifice of Beauty—the great reaction.— Yours affectionately—J. B. YEATS

I think I have already written to you that it is ugliness which created beauty. The purely beautiful only breeds weariness or rather laziness— *vacuity*.

132

My dear Willie—I hope I do not weary you and may I say that I hope you read each letter as it comes? otherwise perhaps it will never be read by any one, which would disappoint me, though perhaps that would not much matter. Still, I have made some distinctions worth thinking about. That Hector was a hero because a man of a few single feelings and of certain opinions—preëminently the good man, the upright citizen— whereas Achilles was only occasionally a doubtful sort of a hero, and at other times the artist and the poet who refused action that he might live with himself in self-centred solitariness. From this distinction follow others, as that the artist and poet should by law of his nature resist his contemporaries in their actions and thoughts, since being different from them he cannot otherwise protect himself, and that this resistance should not be for the purpose of benefiting them or for any other kind of propaganda, but that he be himself.

The emphasis of the orator and the teacher bears no relation to the emphasis of the poet—indeed is fatal to it. If the sick man moans that he be heard we restrain our pity. The nightingale would cease to sing if it knew people were listening—every farmer's boy knows that. The artist rudimentary in the crudest mind has so instructed him. Man in his social aspect is indeed charming, it is the world of interchanging opinion, of sympathies, of beautiful ideas and candid and mutual help. All the virtues belong to it. Continually we seek to perfect it so that its system of rewards and punishments may work with the smoothest regularity. *Art is solitary man*, the man as he is behind the innermost, the utmost veils. That is why with the true poet we do not care what are his persuasions, opinions, ideas, religion, moralities—through all these we can pierce to the voice of the essential man if we have the discerning senses. These are no more than the leafy wood out of which the nightingale sings. If Achilles gathered his intimates about him when he 'sulked in his tent' it was not that they might share his solitude, only that they might keep up his courage while he faced it—also that they might tend on him with food and drink, for the passion for solitude weakens the practical will.

I think also that I made a good point when I pointed out and explained the importance of portraiture. The portrait is to preserve feeling and by concentration give it intensity. Now intensity is not art, yet it is the parent of art and its groundwork. Yet here also the artist must work as a solitary, otherwise the intensity is spoiled by the intrusion of what is alien. It does not come on one with the same strangeness—a strangeness yet with something familiar—one's secret heart answers to it as to a language learned in one's infancy and then forgotten. This is the quality of naïveté so noticeable in the drawings of some of the ancient PreRaphaelite Masters—you find it in M. Angelo, seldom in Raphael, who indeed is not intense. Hector was always right and noble, yet his charm was that he was so easy to understand and follow. Achilles always wrong, but he was always deep, soundless in his depth. The noblest religion, the most perfect morality are not so deep as the human heart and its will.

These are rough-hewn sentences, but I hope you catch my ideas.

In these days social man is well represented. He has invaded us and occupies all the positions and captured the poets. In this congested city we sleep, as it were, fifteen in a bed. Art is solitary man.

I am trying everywhere to find a cheap edition of E. A. Poe's poems. I fancy he was a solitary in his art and in himself.

Lately I read again your 'Cutting of the Agate' and was surprised to find how much I owed to it—in fact I have assimilated it so much that I do not now know when I am writing your thoughts and when my own.

Except for a few bridge players I think I am the only one in New York who does not give all his thoughts and time to the war.—Yours affectionately—J. B. YEATS

TO LILY YEATS

133

New York
Sept. 10th, 1914

. . . We talk of nothing but the war. An old Irishman (older than I am) Capt. Freeman, late of the British Army, maintains that Rothschild owns the New York press and said it is all against Germany. I have just received a pamphlet from Sir Roger Casement standing up for Germany which of course I shall read but if it converts me I won't be nearly so happy. Here the Miss Petitpas and myself are of one mind, and besides Germany or rather its Kaiser have so long been my pet aversion, and I am enjoying the unexpected in finding myself in agreement with England. Sir Roger Casement is an enthusiast—his charm is that he never sees facts exactly as they are. Have you heard of an Irishman called Lehane? He always sees facts even though he is a Socialist and an important man in Ireland, and he is dead against Germany, and says that in 5 or 6 months Germany will have no money and come into the lending world asking the great banks for loans and then the Government being bankrupt will get no loans and the Socialists will get busy and take over to themselves the rule of Germany. But Sir Roger is a charming man and Quinn's friend—he returns to Ireland in a few days and I have no doubt that when he arrives in the Green Isle he will come into the public view. He is afraid of no one and is the soul of honour. When I saw him, he would mutter to himself 'Poor Kaiser, Poor Kaiser,' almost with tears in his voice. . . .

According to Capt. Freeman, Rothschild controls England and France. Germany will not submit, hence the hatred. . . .[1]

TO LADY GREGORY

134

Nov. 19, 1914
317 W. 29. N. York

My dear Lady Gregory—I don't think I sufficiently acknowledged how perfectly you had the theory as you had already the practice 'from things temporal to things eternal'. I am sending you by this post a paper with a poem by Percy Mackaye on Isadore Duncan's 'children', some fifteen now housed at Rye by Mrs. Simeon Ford who is the hostess referred to in the poem. All through this poem we have the note of pain strummed lightly and dancingly—though indeed it is now strummed all around us by what is happening! and poets are saved the trouble perhaps. It is because in every poem this note must be continuously struck that we have come to consider all poetry to be something sad and mournful.

I have been very busy on an article on English character. Here are two great facts as I think of English evolution through the century—England an island and a natural fortress—hence no national army now necessary.

[1] Sir Roger did not return to Ireland, but sailed for Germany. In April 1916, on the eve of the Irish Easter Week rising, he landed from a German ship on the coast of Kerry. He was brought to London, tried for high treason and executed.

And for third fact—no strong central government—the consequence of two preceding facts. Also England being an island was not subject to constant immigration as were the continental nations, so that the destruction of life by plagues &c. had free scope to keep population scanty securing thereby that there was never any struggle for existence. The Englishman had only one enemy, *disease,* otherwise lived free from care, for himself or for his country, no military discipline to vex and harass his days and no taxes and no government regulations of any kind, and no need to struggle for to live since, there being a small population over a wide area, each man had but to stretch out his hand to take what he needed, and like a man living in good society subject to but one control, the opinion of his neighbour legally embodied as we know in the ancient English institution of trial by Jury.

Out of all comes the Englishman's feeling for liberty. Liberty is an English thought, and there it remains—it is not yet in American, French or German thought—for though he has not the idea or theory of liberty common in France and America he has, which they have not, the feeling in his blood and in his bones. An Englishman believes he has a right to do what he likes with himself, which includes his beliefs and whims, and with his property, and property includes wife and children and servants and oxen and asses and the stranger within his gates, and the Englishman is law-abiding, because law in England has for purpose the protection of property, it being the bulwark of personal liberty. Hence also the Englishman's selfishness. In his thick blood, clotted with ignorance, liberty quickly becomes selfishness—uncontrolled except by definite law—hence the Englishman of all time. Hence also that puzzle to foreigners the *British matron,* both the embodiments of two principles, law and selfishness—when a man has a right within the law to do what he likes with himself and his family and none of his neighbours dispute it. That strange irregular contract-breaking sprite sympathy has no chance to speak a word to sweeten his life.

The Englishman stands alone, a Goliath champion for liberty and yet because of his selfishness he destroys the liberty of others' country over which he can stretch a hand.

When an Englishman is a gentleman—a rare species and now almost extinct—he has the liberty without the selfishness, and I hail him as the most charming of companions and truest of friends, Oliver Elton for an instance. And now I come to the last link in my chain of argument. The Englishman gets his gift for poetical creation from his gift for personal liberty—he is self evolved, a law unto himself—what human nature he has is his own and made to suit his own palate—none other being consulted. That is, he has the deep sincerity piercing to the very centre of life and the principle of all things without *which Poetry does not speak to be attended to.* Other nations follow reason and their poetry is the lean music of argument and rhetoric; ideals and noble theories and all the rest, which Americans *follow after, are the enemy* plucking the unit man, the individual out of his sublime solitude to place him in this or that fraternity and be in the bonds of sympathy or antipathy with his fellows. From this noisy kingdom the English, whether boor or scholar, whether poet or not, turns away to follow imagination which is the voice of essential longing, so that his poetry—if by favour of the gods it be allowed to exist in tangible and visible form, is true poetry. We have the cries of the wild beasts and the singing of birds. English poetry is the human cry, it explains nothing, since to explain is to weaken, and that is not its purpose.

A man is most intense when alone. If he seeks company it is to lessen and relax a mood that had become intolerable. Let him keep his courage and remain alone and presently will burst from him the human cry which is poetry, the cry of a spirit at the self-same moment tormented and appeased. The Englishman is unspoiled—he does not keep much company like the efficient German or the sprightly Frenchman—at least it was so in his uncorrupted days.

This letter is really for Willie as well as for you—though my sending it to you is because of your kind words.—Yours very truly—J. B. YEATS

I would have it typed only it is so expensive.

135

317 W. 29. N.Y.   *Nov. 19, 1914*

I send on another letter for Willie who I think is with you. I hope you will read it and like it. My daughters are both suffering in health and nerves because of the war made manifest about them in many ways. Lily is so angry and fierce about it—a sort of laughing vehemence.

In this house is no room for war nerves. It is not the shadow but the substance of its misery that is here—the three Miss Petitpas have their three brothers at the front and lots of cousins of whom some are killed. The brothers being away it devolves upon these three girls to support the parents and a younger son, besides which something having gone wrong in the delicate matter of graft with the policeman at the corner they are being harassed about taking out a licence hitherto evaded—a licence costs 1200 dollars—for these little places have to pay exactly the same for a licence as is paid by the great hotels, which is not their French idea of justice nor is it mine. Meantime they must look pleasant or their customers would go elsewhere—so where is the use of war nerves? but I can't tell you how their eyes snap. God help the Kaiser—if they caught him they would strangle him there and then—they look quite white and there is no mirth. . . .

TO W. B. YEATS

136

New York
Dec. 21, 1914

The chief thing to know and never forget is that art is dreamland and that the moment a poet meddles with ethics and the moral uplift or thinking scientifically, he leaves dreamland, loses all his music and ceases to be a poet. Meredith is musical while he stays in dreamland—Browning also. When they turn away from it to discuss actual life as they constantly do, their lines grown harsh—they cease to sing. Shakespeare never quitted his dreams. The scene where Hubert talks with Arthur about the putting out of his eyes is all a dream—in actual life such conversation would have been impossible. We all live when at our best, that is when we are most ourselves, in dreamland. A man with his wife or child and loving them, a man in grief and yielding to it, girls and boys dancing together, children at play—it is all dreams, dreams, dreams. A student over his books, soldiers at the war, friends talking together—it is still dreamland—actual life on a far away horizon which becomes more and more distant. When the essential sap of life is arrested by anger or hatred we suddenly are aware of the actual, and music dies out of our hearts and voices—the *anger subtly present* in ethical thought—as it is also in most kinds of argument ; how many poems has it laid low? . . .

The poet is a magician—his vocation to incessantly evoke dreams and do his work so well, because of natural gifts and acquired skill, that his dreams shall have a potency to defeat the actual at every point. Yet here is a curious thing, the poet and we his dupes know that they are only dreams

—otherwise we lose them. With our eyes open, using our will and powers of selection, we, together in friendship and brotherly love, create this dreamland. Pronounce it to be actual life and you summon logic and mechanical sense and reason and all the other powers of prose to find yourself hailed back to the prison house, and dreamland vanishes—a shrieking ghost.

137

Dec. 22, 1914

To find out what was the mind of Shakespeare is valuable, but the real thing is to find out what is my own mind when I read Shakespeare or any other poem. If I know the mind of Shakespeare and in order that I may know it better, am made acquainted with the period in which he lived, it is good because thereby I may come more quickly to know my own mind —for I study him and all other poets exclusively that I may find myself. It is the same with nature itself. As artist, as man, seeking what I have called dreamland I am concerned still to find myself and my own mind, and only incidentally am I concerned with the intentions of Nature and her mind. Herein I am the reverse of the historical and the scientific student. They are concerned with what is other than themselves, whereas the artist in us and in all men seeks to find himself. Science exists that man may discover and control nature and build up for himself habitations in which to live in ease and comfort. Art exists that man cutting himself away from nature may build in his free consciousness buildings vaster and more sumptuous than these, furnished too with all manner of winding passages and closets and boudoirs and encircled with gardens well shaded and with everything that he can desire—and we build all out of our spiritual pain—for if the bricks be not cemented and mortised by actual suffering, they will not hold together. Those others live on another plane where if there is less joy there is much less pain. Like day labourers they work, with honest sweat to earn their wages, and mother nature smiles on them and calls them her good children who study her wishes and seek always to please her and rewards them with many gifts. The artist has not the gift for this assiduity, these servile labours—so falling out of favour with his great mother he withdraws himself and lives in disgrace, and then out of his pain and humiliations constructs for himself habitations, and if she sweeps them away with a blow of her hand he only builds them afresh, and as his joy is chiefly in the act of building he does not mind how often he has to do it. The men of science hate us and revile us, being angry with impotent rage because we seem to them to live in profitless idleness, and though we have sad faces we are yet of such invincible obstinacy that nothing can induce us to join their ranks. There are other things about us which perplex and offend them. They always work in gangs, many minds engaged on one task, whereas we live and work singly, each man building for himself accepting no fellowship—for we say it is only thus we can build our habitations. So it follows that they charge us with selfish egotism and insolence and pride, and it is vain for us to say that we work in the spirit of the utmost humility, not being strong enough for their tasks, and suffering many pains because of the anger of our offended and beloved mother. They are mighty men with strong wills. We are weak as water, our weakness is our raison d'être, and now and again when the strong man is broken he comes to us that we may comfort him. We even may make merry together, for we love our fellow men more than we do ourselves.—Yours affectionately—J. B. YEATS

138

Dec. 23rd, 1914
317 W. 29, N.Y.

My dear Willie—In my note yesterday was apparently some confusion of thought. I spoke of art as a means by which a man searches for and finds himself, and afterwards I said that artists were engaged in building habitations in which the spirit might live and enjoy its life in full activity. Yet there was no confusion. When a man builds a house on a site chosen for its beauty making the house also as charming as he can, then he has found himself and also built for his spirit a habitation where it can live at ease. But if a man builds a house, say close to his factory and with all the utilities and lives in it merely because it possesses all the utilities—but outside his appreciation of these conveniences has no other feeling and no affection for his house, then he is of the type scientific or philistine. He is a man untrained in the art of finding himself and his poor spirit if he has one wanders without a house or habitation. The late Dr. Salmon was a great man and a great mathematician but it was well known that tho' he was an infallible judge of every kind of investment he paid no attention to what is called the artistic values being exclusively a man of science and therefore a philistine. Mathematicians are as a rule philistines and are apt to think that there is nothing in life valuable except the utilities, and that what is called efficiency is the chief of human faculties. A friend of mine, a fine classical scholar, told me that in his experience, mathematicians could only talk of the price of things—tell them, he said, what you pay for your boots. I once met Dr. Salmon at dinner and was much flattered by his taking me aside and asking me what I paid for my lodgings—I thought that the great man was interested in me. Professor Dowden, his relation and my friend, undeceived me. He said it was only Salmon's way. All his long life Dr. Salmon sought for scientific and practical truth and has left a distinguished name. Yet at that dinner table had he listened to me I could have told him things that would have opened his eyes to a world of which he had never dreamed and perhaps he would have acknowledged that the tangible is valuable only for the sake of the intangible. There are whole streets in London, whole districts where the people inhabiting the houses are prisoners each in his cell and to walk through them is to breathe prison air since their houses have no grace, no architectural charm, no artistic decoration, nothing to remind or to suggest that there is anything in life except this and that utility—houses everywhere but nowhere a home, nowhere an asylum for the affections—amid such surroundings humanity is withered. Artists exist that these places be destroyed—a kind of prison reform much needed in great cities.

I said above that the tangible is for the sake of the intangible—that is, we nourish the body that the soul may live.

I am quite aware of the fact that in these notes there is nothing very profound or revolutionary, yet I think they tend to make things lucid. We artists do not enough explain our position. We do not undervalue utility—only we would have people see that it is not an end in itself, but a means. A rich man possesses all the utilities, but is he alive? A poor man with few of them may lead a life rich and sumptuous with experience.— Yours affectionately—J. B. YEATS

I39

My dear Willie—So true is it that people of artistic temperament are for ever seeking to find themselves, that it is even true of our lovers. An artist in love is seeking himself and the girl he loves—if she be artistic, is seeking herself—the practical person, man or woman, is just trying to obtain that convenience, marriage, and it is the safest kind of marriage, even though it be a humdrum affair. An artist in love is a vehement creature. At one time he finds in his sweetheart's eyes and heart and soul all of himself and more than himself—at a single bound attaining to the artist's heaven and then he fails, or thinks he fails, and like Milton falls back into a gulf of anger and despair.

> 'And in her eyes I find
> A wonder, or a wondrous miracle,
> The shadow of myself formed in her eye;'

> . . . . .

> 'I do protest I never loved myself,
> Till now infixed I behold myself
> Drawn on the flattering table of her eye.'
> *King John*, Act II, Sc. 1.

Perhaps the happiest kind of marriage in our mortal state is where the artist weds with a philistine—at any rate marriage remains for the one who is philistine an abiding convenience, and though the philistine cannot come up to expectations, still on the philistine's side there need be no spurning and there will be none, as long as the marriage is a recognised convenience. Happy is the artist who marries a philistine wife. He is a bird in a cage and will not sing as of yore—still it is a cage supplied with all the conveniences. It is of course a humdrum happiness and Milton would have none of it and his proud spirit disdained the laxities and facilities of free love wherein no man yet ever found himself, dropping the experiment at the first hint of failure.

It is my belief that all great artists have developed their genius by the ways of discipline—otherwise there is no meaning in what I have said touching the probe of pain. Let the minor genius go his light way and enjoy his life—the great nature cannot so live, he is never really in holiday mood, even though he often pluck flowers by the wayside and tie them into knots and garlands like little children and lads out on a sunny morning.—Yours affectionately—J. B. YEATS

Who was the French cynic who said that lovers can go on talking for ever, because they are always talking of themselves?

FROM W. B. YEATS

140

Here W. B. Y. writes to his father of the first part of his autobiography, published under the title Reveries over Childhood and Youth.

Coole Park, Gort, Co. Galway
Dec. 26, 1914

My dear Father—When I got the last letters and the old letter typed from my typist—there are still a few to come. (One typist gave up the job) I will be able to see her, and so comment on them before your thought has gone on to something else. They always interest me deeply. Yesterday I finished my memoirs I have brought them down to our return to London in 1886 or 1887. After this there would be too many living people to consider and they would have besides to be written in a different way. While I was immature I was a different person and I can stand apart and judge. Later on, I should always, I feel, write of other people. I dare say I shall return to the subject but only in fragments. Some one to whom I read the book said to me the other day 'If Gosse had not taken the title you should call it "Father and Son".' I am not going to ask your leave for the bits of your conversation I quote. It is about 17,000 words which is just the right size for Lolly's press and will prepare for my quotations from your letters. There is a great deal about my grandfather in Sligo and I have grouped round Aunt Mickie some passages about our ancestors. Later on I speak of Wilson and Potter (I would be glad if you could write me your memory of his death. I have given an account as I remember the story. Farrar came and told us.) Then Dowden and O'Leary and J. F. Taylor gives me short chapters. The book is however less an objective history than a reverie over such things as the full effect upon me of Bedford Park and all it meant in decoration. Everybody to whom I have shown the work has praised it and foretold a great success for it. You need not fear that I am not amiable. I shall illustrate it with a photograph of Jack's *Memory Harbour* at any rate.

I came over here two days ago to see Lady Gregory about the theatre before she starts for America. Thanks for your recent letters, Lady Gregory has read some of them to me but I must get them typed. The week after next I go to the Sussex Cottage and Ezra Pound will be my secretary. He brings his wife with him this time. She is very pretty and had a few years ago seven generals in her family all living at once and all with the same name—Johnson, relations of Lionel Johnson.—Yours ever—W. B. YEATS

TO W. B. YEATS

141

New York
Thursday [1915?]

My dear Willie—I strongly advise Lady Gregory and you to accept any invitation coming from the writer of enclosed letter. I twice stayed with them at their charming old country house on the Hudson. They are very young—married when she was 17 and he 19, and have now two little babies. They are very intimate with Ned Shelton (successful playwright), Van Wyck Brooks and other young literary people who have been wont to come to their house at week ends. They amused me immensely—she all piquancy—a peculiar piquancy—made up of youth, courage, a considerable touch of temper and puritan uprightness—a real charm as it were *in spite of herself*, also in spite of herself very womanly. American women are too much made up and decorated with a carefully sought out preparation of the *obvious*—this little woman shines out among them because she is always herself and *shows* a *delicate fragile* distinction. Her husband is handsome and tall and very easy going and innocent—all his interest being in ornithology—he killed off all the English sparrows with the result that he has been able to count 36 different species of birds round about his house. He will talk for ever of his father, who gave up a distinguished position in Egypt to become a disciple of Tolstoi, and would have given away all his wealth, only Dowager Mrs. Crooks his wife, a clever genial and witty woman of the world, interposed. Old Crooks died a few years ago, and is adored by the Socialists and Radicals and political dreamers, who collect his books, and verses.

The young Mrs. Crooks intends her husband to become eventually American Ambassador at Paris. That's *her* intention, as he knows many languages, and like a good American he has to obey her. I used to advise Ned Shelton whom I liked very much to make a close study of them for endless plays might be written around them.

I shall be greatly disappointed if Lady Gregory is not amused with them, and does not like them—they are both extremely well bred. American breeding when good is the best in the world. A princess here is like a princess out of the wood—she has the dew of the morning on her hair and on her brow, a Diana rather than an Aphrodite—and she carries a spear.

Of course I know that I have taken in thus praising them the *surest* means of making you very critical, still I will risk it.

I am greatly delighted to hear of the success of the *Well of the Saints*. I wish you had sent me on papers.

Mrs. Ranum tells me she has written to you on behalf of the 'Sun'. She dines here at my table almost every day—she is young and pretty and very efficient and clever. She lives in New York, her young husband a professor living at Cornell—. They 'are devoted to each other'. Yet this is the arrangement. In any other place but New York, it would be a surprise. Where is Mrs. Grundy?

142

New York
(undated, 1915 perhaps)

. . . In G. B. Shaw's original assaults on Shakespeare he called his ideas 'trite'. Of course they were trite, none other are admissible in pure poetry. The muses are the daughters of memory. Bring an old man into the place of his birth and show him the 'improvements'. Would he not be shocked, and notwithstanding the latest improvements in plumbing would he be reconciled. . . .? 'Cut out the magnanimity,' said Keats to Shelley. . . . By magnanimity he meant the new philosophy of the abstract which even Shelley could not make poetically iridescent though it was with the colours of the rainbow . . . this free verse is to me a constant puzzle—It is good so far as it goes. It seems to me to be the accentuation of the lesser rhythms which are employed by all of us in our daily conversation, but a rejection of the greater rhythms. . . . In Shakespeare's sonnets we have abundance of the lesser and the greater rhythms, he brings them again and again into juxtaposition and sharp contrast. This free verse movement is a deposit of the democracy, whose gregariousness is happy only with lesser rhythms and does not like the gentler rhythms of Poetical Beauty, for these impose silence and wonder, feelings repugnant to democracy which likes babble and noise. The gentler rhythms come out of the heart of

silence. . . . The intellectual awakening of the French revolution has not
yet really borne any poetical fruit, however much it may be a matter for
mental exercise, it still is alien from poetry, as it was from Wordsworth
and Shelley. Shelley's effort to turn it into poetry was a failure. . . . How
different is Hugo when he turns away [from the multitude] and in the
words of my definition glorifies Experience, [then] like a sword of finest
temper one of his lyrics can pierce my armour of sloth or pride or apathy
and pierce to the marrow of my bones. . . .

143

(1915)

Indulged facility seems to me a good phrase and should be made current
coin. A painter producing what does not really interest him will fall back
on facility and produce to order 'modes of thought and of expression
accepted among the best people'. I remember some figures of what is called
abstract beauty drawn by Herkomer that elicited the admiration of Edwin
Ellis. Supremely clever himself he worshipped cleverness and cleverness is
another name for facility. German sculpture and architecture is I should
say of the indulged facility pattern, since the artists produce these things to
order and without any other interest. Had there existed in the time of
Dickens another Queen Bess and had she demanded of him that he created
a beautiful woman—out of his wonderful cleverness he would have
accomplished his task and doubtless his admirers would have considered
that he had surpassed himself. For people do admire an indulged facility.
Edwin Ellis is not alone, particularly in crowded cockney London,
where no one has time to be much interested in anything. G. B. S.
would not have attempted that job—in fact could not—laughter and self-
mockery would have choked him.

144

N.Y., 1915

. . . Outside mathematics and science, there is no such thing as belief
positive; yet there is a certain intensity of feeling whether of love, hope or
sorrow or fear which we label belief; with the solitary man this remains a
feeling and is something personal, and therefore the very substance of

poetry. With the companionable it crystallizes into opinion which is the substance of prose and is conceived and brought forth in emulous or angry contention. To keep his faith alive, Carlyle was obliged all his long life to be incessantly scolding and prophesying and speaking to the people. Coventry Patmore was a companionable man, and consequently a poor believer in the dogmas he so intolerantly professed. Always did he write in the heat of hatred, the most companionable of all the passions. The man who hates is the furthest from being a solitary and is a man dependent on having about him the people he hates whether in actual presence or in his mind's eye. In my own life, I knew a well educated and rather pretty woman, who was the most hospitable soul alive. Why thus hospitable? Because she was burning to meet people whom she might contradict in incessant wrangle; we were given a Circean welcome. In the poet of 'The Dreadful Night' we have a true solitary; Landor also; although in his case it was perhaps the result of a conscious effort; Browning always a companionable man, a sublime showman with a voice of titanic volume, sometimes incoherent but always dominating in his energy and learning; evermore would he stand in the public eye. There are times in the life of every man when he is visited by the solitary spirit; so it happens that occasionally Browning sang melodious syllables. Coleridge was solitary; whether he wrote or talked, always in soliloquy: hence that personal charm which seems to have fascinated everyone except the splenetic and self-willed Carlyle.

The old hermits were right in their instinct for the desert since it meant a living to one's self, wrong in that it meant a separation from human voices and from the faces of men, women and children and an uprooting of the human plant from its natural surroundings. . . .

Have you read any of Hardy's novels? Judging by one of them I have just been reading and by his portrait and the looks in his eyes, I would call him a true solitary. Meredith seems to me one of the companionable; his nerves always stretched in social excitement, soothed or irritated by the people about him, so that he is much occupied argumentatively in communicating with his fellow creatures. He seldom trod the narrow path of the elect of poetry, but valiantly walked abroad with his companions, a talker, and a lecturer, and a master of incisive speech. In Hardy's sentences there is always an undersound which is the croon of poetry and like the noise of the sea breaking on far away rockbound shores.

Throughout the world of poetry and art do we not find at the present time a wealth of expression with a poverty of meaning, and is not this

because the companionable are far in excess of the solitary? The method of
the companionable is to find some truth on which all men agree and by
harping on that to rouse his fellow mortals to spiritual excitement and
intellectual effort. Carlyle, for instance, knowing that all men hated lies
proceeded to show that the world was living contentedly with every kind
of sham. All the meaning as regards thought and idea and philosophy in
Carlyle might be contained in a few pages, but what a wealth of expression expended in the presenting of that meaning. In Blake, as in all the
great poets the wealth of meaning beggars the wealth of expression; even
though the words are strained to their utmost capacity, and every variety
of rhythm and verse and intonation and mental attitude and gesture be
pressed into the service, it is only after much study that one gets the
meaning, and even this does not suffice unless there be kindled in us a mood
identical with that of the poet. For the meaning is not a something to be
communicated or explained, but to be revealed, a vision and a dream—no
more; we see it or we do not see, that is all—What can be communicated
or explained is prose.

TO ELIZABETH YEATS

145

New York
Feb. 17, 1915

. . . As to sleep. I have always known only one way of procuring it—by
walking exercise. Here in New York, I get no sleep unless I walk, and
walk a good deal—every day in snow and slush, the wind piercing me to
the marrow I trudge out along these *beastly streets,* and in summer I do the
same, sweating from every pore. I also have reduced my consumption of
meat to a minimum—day after day. I only eat the leg of a chicken; my
breakfast boiled milk and very little coffee in it, and bread and butter, and
an orange; my lunch, vegetables and gravy and an orange; my dinner,
the aforesaid leg of a chicken, vegetables, salad and an orange or apple; at
dinner also I drink a bottle of Californian claret. Yet even with this diet I
must go for walks. The Americans *never* walk. In winter too cold and in
summer too hot—but I must walk—walking was with my mother a fixed
idea. If you said your eye was itching, she would look at you anxiously,
and say, 'it is bile, you need a walk'. In her youth the doctors discovered

walking. Abernethy the famous London doctor (he was a rough man from Derry) would say to a fashionable Countess, 'Sell your carriage Ma'am and buy a hoop'. Abernethy should live again and come to New York we should then not hear so much about 'American nerves'. I could have nerves if I liked. I know better.

. . . I was at an At Home at —— last Monday. It is astonishing how uninteresting the —— seem to be—the surprising thing being that they have so little intelligence. —— proposes herself to be an enthusiastic admirer of Tagore. Yet she looked blank with astonishment and no doubt horror, when she learned from me that he is a Hindoo. They all talk Literature, and the drama, yet on these subjects they have not the most elementary knowledge. *Practical life* is what they really enjoy, and if they would keep to it, they might be most entertaining, and their nicest quality is a spirit of kindness. It is in all of them—notwithstanding their value for the dollar, of which they have so many.

—— can talk and be very interesting with her good sense. If we had her a while in Dundrum—we would make something of her. She tells me that she is perfectly certain that Isadora Duncan is mad, she gathers this from what Isadora has said to herself—of course due to the death of her children. Old —— appears at these at homes looking a human icicle. . . . All this ill humour in me is probably due to the fact—that the people at these At Homes are young and won't listen to me or even look at me.— In N. York, people make you feel your are old first of all by the fuss they make about you and then, having done this 'devoir', by the way in which they utterly neglect you. This is done better in the old country.—Yours affectly.—J. B. YEATS

TO SUSAN MITCHELL

146

New York
(1915)

. . . The *New Republic* is edited by a group of young writers, all supposed to be awfully clever. They are having a fine time, and their magazine is greatly lauded—all the superior people take it in. I might think more highly of it but they without a moment's delay refused some articles and stories I did them the honour to submit. It is reported that the magazine is

financed for three years by a rich American woman. I think all American
magazine writing far too frightfully clever. It is as if a man had by mistake
hired an acrobat for a footman, so that when he asked for a glass of water
it was handed to him by a man standing on his head.

TO W. B. YEATS

147

New York
[undated, 1915]

The poet is not primarily a thinker, but incidentally he is a thinker and
a stern thinker, since the source of his magic is his personal sincerity. What
he says he believes, and from this it follows that he must have few beliefs
and those of the *simplest,* for time will not allow him to be travelling over
the whole world of thought—that is, for the professional thinker. Yet the
brilliant talker and rhetorician can do this. Macaulay, for instance, out of
his facile habit of belief could proceed everywhere, except [to] poetry.
Carlyle was such another, only with the difference Macaulay flattered his
audience whereas Carlyle insulted it—yet neither had the real instinct for
truth, the primal deep-lying sincerity, which is the poet's virtue. . . .

TO SUSAN MITCHELL

148

317 W. 29. New York
Sept. 20, 1915

. . . The Irish took to hatred when they deserted the statesman Isaac
Butt for the politician Parnell. Hatred is a prison where people can only
rave and foam at the mouth and tear their blankets and attack the keepers
and yell obscenities, finally to be quelled and put in punishment cells. The
many fine movements in history which have so ended! Hatred has got
hold of socialism in New York. An educated reflecting people like the
Scotch would never have deserted Butt, and they'd have won, or the Butt
methods would have won. Parnell was not a great man, I remember at
school certain boys who had a natural leadership and who always had a

certain following, and I remember also that they were never otherwise interesting and never by any manner of means intellectual. A certain combination of egotism and vanity and activity and courage did the trick. Much intellect and indeed any breadth of intellect would have spoiled them for the purpose.

Lady Gregory was immensely impressed by Mrs. Parnell's life. But then Parnell was an Irish aristocrat and he won a woman's love. So as Irish Grande Dame and as weak woman she was bound to admire him and the book. . . .

149

New York
Sept. 21, 1915

. . . Ireland must help England—their grievances are against the Irish Protestants especially the landlords and against the English middle class, and those beastly non-conformist ministers. After the war will come some great social movement, in which the Irish must help *their English brothers*— who certainly won't be the middle class their old enemies. The English workman is against the Germans, therefore the Irish nationalists should be against the Germans.[1]

When a Socialist tells me, Patriotism is nonsense—I reply—that is as if you told me all old women were the same even tho' one of them happened to be my own mother. . . .

TO W. B. YEATS

150

N.Y.
Oct. 6, 1915

I knew Seeger. He was from Mexico, though his family are of New England. His courtesy, unlike that of most Americans, was grave in quality, remote and dignified. He was very young and handsome. He told a friend of mine who met him in Paris that he would not be tempted to leave Paris by the most (?) appointment, and this although in great poverty, hardly

[1] In the Great War Yeats's feelings about England greatly changed. He also had the old-world Irish nationalist's sympathy with France.

able to make ends meet. He joined the Foreign Legion of France from love of France, a lesser motive would not have tempted a man to whom war must have been odious. In his life as in his art a man of the finest feelings. (His) is the only war poem I have seen that is interesting, since in it only do I find intensity and the self-command that is intensity. These drawings are not really like, but they suggest the type (sketches). He had a habit of looking downwards. His eyelashes, long olive eyebrows, a perfect arch. He talked without any hurry, never impatient, though sometimes a little eager. . . . When last on furlough in Paris, for the three days it lasted, he was invisible—with a girl, said his friend—it may have been to write this poem. He seemed to know Spanish. I liked to hear him talking it.[1]

TO OLIVER ELTON

151

N.Y.

Dec. 17, 1915

You asked me long ago for a letter, and I have wanted to write very much, out of friendship. Yet what can one say?—I am living as we all are in a house chronically on fire, and the firemen are here, and because they are risking their lives for me very profusely I am expected to put up with their domineering ways and brutal manners.—I want to live, and they are ready to die for me—so I must submit, and, that I may live at all, must give up everything that makes life worth living. That is how war appears to me. I praise these firemen and hymn their valour just to encourage them and keep them going—I even tell them that war is [a] good thing in itself and that we shall all be the better for it—*but I don't believe this.* . . . As to literature proper, it will have no effect—the robin redbreast, once this hurlyburly is over and gone, will again sing his reedy note, and the blackbird and thrush from the tops of the trees their songs of pride and vaunting, and the nightingale his passionate warble out of the depths of the grove; that is to say, the poets, of which (*sic*) these birds are the symbols. Poets deal with what I call ultimate human nature—descending into the depths. Doubtless there will come changes in the social structure

---

[1] Alan Seeger was killed in Flanders. The poem referred *t*o appeared in the *North American Review* (October, 1915), and was called 'Champagne' (17 verses, written in Champagne, France, 1915).

and then will come quantities of rhetoricians writing in prose and verse—but the real poets, avoiding the transient and the ephemeral, will concern themselves with what they have always concerned themselves [with]—*ultimate human nature.*

What, you will ask, is ultimate human nature? Do you remember the end of the *Cenci?* and how the women *prattled of trivialities,* merely to distract each other's attention from the death awaiting them? All through *Hamlet* the theme is the ultimate man—and one likes to think of the sea-kings and the sirens who dwell in the depths of the ocean. Soldiers are artificial men, made for a purpose, and so are most men—poets are the only men who are true and natural, for they have the secret of being musical with [? within] themselves, like pretty children whose very tantrums are delicious. Why are such children seemingly doing right in our eyes? Because we recognise their *wisdom.* The greatest sage cannot be wiser, if wisdom be, as I think it is, the being true to yourself and to your knowledge (knowledge in the child limited, in the sage also limited). Soldiers though they be heroes are wise according to the wisdom of others, and so it is with the loud multitude for whom the rhetoricians labour in their vocation. The poets remain the protesting voice for the other wisdom, the true wisdom, that of human nature, which would get out of its cave of false honour—and real dishonour and defeat;—seeking the liberty to be itself, so that every intuition and instinct might bear blossom and fruit. . . .

—— is all ego, nothing else but ego, incarnate ego. If his wife is intelligent and also loves him I should like to hear her talk about him. For love, real love, means knowledge—not, as people think, amiable prejudice and wilful ignorance, though it may mean no sense of right and wrong when the loved one is concerned. A woman in love with husband and child is in this like a poet. She would know everything; she cannot know enough. How does intensity show itself in a poet? Is it not in his profound knowledge of the finite? And we listen to him because we feel he *knows:* by the same mark we know the loving wife and the loving mother. These people don't praise or admire their 'darlings'—they can't—they are not like the foolish man who admires himself. A man may love himself, yet even this love is so great a passion that it has no patience with the insincerities of self-admiration.

TO JOSEPH HONE

152

J. B. Yeats was a principal speaker at a debate on the Playboy *following the disturbances in the Abbey Theatre in January 1907. His son has given a rather different account of what happened in the poem 'Beautiful lofty Things'.*

> *'My father upon the Abbey Stage, before him a raging crowd:*
> *The land of Saints, and then as the applause died out,*
> *Of Plaster Saints, his beautiful mischievous head thrown back'.*

New York
29th December, 1915

... Of course I did not make a speech in favour of patricide. How could I? Here is what I said. I began with some information about Synge which interested my listeners and then: 'Of course I know Ireland is an island of Saints, but thank God it is also an island of sinners—only unfortunately in this Country people cannot live or die except behind a curtain of deceit'. At this point the chairman and my son both called out, 'Time's up, Time's up.' I saw the lifted sign and like the devil in *Paradise Lost* I fled. The papers next morning said I was howled down. It was worse, I was pulled down. .... The sentence about the curtain of deceit flashed on my mind at the moment, and was a good sentence, but manifestly a blunder, although I did enjoy it. .... Among my ancestors was a man called Voisin. He must have been a French Huguenot—that's the man I'd like to have met. He dyed the whole family in a sort of well-mannered Evangelicism, at least I cannot otherwise account for it among a family so intelligent as my father's family; it's being well-mannered points to a French ancestor.

Do you see your cousin Nat Hone, the great painter. If so tell him I often see his pictures here at John Quinn's, and they are in fine company, for with them are some of the greatest of modern French and modern American (John Quinn has a real knowledge of art) and I think they 1ower among them by depth of feeling and their poetry. I visit them constantly, and sometimes one is my favourite, and sometimes another. Just now it is a picture in which there is a rainbow, a faint little bit of colour in a brown seascape.

Kuno Meyer

TO LILY YEATS

153

Kuno Meyer, charming translator of old-Irish poetry, was in America seeking Irish sympathies for Germany. He had written to J. B. Y. that 'it would be perfectly dreadful if people were to regulate their intercourse or choose their friends according to what they might think about the Lusitania *or any of the other calamitous incidents of the war.'*

Jan. 1st, 1916

. . . Kuno Meyer made many attempts to get me to go and see him, but I resisted every time. I told him I would not forget the *Lusitania*—that it was between us a skeleton out of the cupboards . . . I had an invitation to tea from the Colums, but I managed to get out of that, for I feared that persistent Kuno Meyer might turn up.

TO OLIVER ELTON

154

Jan. 16th, 1916

I am too old to learn. I lean on my amour propre, though I do not, and never have, in the English manner worn amour propre like a royal decoration on my sleeve.

TO W. B. YEATS

155

July 26, 1916
317 W. 29 St., New York

. . . We know that a real artist could suggest a crowd by painting only their figures, and another could not paint a crowd even tho' he had carefully painted fifty. With a single line Blake or Shelley can fill my vision with a wealth of fine things.

All this is very elementary, yet it needs to be insisted on just now with these cubists and others. The doctrine that poetry and art are imitative is forgotten.[1] I am not sure if it is not decried, it is too humble a doctrine for these high fliers. This war by its mightiness and the enormousness of the conflagration may dispose certain people to think that everything old is old-fashioned. . . . The only man that never alters is the poet for he is that deep-lying human nature which cannot alter, tho' I admit that he may become freer, which is not to alter but to become more itself. . . . If old Homer's spirit visits the trenches, he will find many marvellous things, but not marvel at the courage or heroism or cowardice either. In these he's at home, and he will know all about the suffering women and about the generals and the statesmen and their crafty ways. . . .

156

New York
Feb. 2, 1916

. . . My theory is that we are always dreaming—chairs, tables, women and children, our wives and sweethearts, the people in the streets, all in various ways and with various powers are the starting points of dreams. As we fall asleep we drift away from the control and correction of the facts into the world of memory and hope—for all night long and all through our sleep we are still dreaming though the dreams be hidden deep in the subliminal consciousness under the cloud of sleep. As we drift back into consciousness we become aware of the dreams, note them and observe them until a fuller wakefulness brings us once more into contact with actual fact. Sleep is dreaming away from the facts and wakefulness is dreaming in close contact with the facts, and *since facts excite our dreams and feed them we get as close as possible to the facts if we have the cunning and the genius of poignant feeling*, and since it is true that certain facts, or facts seen in a particular way, may injure our dreams so that they pain us, we acquire a knowledge how to handle them so as to deprive them of their power to do mischief. With what deliberate self-deception, with what sophistry does a lover approach his sweetheart, and at the same time with what penetration and power of knowledge. All men are artists from morning to night and all night also, creating phantasy, and we who are artists do deliberately and with science and conscious purpose and a great ambition what the others are doing without knowing it. In wakefulness and in sleep when

[1] For W. B. Yeats's reply see letter 161.

we act, when we think, we are each of us shrouded in dreams—when the soul departs dreams leave us, and not till then.

All great poets and artists are rich in the finite—art they say like everything progresses—but I ask in what direction?—by *getting closer to the finite*.

There was a time when faces and hands and feet were represented only in profile, and till a short time ago shadows were rendered as merely brown. After long contention people recognized that they were blue or purple—and why was this an advance in beauty? Because it was a truer and a getting closer to the finite. M. Angelo beat the ancients because of the *palpitating* quality of his marble flesh.

These artists who say that representation of the fact hinders art are sinning against the first law of art—for *art is imitation*—and art is concrete, because you can only imitate concrete things. . . .

157

Feb. 10, 1916
317 W. 29. New York

My dear Willie—The ethical doctrine most popular in America is expressed by the word *service*. Every man, woman and child is brought up with the idea of service and it is fatal to sincerity. In America there is no such thing as sincerity. The effect of democracy is that each citizen regards himself as holding, by virtue of his citizenship and his vote, a kind of *public position*. Socrates in his *Apologia* says that he soon discovered, that in democratic Athens he could not serve truth if he usurped a public position, for which reason he forsook all opportunities of public service and devoted himself to a private life in which he sought for truth, pure and simple. The head of a great Railway or other big commercial concern must, if he is to do his duty to his clients, throw overboard nice ideas of honour and honesty and employ the accustomed methods of graft and bribery, making any [indecipherable] which he does not avow. The Editor of a paper enlisted in some propaganda of socialism or philosophical anarchism finds that he must look askance at truth, as these men do at honesty, overstating and understating matters in a way that must ultimately blunt all their susceptibilities, which are of the very essence of fine discretion, and which also are at the root of that enthusiasm which is the soul of poetry. If a poet preserves his susceptibility to truth, poetic enthusiasm remains to comfort and inspire him even though he has parted with every other honourable quality. I was greatly struck with your description of Arthur Balfour.[1] It is the description of a leader of men. People think of leaders as men devoted to service, and by service they mean that these men serve their followers. Of this kind of leaders, President Wilson is not so much an instance as its characterization, since he makes too obvious and indecently frank his desire to serve his followers. *The real leader serves truth, not people, not his followers,* and he cares little for authority or the exercise of power, excepting so far as they help him to serve truth, and we follow him because we too, when our attention is directed to it, would also serve truth, that being a fundamental law of human nature,—however unfaithful to it we may often be when misled by passion or self-interests. Your grandfather Pollexfen was my idea of a leader, though—not being a man with a large mould of intellectual power—only in embryo. Authority and the exercise of power in itself distasteful to him, but his sincerity absolute— such men gain a ready audience. Their commands excite no anger, since we are not brought face to face with an Ego. They and all of us are serving a mistress who really issues the orders we obey. Were President Wilson a real leader, he would, like Socrates, devote himself to the truths of public conduct, such truths as fill to the utmost curve the amplitude of the mind, and Americans would have followed him as sheep the shepherd. Of course, by truth I do not mean logical or scientific truth, but the something which is the core of personal sincerity and a mystery that reveals itself only in deeds or in the works of Art. Logic and Science are public inspectors who analyse and approve. Poets must possess by nature and must cultivate this kind of sincerity. Otherwise the spell and the leadership will leave them.

We have the doctrine of service, and it is, I think, largely due to the women, so powerful in America where they write the poetry, and are still, and will remain for generations a *servile race*; and the women who are most subject to the doctrine, are the intellectual and what are called the emancipated women, for they make explicit what hitherto is only *implicit* in women's condition. Following her lights, woman cannot grasp the idea of individualistic sincerity, and because of democracy and its anxiety, her idea of virtue is service, whether as master or slave—for some rapid and easy method of forming and tasting opinions. We have adopted reason or logic for masters. Now reason cannot be master—its office is to be critic. A man loves his mother, and reason tells him she is not so good-looking as other old women and not so clever or accomplished, and a feeling deep within him makes answer that reason lies in its throat or if he listens, as he

[1] See note to letter 196.

might do, it is not that it may destroy his filial affections and preferences, but rather that he may acquiesce in a dear mystery beyond his power of understanding. In questions of conduct, as for instance, in patriotism or family affection and in a thousand other directions, the man who follows reason will wander along a stony path, and the poet who does it would drink in a well where there is no water.

How far is it the fact that cubists and free verse people are heretics of this kind?—Deserting the dark mysteries of real poetry and art to uphold something which promises them an easy victory in wrangling contention with bewildered opponents. They are out for the victories of logic, and if we cannot answer them, we know that they are wrong and hate them and shall, (please God!) continue to hate them. A poet must be, before everything, a servant of truth, and they are servants or rather the kind soldiers of logic. It is only in the unrestrained familiar conversation of truth, naked and unashamed, that the poet can draw easy breath. He must, as it were, walk affectionately, with her arm through his—then he can write poetry in which will be the heartbeat and the warm breath and the fragrance of her presence. Am I growing too dithyrambic? Yet, I do not think so, for to describe the relations of a poet to truth, one must resort to figures of speech.—Yours affectionately—J. B. YEATS

Have you noticed that when we talk of a man of genius, one tries to explain his failure? When one talks of a man of talent, we try to account for his success, this is apropos of my conversation about Dowden.

158

317 W. 29, N. York
Feb. 24, 1916

. . . The pro-German anti-British Irish are moved by spite. It was spite to which Parnell appealed when he ousted Butt the statesman. Butt was a man of genius, that is a man of vision. He looked beyond the mists of time and saw an Ireland educated to govern itself. What does Mrs. —— care about an educated Ireland? She has not time for such thoughts, she wants to humiliate England. Butt called it 'the policy of exasperation'.

I 59

Feb. 27, 1916
317 W. 29, N. York

My dear Willie—I think I am entitled to call myself 'an inheritor of unfulfilled renown'. I told Colum and his wife the whole plot of my play—I never saw people more delighted and Colum says that it should be written. Percy MacKaye if he begged me once begged me twenty times to write it—he called it a psychological comedy, and here I am working at my own portraits, and in possession, as I believe, of a matured technique that would place me high among portrait painters . . . but next month I shall be 77—senectus and old Father Time stand in my path and old Time shakes his hour glass—as if he would hurry downward the few grains that remain.

I think there is always with me a residuum, a something at the bottom of the 'cup of my sorrows', and that something is a conviction, an intuition inseparable from life—that nothing is ever really lost, and that if we could see our world and all that takes place on its surface, and see it from a distance and as if from the centre of the sun, we should find it to be a fine piece of machinery working to certain ends with an absolute precision. I had in my only philosophy a faith founded like that of Socrates upon the basis of my conscious ignorance—it is a sort of sublime optimism, and I am well satisfied with my ignorance as my betters are with their knowledge—and I call it sublime because it soars to such heights, that these logical people cannot reach it with their arrows, and I believe if the truth were known and confessed, that this doctrine of a conscious ignorance is, at this present moment, the abiding solace and hope of all my fellow mortals. Grand majestic spirits will spurn it, but passive, inactive beings like myself, and all of us when the time comes that energy can no longer help and pride is humbled, will return to it as a last hope, and as indeed the only one left—and so true is it to my mind that I feel I am writing only platitudes; moreover, *I think it is only doctrine for poets*.

Have you noticed that poets use ideas in a way quite different from prose writers—the latter treat ideas as matters in which they believe, as scientists believe in the law of gravitation. With poets ideas are consciously or unconsciously part of their technique and of the machinery of poetry. We do not know and we do not care whether Wordsworth actually believed in Plato's doctrine of prenatal existence, the idea is not really an integral part of the poetry. Did Shelley believe in what Keats called his 'magnanimity', fine ideas, which came to him second hand from the cold brains of Godwin. At any rate, his verse when he writes about these things is very different from when he writes concrete things. The callow American poet is all for ideas, if these are true and fine, then the poetry is true and fine etc. To ideas outside those of science and mathematics, we extend only a half belief. When I proclaim that the soul is immortal, what am I really thinking of? This and that person who is dear to me, and of the sad reality of death and also of the reality of my own longing—and when I write of immortality, apart from these, the verse will grow languid as my beliefs, for in my terrible sincerity in presence of any sufferings, perforce, I will avoid the emphasis of a real belief. We know that it was the practice of Socrates and his school to affirm nothing and to know the boundaries dividing the regions of belief and half belief—'Men of Athens, we now separate you to your various vocations, and I to die, which is what I know not'. Those are the last words of his Apology.

Let poets, by all means, touch on ideas, but let it be only a 'touching' and a tentative groping with the sensitive poetical fingers. It is bad poetry which proclaims a definite belief—because it is a sin against sincerity. Wordsworth was full of 'beliefs' and ideas—yet always is it evident that he knew them to be only longings—and so it is with every poet that writes of ideas. It is a fault with Browning that he is too confident—he was at heart a practical man, and after the manner of his sort must have even in matters of the spirit definite grounds upon which to work—. People talk with complacent superficiality of vagueness and a mere suggestiveness as necessary in poetry. But this is only true when they enter the regions where we all spend so much time—the blissful regions of longing and half belief—here not the certainties of joyous conviction are audible but the plaintive longing of half belief. Nay, there is not even this —only a faint hope—and for this there is as far as I can make out no foundation except the consciousness of mortal ignorance.

Religious poetry is poor and always will be so—because it asserts a definite belief where such a thing is impossible. The deepest feeling in the human heart, its sincerity, will not accept this kind of comfort. We turn away from it, sick at heart, and no amount of self flagellation can cure the sickness. The Catholic Saint suffers from an incurable sadness—wearied with attempting the impossible.—Yours affectionately—J. B. YEATS

TO RUTH HART

160

317 W. 29th St.
March 4, 1916

There are many lovely things in America, and I would advise any Englishman as soon as he has finished his University education to come here that he may cleanse himself of English vulgarity. But 'the woman is very loud' as a French maid that I know said to her master, and when he replied that it was 'American brilliancy', she replied, 'Then they should go to the centre of the wood'. I think the young American very superior to the young American woman.

The French maid was for a while at Lord Howth's, and speaks affectionately of Shielmartin, etc. She dresses like a countess, but her English she has learned from English footmen, and it is most amusing when she talks of "is Lordship's order', etc. She is my fellow lodger and is most intelligent.

. . . When I return, it will be like a new world—and I shall come upon you full of strange surmises, not to say apprehensions

FROM W. B. YEATS

161

18 Woburn Buildings, London, W.C.
March 5, 1916

Dear Father—I cannot reply to your last letter, the one with the amusing picture of Wilson, favourite of heaven, for I have sent it to the typist to be copied.[1] I am handing the letters over to Ezra Pound, who is to make a first small volume of selections for Lollie's press, I thought he would make the selection better than I should. I am almost too familiar with the thought, and also that his approval representing as he does the most aggressive contemporary school of the young would be of greater value than my approval, which would seem perhaps but family feeling. It will also enable me to have a new book for Lollie sooner than if I did the work myself, as I shall be busy writing at something else and my sight

[1] For J. B. Y.'s views on President Wilson see Letters 157, 165.

makes my work slow. In the last letter, but one, you spoke of all art as imitation,[1] meaning I conclude, imitation of something in the outer world. To me it seems that it often uses the outer world as a symbolism to express subjective moods. The greater the subjectivity, the less the imitation. Though perhaps, there is always some imitation. You say that music suggests now the roar of the sea, now the song of the bird, and yet it seems to me that the song of the bird itself is perhaps subjective, an expression of feeling alone. The element of pattern in every art is, I think, the part that is not imitative, for in the last analysis, there will always be somewhere an intensity of pattern that we have never seen with our eyes. In fact, imitation seems to me to create a language in which we say things which are not imitation.

At the present moment, after a long period during which the arts had put aside almost everything but imitation, there is a tendency to over-emphasise pattern, and a too great anxiety to see that those patterns themselves have novelty. I write all this not because I think it particularly striking or because I think you have no answer to it, but to suggest to you some new thoughts which will come to you from meeting it.

I return to London to-morrow, mainly to get rehearsed and to get ready for rehearsal a little play in which the principal characters wear masks designed by the painter, Dulac, it is an experiment and is to be played in Lady Cunard's drawing room.[2]

We have had all kinds of copyright difficulties, the usual ones accentuated by war time, over the autobiography. You have probably therefore, not yet received your copy. I saw Lady Gregory a couple of weeks ago on her return, and looking very vigorous, she is now in the West of Ireland again, correcting the proofs of the big book on fairy belief, which I have annotated copiously.—Yours ever—W. B. YEATS

TO LILY YEATS

162

March 6, 1916

. . . When I go out for a walk I spend a long time in the Pennsylvania Railway Station which is quite close to this. I find comfort and pleasure in such vastness all heated with electricity—with shops etc.—and no train in sight and no steam whistles audible, for they are all underground reached

[1] See on this subject Letters 155 and 156.   [2] *The Hawk's Well.*

by stairs. People are always hurrying to and from trains—no matter how many, lost in the wide space; their footsteps making a pleasant bustle, while negro porters dart about offering their services. . . .

TO W. B. YEATS

163

April 28, 1916
317 W. 29, N. York

My dear Willie—People have an idea that poets live in disorder, and feed upon it. If they feed upon it, it is only that the pain of disorder sets their intellects to work in bringing to it order, so that in the ensuing silence and quiet, they might have leave to sing. The poet is an orderly man, because he allows no single feeling to remain single, forcing it into harmonious relation with all the other feelings. He is a whole man, whereas others are only sectional, his anger that of a whole man, his love that of a whole man, his inner life crowded [and] complex.

Self-control is the essence of his being. Sailors who have graduated in the University of the seas and ships and become captains and mates have generally personalities. The discipline of the forecastle which is that of self-control breeds them in the right way. Solitude and silence and much self-communing in a world where everything depends on self-control, compel him into personality, a real personality, though it be of the simplest.

To be effective among sailors a man, whether as captain or mate or mere comrade, must feel and the others must feel, that what he does or says is sanctioned by every section in himself, if one feeling one section is left out, the personality is incomplete, and its absence is an irritation and fatal to his influence. John Pollexfen's stories about his life at sea were interesting, because they revealed and illustrated this doctrine. He once said to me that with him it was always a trouble that he must have time to think, that thinking was never a logical process, but just a consulting together of the various instincts that constituted his personality. If there was logic at all, it came afterwards. He first 'made up his mind,' and then expressed it, perhaps, by means of logic. Without the personality and with logic only, a man is merely a sea lawyer, whose opinions carry no weight with friends or foes, what Hamlet meant when he said 'Words, words'.

Yesterday, I was present at a rehearsal of three of your plays by a Ladies' school—a lot of nice, immature girls sang as larks. *Deirdre* was one of the plays, and it was amusing to see the lines that were left out. Years ago, they gave a play of yours, *The Land of Heart's Desire*, and made 800 Dollars, which they gave to a hospital, and helped the publisher to sell a hundred copies of the poem.

At the head of the school are two women, the most human possible. The girls made great hash of it, and I did not hesitate to tell them so, but everyone is in earnest and eager for advice, and none of them had seen the Irish plays acted. I thought the singing very good.—Yours affectionately—J. B. YEATS

TO LILY YEATS

164

New York
May 17th, 1916

... So Lord Justice Holmes is dead. Several years long ago he dined with me when we lived near Sandymount. A few days before I left Dublin for London in 1867 he invited myself and four others to his poor little lodgings in Nelson Street, and all the men except myself became Judges of the Supreme Court in Ireland—one was judge in Jamaica—with great incomes and carriages and property—and except Hugh Holmes all died long ago and are forgotten except in the fond memory of their children and grandchildren. Am I not entitled to think myself the successful man among them? At any rate I am inclined to think that any one of them would have bartered away all his honours for my length of days—even if they did not have my brilliant offspring, yourself included. If only I had grandchildren. . . .! [He was to have them.]

Quinn says that at the coming election it will be hard to beat Wilson, and that Roosevelt, he fears, won't be nominated. He will be the favourite of history and has a great intellect, but he has scared the country. America may plunge into war but will never vote for it, and to vote for Roosevelt would, they think, be to vote for war. I myself think that peace is safer in Roosevelt's hands than in the fumbling hands of Wilson. . . .

These executions are having a considerable effect here. The strongest element in this country is a humanitarian sentiment outside the 'cowardly' South where they lynch negroes.[1]

[1] The executions referred to were those that took place in Dublin after the Easter Week Rising in Dublin of 1916.

Pittsburgh Lecture—Home Thoughts

TO MRS. HART

165

My dear Mrs. Hart—I was so pleased to get your message in Ruth's letter, that I must write to you to thank you for it. I am always thinking of coming home. A year ago when Willie was here he wanted me to start for home with him, he paying all expenses and saying that it would be only for a vacation after which I could return. I am afraid to go home. It was so hard to make a living—here there is always something to do. I lecture, I write, I do portraits—my lack of practical instinct for success pursues me even here. I paint better than most people, but 'most people' can turn their talents such as they are to a practical success. Were I younger, I think I would betake myself to the lecture platform, preparing for it by reading and collecting knowledge. I have a sort of Boanerges gift. I can shout and gesticulate and make pantomime gestures and smile naturally in the right places, telling an anecdote here and there—and do all the necessary things for platform lecturing. I lectured at Pittsburgh last Xmas and my chairman (a lady) has since written to me to say that my lecture was one of the most brilliant lectures of the year—and I had for rivals Masefield, Noyes, etc., in fact every one of the distinguished men from England, and since that I have given a better lecture here in N. York, and got more enthusiastic applause. I have also a book coming out next Xmas published by my daughter at her 'illustrious' Press, the Cuala Press.

I was delighted to read in Ruth's letter all about your sons and daughters and their happy marriages. When I left Dublin they were all just growing or just grown up, now they are serious responsible citizens fathers and mothers of families, and you yourself in such good health and spirits, Ruth says. Were I at home, I would persuade you to sit for me. The *best painter in America* wrote from Dublin when he saw my work in the Modern Gallery and the Abbey Theatre, that I painted better portraits than Orpen or than Sargent (and he studied both in Paris and Madrid, spending years there—he is considered a very fine critic).

I am thinking seriously tho' vaguely of returning when the war stops, or perhaps in any case before next winter. Every winter threatens to end my life, and I don't want to die without seeing Ireland again. I was sorry to hear of Hugh Holmes' death, it is curious that tho' I have not exchanged a word with him for about thirty or forty years, yet I *felt* his death; he used to dine with me sometimes during the first two years of my married life—and so he belongs to that period, that long-vanished dream of my youth and marriage. I lived in a small house at Sandymount and Willie was a baby; at that time we were both poor, and he very poor living in a lodging in Nelson St. A few days before I left for London I spent an evening with him. We were five in number, and all but myself became judges and one Chancellor—and now I am the survivor—does that make me the *successful* one —better any sort of a living artist than a dead judge?—I don't think so; but still there is a smug if contemptible satisfaction in being alive. At any rate perhaps if I had not been an unsuccessful and struggling man, Willie and Jack would not have been so strenuous men. For the girls it is another matter. Masefield told a lady I know that he thought my daughters the most interesting women he knows. I wish I could show you their letters . . .

I suppose Howth is as beautiful as ever—what does it care whether the war goes on or not? Even the terrible domestic tragedy, the rising in Dublin does not affect it, nor Mahaffy's becoming Provost at last—but the enterprising builder is its ever present enemy. When I return I shall look out for his ravages. The fact is there are too many people in the world. This war itself would not have come, but that the German nation swelled to such proportions—and Howth would keep its solitude, but that Dublin grows apace.

We are all dreadfully angry with the President. In the words of a friend of mine, an Irishman, 'he has debauched American public opinion and made us a nation of cowards'.—My hope is in Roosevelt.—Yrs affectionately—J. B. YEATS

The feminine world of N. York is just now interested in the rumour that the President's wife is to have a baby. She is rich and elderly. The ladies are more interested in this than in the war, and this is the eternal feminine, supposed to be banished from N. York, for good and all.

This President is a confirmed sentimentalist; hence his memorable phrase, 'America is too proud to fight', and the other day he wrote 'Europe is war mad'—*war mad*—when the greatest war for the greatest issue in history is being waged, and England engaged in perhaps the only creditable war she ever entered on.

Never trust a sentimentalist. They are all alike, pretenders to virtue, at heart selfish frauds and sensualists; against him we have Roosevelt, a man of highest courage and of passionate sincerity.

I am told that all the Southerners are cowards who have never recovered from their defeat and losses in the civil war—and it is alleged by Roosevelt that the Wilsons who are from Virginia were always cowards and that they did not take part on either side in that war. There you have Wilson; a sentimental coward. I am told also he is very lazy—the lawyer who represents in legal matters the French Government told me this. I am a physiognomist and damned him from the first.

TO JACK B. YEATS

166

August 19th, 1916
317 W. 29th, New York

My dear Jack—It is a good morning. Such as we get weeks of in the Fall—the windows all open and quite quiet at the back of the house, and no squalling children since there are no children in N. York. So I naturally being in good humour which is favourable to the affection, think of you and the perfect wife. *Do* write to me. Hereafter when I have become a silent member of the Company existing only in memory, it will be pleasant to think that you have written to me many times. So do write.

An old man should think of the past, but I am all interested in the future. I watch the post. I have an idea that any moment a Commission may come to me—my success at Pittsburgh has raised all my hopes and I trust myself. Do you know that often when I am in low spirits I take up your illustrations to the Hannay book, and each time I get a fresh impression of their loveliness and their actuality—and a sort of poetic truthfulness—you satirize but with such a kind heart. York Powell as you know once said you had a mind like Shakespeare's—I like also the way you 'progress'. You do not stand still—a man of genius should be like a growing boy, who is never, never, and never will be a grown up. He must have a new style and new methods, not for fashion's sake, but because he has outgrown the old ways. People are offended with Willie because he won't go on writing [word indecipherable] and Lyrics. They are fools for their pains, and I anathematize them—I hope you take things easy. *I failed because I worked too hard.* I let myself be driven by that foul witch, an uneasy conscience, which is only another name for *Fear*—who is the demon of life, and the great source of all or almost all its crimes and its criminals. Since I came to N. York I have taken things easily, *never worked at any thing a moment longer than I was interested in it,* that is the secret—*never interest yourself in anything you don't care about.* This is not the rule for conduct, but is the rule for art, and for artists in their work.

I have two lectures before me—certainly one lecture to be delivered in a large Hall taken for the purpose. Quinn guaranteeing the rent, Mr. Sloan working it up and taking all the trouble. The Americans are the most human, that is the most affectionate, sympathetic, and helpful people that ever lived under the wide sky—and in America the sky is very wide indeed—100,000,000 people all human and [word indecipherable]. The Englishman does not try to be human, he does not know how, he has forgotten. He wants—God bless his simple heart—to tread the narrow path of duty, and how narrow it is. Solemnly he talks to his wife, solemnly he whips his boys. Solemnly he pays his bills.

These three French women work harder than any other women I ever encountered and yet they are as easily pleased as children and when I go away they will all kiss me and cry their eyes out, and mourn for me and waft me on my way with good wishes, they are human and therefore fond of other people. One of their guests is now in Hospital dying as we think of dropsy. She lived here a good deal. The Petitpas who never leave the house except for some pressing need, go regularly to see her and always bring her food and fruit. For they are convinced that in the hospitals people don't get enough food.

TO LILY YEATS
167

Sept. 15, 1916

. . . 100 cities contended for the honour of being Homer's birthplace and the question was never solved, and now it may be debated whether Willie (whom the Pollexfens used to hate declaring over and over again that he was just like his father) is a Pollexfen or a Yeats. The fact is he is both, one side of him not a bit like the Pollexfens and the other side of him not a bit like Yeats. I do so wish you had known my uncles Thomas and John—you would be proud to have their blood. They were so clever and so innocent—I never knew and never will know any people so attractive. . . . They were both so tolerant, so indulgent which you felt was part of their cleverness. . . .[1]

[1] Uncles Thomas and John were sons of Parson Yeats of Drumcliffe, the parish in which W. B. Yeats wished that he should be buried. 'In Drumcliffe churchyard Yeats is laid . . . An ancestor was rector there . . . Long years ago. . . .'

TO OLIVER ELTON

168

N.Y.
Sept. 25th, 1916

A young lady (I only met her once) told several of us at dinner that she and her husband and her friend and her husband lived in the woods naked —I asked, absolutely naked? and she answered, absolutely naked, and when I asked why she said it was so convenient for bathing in the lake!

TO LILY YEATS

169

October 5, 1916

. . . A few days ago I was introduced at dinner here at Petitpas to an elderly man—Mr. Herbert. In 1872 when I was at Muckross Killarney he was then a very little boy, and now he is here for 34 years, holding some municipal office, married to an American with a married son—his father Captain Shaw Herbert long dead, and Muckross, an estate of 160,000 acres sold to strangers. His uncle was the owner of Muckross. It was for me a curious meeting. He said my portrait of his father is still treasured by the family—to my surprise—for I was only two or three years an artist, and it was very bad. He has an American accent which would have shocked the people of Muckross. Here his wife wanted me to come and stay with them in the country—he is very like his father but with a square head and without the aristocratic swagger. He was not bred at Eton and has not been an officer in the Grenadier Guards. He was mournful over the loss of Muckross. The Herberts of Muckross are now only a memory.

TO SUSAN MITCHELL

170

New York
Oct. 12, 1916

. . . As I am in my second childhood—or ought to be—you must excuse me if I am too garrulous. But I am reading again *David Copperfield*—

and so want to write another sentence about Dickens. That book is all a dream; everything in it is taking place in an impossible world—made out of *desire*—and if there is any of the actual world—and there is much—it is only because desire has to build its dreams out of the only materials to its hand. Do you remember a drawing by Leach? Outside a bedroom door is a group and all are busy in throwing against it pails of water. There is the pompous butler, the spick and span footman, and the page boy, there is also the fluttering housemaid, and there is the materfamilias superintending the whole performance—in the crinoline petticoats of which there are many, with the drawers coming well down over her shoes as was then the fashion—and the legend below says, that it is all because Jackey is now a midshipman and can't sleep without the noise of the waves; this is good wit and delicious, *because it is impossible*. The world is vanity saith the Preacher—it isn't. God made it, it is reality, and art and poetry are vanity; that is, they have no existence outside man's imagination—and what is not this kind of vanity, is neither poetry nor art or humour or anything else that is important. By logic and reason we die hourly; by imagination we live. A man loves his wife—is it the real woman he loves? He has long ceased to see that woman, tho' every one else does, except perhaps her children who have a dream mother as he has a dream wife.

You know better than I do—but I think Miss —— drove out Dan Cupid, as Betsey Trotwood drove out the donkey from her patch of ground. I wish it had been otherwise, one's first glimpse of happiness, one's entrance into that dream world, comes by falling in love. Ask your own heart if I am right. If you were not a woman and under conventions that beset the woman what love poems you would write! how do I know this? Because I am a physiognomist. I think I see you laughing, as I am now, and when we laugh we forgive—and so you will pardon my impudence.— Yours affectly—J. B. YEATS

Have you noticed Miss —— well? she has known sorrow and indeed lives with it, but she has never known happiness, never heard of it—that fairy wand has never touched her intellectual brow, and that's where she parts company with so many of us, who think as fools.

Reminiscence of School Days

TO OLIVER ELTON

171

N.Y.

Oct. 18, 1916

When a very little boy I spent two years at Seaforth [*near Liverpool*], where I was at a school kept by two old maids. There was 'Emmer' (Emma) and Betsey and Anne. We were ruled by the fear of Hell and 'Emmer's' birch. Yet Emma remains in my mind as something attractive—a stern face hiding a tender heart [*sketch*]; it was hidden, but we discovered it, being small boys and on the look-out for it . . . there is a lot of poetry in a little boy.

Anne I forget. She died. [*sketch*] Betsey, in whom was nothing tender, outside or within. I hated Betsey, who caned me for nothing. (I can't remember the back of Betsey's head.) All the boys except myself and one or two Irish boys were destined for Eton or some equally glorious place. During a thunderstorm operations were suspended—I mean we sat still and did no lessons, and the ladies occupied themselves in silent prayer— at least so we thought. There was a big brother (he was in the coal trade) who sat at meals and sometimes caned the little boys at the table; which I could see enraged the sisters. On Good Friday we fasted; that I remember, being like the rest a greedy boy. I just remember, it was a portion of minced mash. I was desperately afraid of Hell—yet the fasting was near and immediate.

172

Nov. 1, 1916   N.Y.

I agree with you that there is a great deal of the statesman in George Russell [AE]. . . he is an open-air man, he keeps his windows and doors open, he keeps open house and welcomes ideas. Yet he is not quite big enough. There are more things in heaven and earth than are dreamt of in his philosophy. I used to tell him he was still a *Portadown* boy; Portadown is the little town where he was born, and it is an Orange town. There is just a touch of the mediocre in his mind, as there is in Shaw's and in all these Co-operative Socialistic people. The fact is, a man cannot go into public life and mingle in any of these movements without danger of the mediocre. To keep out of the mediocre one must keep the simple eye and love only truth. To wholly escape it a man must stick to literature, if that, as in Russell's case, be his forte, or become a scientific thinker. Russell seems to me never to put any thought into his poetry, for which reason it remains of light calibre; in fact, a mere wisp of summer cloud, and like a summer cloud, it may promise fine weather—or it may be portentous of a thunder-storm.

173

Dec. 6, 1916   *N.Y.*

Why is Meredith obscure and hard reading?—First of all, his criticism is very profound and learned, and all embossed and garnished and encrusted with strange allusions of learning and philosophy. And then whom does he criticize? The personages in his books. And who are these? Faint adumbrations, arabesques, phantoms—he has never *seen handled or tasted* one of them—and naturally neither do we—so criticism about him is criticism about something in the void. Dickens with his breath breathes the breath of life and reality and power into all his characters and into the houses where they lived and the streets they frequented. Is there in all the many volumes of the immense George Meredith a single being so alive as that honest creature Micawber? There's something to criticize. It is enough for me to call him that 'honest creature'; and so it is with all Dickens's creatures. *David Copperfield* is pervaded by love—love for real beings—and the love so vivid, because Agnes, Dora, the old aunty Peggotty, David's mother, Traddles, are real, and trembling with life and soul and being—as real as life or as Shakespeare's creatures.

174

Decr. 10th, 1916

I have just read *Dombey and Son*. There is more genius in it than in *David Copperfield*, but also pages of dreary farce and dreary romanticism, and yet it is superb in parts and the man has a poet's heart whereas George Meredith had only a critic's.

175

Dec. 13, 1916   *N.Y.*

Among the obscure French people I meet there is a great disposition to complain of England. It would be a surprise to see how I stand up for your villainous old country, maintaining that she is a true and loyal comrade in this war. Not that I credit her with any noble aspirations after the good and the beautiful, nor that I have any faith in what is called the English gentleman. He is always thinking of his own order; he has no other criterion. But I do trust the English people outside that magic circle of 'gentlemen'. It is they who are waging this war; on them I keep my attention, and so do you, I fancy.

176

Dec. 19, 1916   *N.Y.*

I must write again on this matter, Compare the sentences that come from Dickens with those minted by G. Meredith. 'Minted' is the word, for they are of shining metal—and all so difficult, coagulated, clotted, and scored like so many rough rocks and stones—through which, I acknowledge, there does flow a thin rivulet of genuine crystal poetry. But the stream is no more than a rivulet in parched summer-time, while the rocks and stones that impede are big enough in all conscience—all made out of the critical intellect, which is cold as winter. And when, as he occasionally does, he steps aside to try his hand at a piece of invention, how poor that invention is compared with the rich copious invention of the great creature Dickens.

TO MRS. HART

177

317 W. 29 St., N.Y.
Jan. 8, 1917

. . . The last two years my son is making some money. A poet lives very frugally and he especially, and so he has assisted me materially, and now my ambition is to be quite independent of him. . . . Last summer I painted 4 portraits in a town near Pittsburgh, all life-size and full-length.

and I was a personal success. The *house was small,* and I stayed 7 weeks, and yet the inmates liked me, and have said several times over since how much they missed me. Last Xmas I lectured in Pittsburgh to a club before which everyone of importance had lectured the same year—Masefield, Noyes, Granville Barker, etc.—and I was told by several people my lecture was one of the best given them. . . . The chairman liked the lecture so well that she gave me the commission for the portrait. That a man should paint well who lectured well is hardly good reasoning. . . .

TO OLIVER ELTON

178

N.Y.
Jan. 9 [? *1917*]

I am glad you are in pleasant quarters—a garden and retirement, close to the river—and this, in England, at the present moment! I will do the Englishman full justice; he does not lose his head, even now; he ceases neither to love his children nor his wife nor his garden nor his poetry. Would this happen here? The American cannot possess himself in peace and so his poetry and literature are all for the newspapers, and the poetry he has is whistled down the wind. His whole talk is of joy and happiness—talk, as I tell him, only fit for athletes and football-players—a shallow vulgar paradise easily come at by anyone except the true artist and poet, who seek a something quite different. What it is, we will tell him when we have found it, and even then he won't understand, since we speak a strange language out of the strange country of pain and desire. With us pain and pleasure come together and cannot be separated. The greater the pain, the greater the pleasure—the immortal and the mortal in everlasting embrace—a nuptial embrace—not sterile.

179

N.Y.
Jan. 21, 1917

I look forward confidently to a millennium. We cannot put any restriction to man's power over his fate and fortune. Some day, production will have reached such degrees of power that making a livelihood will be as easy as cooking eggs. At the same time, children shall appear as they are wanted; and instead of living as we do now congested in cities—fifteen in a bed, I call it—we shall be scattered, and cultivated. Not by living gregariously but in a qualified solitude can man reach his full stature—and instead of being altruistic rhetoricians and fussy philanthropes we shall sing like the nightingales. And in this delirious dream, as I fear it must appear to you and to most people, the whole question of sex will undergo a change. For I am an old dusty sundried conservative in some things, marriage for instance. Marriage is the earliest fruit of civilization and it will be the latest. I think a man and a woman should choose each other for life, for the simple reason that a long life with all its accidents is barely enough for a man and a woman to understand each other; and in this case to understand is to love. The man who understands one woman is qualified to understand pretty well everything.

180

(No date, probably 1917)   *N.Y.*

In my mind art that includes poetry is what really matters—it holds the place Religion held and is Queen of the Sciences. . . . I would say that there is ordinary art, without poetry, and wonderful it is—Sargent for instance—most artists are of that kind; and there is extraordinary art, art with poetry. I think I can appreciate both, but with my whole soul the latter. At any rate it is the rarest, and it is not learned in art schools. A rare flower, and the secret of its planting and growth known to none of the gardeners. I think it is wind-sown, and sometimes hot sun favours it, and sometimes the coldness of an Alpine valley. No one knows; indeed it is often sown but withers away, the climate not suiting it.

181

(No date, probably 1917)   *N.Y.*

. . . Of course it is true that the autocratic intellect of Germany has been busy for a long time with this question of well-being; but it works, like a policeman, with some narrow theory to guide it, compelling people to accept what they only half understand; whereas the democratic intellect goes to work modestly, learning facts and listening to everyone, and not attracted to any theory in particular; urged sometimes in one direction and sometimes in another by varying emotions; always progressive along a road that grows continually at once wider and straighter; and for its methods of administration using persuasion and avoiding force. In a few years the American will be the most humane man in the world, and the most creative and diverse, whereas the German, if the war does not alter things, will become the most brutal—scientifically brutal—and the least creative. Peace and its victories [are] the natural outcome of things American, as war is of German methods.

182

N.Y.
April 24th, 1917

Emerson said that every man is a man of genius if he only knew it, and this has had a most deleterious effect on American civilisation—it is protestantism gone mad. So the little ego that is in each of us is here sometimes as big as Goliath himself, especially among the artists who think they have a prescriptive right to be egos, and so the artist colony has among them a lot of pacifists—that have no education and so have no power of thinking and their pacifism is like a loaded blunderbuss in the hands of a child. . . .

Emotionalism is bad because of its lack of seriousness—Walt Whitman does not believe half what he says—it is all spectacular. The true poet is like the statesman and has a cold heart notwithstanding its abiding ecstasy, and so more serious than any statesman. Minor poets are emotional and so are heroes—none of them have the high seriousness of poetry and statesmanship.

FROM W. B. YEATS

183

May 12, 1917   *Coole Park, Gort, Co. Galway*

My dear Father—I think I must have had all your letters. You speak of anxiety on the subject in a letter to Lady Gregory. . . . I have had all these typed and they are on my shelves in little packers all in order and dates. I think I shall be able to run a new series of extracts, through a review Ezra

Pound edits and this should bring you a little money, though I doubt if Ezra can pay much. I am delighted that you tell me you have written so much of the biography. Do not attempt to send MSS. till after the war. Apart from submarines, there are all kinds of restrictions, and I think MSS. as apart from letters, can only be sent through publishers. . . . I keep hearing praises of the little book of your 'Letters', but as yet have seen no reviews. I came here to take over the Tower, Ballylee Castle.[1] I shall make it habitable at no great expense and store there so many of my possessions that I shall be able to have less rooms in London. The Castle will be an economy, counting the capital I spend so much a year and it is certainly a beautiful place. There are trout in the river under the window. Jack can come there when he wants Connaught people to paint. I have finished a little philosophical book—60 pages in print perhaps—'An Alphabet'. It is in two parts: *Anima Hominis* and *Anima Mundi* and is a kind of prose backing to my poetry. I shall publish it in a new book of verse, side by side, I think. Reviewers find it easier to write if they have ideas to write about—ideas like those in my *Reveries*. I have just made a revision of my *Player Queen*, a prose comedy, and Mrs. Campbell talks of playing for the stage society. It is very wild, and I think, amusing.

I wonder would you be easier in your mind about your letters if you kept a record of the dates and sent them to me. I would then let you know if they reach me, or you might number the letters.—Yours ever—
W. B. YEATS

I am told one should sign in full for censor.
WILLIAM BUTLER YEATS

TO W. B. YEATS

184

July 2, 1917
317 W. 29. N. York

My dear Willie—I think the collective mind is the evil one—it changes a generous man, like John Quinn, into a martinet, sometimes cross as the ? , and it has turned the English man, the honest fellow, a little mad, of Shakespeare's day into the sepulchral bore and hypocrite as we know

[1] A Norman tower in Galway, renovated by W. B. Y. after his marriage, in which he spent several summers.

him in all the later generations. I have just been diligently reading in Turgeniev's memoirs of a sportsman—and have been impressed by the fact that the Russian peasant is like the Irishman—the Irishman of every kind and class, who is not west Briton. These men, Russian and Irish, are individualists, and interested only in individuals, in the poet, in the fighter, the lover, the witty talker, the man who sings, and indeed, in any strange fellow. I think it is a great matter for Ireland that she is a small Island, and that she refuses to take any interest in the great affairs of the British Empire. She is like a child lost in a great Fair, who being naughtily intrepid is not at all frightened, and on the contrary, delighted to be lost. Thus, we have escaped the collective mind, which for so many years has dulled the lustre of English life and tarnished the brightness of its poetry. I wonder whether the revolution and the creation of a Russian democracy will destroy Russian literature. I wonder also, whether it was not the smallness of Athens and the minuteness of its public affairs which explains the greatness of its literature. Whereas the Normans having great affairs to transact and being forced, therefore, to engender the collective mind of public law and duty and statesmanship, lost the individual mind. The collective mind of great nations, oppressed at the same time that it is invigorated by its responsibilities, substitutes for the individual mind which left to itself feeds upon the *little histories* of the individual life—at once absorbed and tolerant, unlike the collective mind which is intolerant and not absorbed at all except in the intolerant forcing of life—a dull spiritless employment.

You will acknowledge we have not the collective mind in Ireland. The English reproach us with a lack of seriousness—that lack is the lack of the collective mind. Any day we prefer a ghost story or a Fairy tale to the *Times* newspaper, aye, and to good books like Macaulay's history—doubtless in time, and with much labour and sorrow and with the aid of the great reformers, we shall acquire this collective mind, and be as dull as the House of Commons and as serious as the Bank of England. Aristotle's doctrine that poetry is imitative means that there must always be present what can be seen, touched, handled—that there must be imagery—there must also be music, great poetry means a maximum of imagery and a maximum of music. In Whitman, we have a minimum of imagery and of music, but he is popular because his poetry stands for an effort to make the collective mind poetry, yet, his imagery is faint and phantasmal and his music slight and monotonous. Had he been an Irishman or an Athenian, he would not have cultivated the large views of the collective mind, but talked out of the individual mind some of the singularity of his own history and experience and America imbued with the collective mind, would have found him trivial—not once all through Homer does the collective mind show its pallid front.

The moral of all this is—let the big Empires perish and the small nations flourish. If a schoolboy comes home for his holidays and finds the whole family engaged in a great lawsuit, he must pull a long face and order his conversation aright and repress his exuberance, and if he plays cricket, do it as a task, not as play, and thereby prove that he is no trifler—in a word, he must acquire the collective mind, and show himself to be a serious little boy. It spoils his temper so that his mother is afraid to kiss him, and he is not happy so that no one wants to kiss him—but, no matter—he is a serious boy, and will grow up a serious man—all his conversation about serious things, and we, Irish, will laugh at his serious face, as possibly Athens laughed at Rome.

In one thing the collective mind is abundant—the poetry of discussion and eloquence, the intolerant contending with the intolerant emotion, with its false ways and insincerity takes the place of feeling, and with the emotion of anger predominant and stiffening into hatred, yet feeling absent, that is the individual mind brooding over its sinfulness and fate is absent—the East wind of the collective point of view rising and drying up the intimacies and the singularities of the individual soul, full of longings and secreting its honey of a strange poetry, which the bee of industry may or may not gather to be hoarded in the bee hives. . . .

TO OLIVER ELTON

185

July 16, 1917   N.Y.

Do you know, I have grown very superstitious, and believe the war will end very soon, because astrology says so. For one thing, all the other oracles are silent. I used to know here in N. York a dear old woman, who for two dollars would tell your fortune. I could bring you to her and after an hour's talk you would emerge, looking like Horatio on that celebrated occasion. I brought Willie[1] to see her. They talked together for two hours and were as pleased with each other as children. When he asked her how

[1] W. B. Y.

much he should pay her, with a most expansive and touching gesture she flung her arms open and said, 'Nothing'.

She is little and old, and noble in her face, and, I need not say, a lady; educated, and well read in occultism. I tried again and again to get her to sit for a sketch, and the damned police were always harrying her, and she has been driven away, to where I don't know. This [*sketch*] is exactly her attitude and look. She has a lovely little daughter, the image of her mother as she was. And she once was rich and lived in good society. Willie was tender and deferential with her, and so would you be; and her face shone with pleasure.

TO LILY YEATS

186

August 24, 1917
317 W. 29 St.

. . . You asked me who old McGusty was. He was an old solicitor always employed by my uncle and the family. He was miserly, and they were always telling amusing stories about him. . . . I suppose he drew up my mother's marriage settlement. It was old Sis, Mrs. Clendinning, my grandmother's sister who told me that 'the old uncle' had been Goldsmith's friend. He was examining chaplain to the Bishop of Dromore (who was Percy the editor of the Percy *Reliques*) and rector of Tullylish which he vacated that my father might succeed. Sis often stayed at the Bishop's and told me she had often heard him talk of Johnson and Goldsmith. . . .

TO W. B. YEATS

187

Sept. 19, 1917
317 W. 29. N. York

My dear Willie— . . . I have always maintained that every man of sense should keep in his library a box of strong cigars, saturate each cigar with some drug soporific, so that if anyone said such a sentence as 'Excuse me, Sir, but what you are saying now is quite inconsistent with what you said earlier in the evening, etc.,' you might reply: 'Sir, your views are very interesting. May I offer you a cigar? It is of a special brand that I only give to my most valued friends.' Ah! with what pleasure one would watch the gradual lowering of the eyelids and the falling away of the mouth and the paling of the lip as one waited for the blessed silence.

Oriental philosophy is like that cigar. That is why we turn to it. Sir Philip Sidney wrote that poetry cannot lie because it affirms nothing, and if you affirm nothing, what becomes of the fighting intellect? Either it conceals its instincts, or is converted, like a heathen king listening to the preaching of St. Augustine.—The man with the logical mind does not— for he cannot—read poetry . . . —Yours affectionately—JOHN BUTLER YEATS

188

[*1917*]

My dear Willie—Ophelia is all phantasy. I have met many women who talked phantasies, but it was only talk and pose for the sake of effect. Ophelia's phantasy is genuine and makes her a solitary (she remembers the people only because of her natural kindness and gentle breeding), and therefore out of every one's reach. She is for ever talking of his father, yet the name only floats on the surface of her phantasy, for 'she is incapable of her distress,' and of course, she did not commit self slaughter. She had not enough relation to life to want to leave it, hence, the poignancy of her distressful state—by her loneliness she reaches the highest altitudes of beauty and loveliness. She no longer suffers, that is past. Why a loneliness unattended by pain should melt every heart with pity, I cannot explain— I cannot even guess. It is no wonder that the 'churlish priest' should award her 'maimed rites'—it is the instinct of tyranny to destroy, and tyrants hate those they torture. . . . Yet only a priest could hate a young girl so lovely. The priest, not allowed to be a man at all,—her beauty was a fresh offence, a curse and a temptation. The interesting thing is that Hamlet is full of a similar phantasy or ecstasy, only when Ophelia is mad in the doctor's sense as well as in the poets', Hamlet is mad as poets are mad. Irving did not know this, nor Forbes Robertson either—most careful, both of them, that every one should recognise Hamlet's sanity. I remember Irving perfectly—I do not so well remember Robertson. I would give anything to be a young man and an actor for I would give Hamlet such a whirl of phantastic energy as would capture the town. Irving makes him pause and have visitations of sentimental regrets, entirely out of accord with his phantastic passion. He was the gentleman and a prince and could at times, regret his lapses from courtesy, but even this regret was only skindeep. He was too carried away by impetuous dreams to think about anything else except for a moment. He has also the phantastic man's desire to put everything he thought at once to the touch of practice, which is the explanation of his strange appearance before Ophelia, when he bade her to get to a nunnery. Like Ophelia, Hamlet was 'incapable of his own distress' as are all men when they are 'phantastic'. I think Hamlet's close attention to good form and his absorption in a kind of dry logic, very characteristic of the state of phantasy. It is characteristic of genuine phantasy to believe that what is in complete accord with [his dream is] what is true.

189

New York
Jan. 23, 1918

. . . I am rather glad that this kind of letter goes to your club and not to your breakfast table. At the club one may be all intellect and not so I fancy when one breakfasts with one's wife. (Then) intellect is out of its place and opportunity is just a howling wilderness and if a man does not know it his wife does, particularly if she be herself an intellectual woman. . . .

I have spoken of humility as the artist's portion—nowadays when everyone is drunk with the hot valiancy of democratic enthusiasm, it is necessary to apologise when saying a good word for humility. . . . Humility is the portion not merely of the artist but of every man who is of sound health and judgment, for what is an artist but a man who is conscious of himself? (As we know it is not enough that a man should be an Irishman. He must be an Irishman conscious that he is an Irishman.) Humility is the portion of every true man and of every true artist. As to the pomp, the ceremony, and the retinue with which great men and great artists have surrounded themselves from time to time, it is only a sort of 'swagger' whereby poor mortals would persuade themselves that they are as the immortal gods. In every king's household and in every great man's retinue is some 'honest' counsellor who does not admire, some Horatio or Kent who just because they do not admire may be taken for friends and lovers. When I see people living on admiration—a husband with his wife or a wife with her husband or a vulgar rich man who assails us with ostentation or display—or a Henry Irving who could not bear the proximity of anyone who did not admire (yet even he had an 'honest' counsellor in Ellen Terry), it is as clear as daylight that what they all suffer from is the ache of conscious failure, and because at heart—if only they but knew it—they are humble-minded men and students. (Don't you think there is something very touching about a vain man? He is all one ache for your praise, would sell his soul for it—Of course you cannot trust a man who will sell himself for a compliment.)

TO OLIVER ELTON

190

N.Y.
Feb. 23, 1918

The world will not be right till poetry is pronounced to be life itself, our life being but its shadow and poor imitation. But when will that time come? It will come when *we live to play*—and when will that come? When science and intensive agriculture and intensive production and perhaps birth-control shall have obtained such a hold on things that poverty shall be as far away as the black plague of the middle ages.

We live to play: that is my slogan, under which we shall set about the real things of life, and be as busy, and in the same spirit, as is nature on a morning in spring. We shall be human beings, and not mere doctors, mere lawyers, mere tradesmen:—lovers, husbands, wives, children, fathers, and friends. These are the figures that will emerge, and civilization [will] come with them. We shall live proudly and exultingly and die in the same mood; so much interested in other things that we are no longer interested in ourselves. You know, however the body decay, the spirit is always young. In all this there is not a word of rhapsody. Of that I am quite sure, for Time will set its seal of actuality on everything I have said.

TO W. B. YEATS

191

New York
March 12, 1918

. . . The poets loved of Ezra Pound are tired of Beauty, since they have met it so often in plays and poems and novels and in ordinary life—always so much the same that they know its tricks, or think they do. It has ceased to be unintelligible, so very naturally and inevitably they turn to the ugly, celebrating it in every form of imitation. And they will continue to imitate it until they have found the trick. I am tired of Beauty my wife, says the Poet, but here is that enchanting mistress Ugliness. With her I will live, and what a riot we shall have—not a day shall pass without a fresh horror. Prometheus leaves his rock to cohabit with the Furies.

Of course, since every poet is primarily mortal man, it follows that while he is imitating and assembling ugliness, he becomes filled with pity. He exchanges for the enthusiasm of beauty which is love that other enthusiasm for the ugly which is pity. But pity is not love. Ezra's Poets are like the dogs that licked the sores of Lazarus. Pity is only pity. . . . You remember how in Balzac's *Lily in the Valley* the heroine could not—it was for her impossible—take her lover's advice and put her terrible husband under the moral constraint of her will, using against him her strength over his weakness—her goodness against his evil.

'Ne devrais-je pas faire mentir mon cœur, déguiser ma voix, armer mon front, corrompre mon geste? Ne me demandez pas tels mensonges.'

'Mais s'il vous tue?' said her lover and she answers

'La volonté de Dieu sera faite.'

. . . In the wide universe man alone is capable of insincerity. Why is human sincerity so potent? When we solve that mystery we shall know Everything. The mere suggestion opens up vast perspectives. Why is it that human sincerity always excites love? Can it be as the poets suggest, that in ultimate analysis it is itself love.

. . . .

Let me add a postscript. I think it will be admitted that we do not care to imitate anything that we understand. The desire is dead. Lovers in the closest intimacy would not know Everything, and women, how secret they are! The simplest among them would keep something back; if all is discovered she is lost. It is the meaning of her modesty. And public men know it—not always. Gladstone explained himself too often and too copiously, not so the subtle and the wily Disraeli. Royalty practises it as an art, and poets hate logic. The charm of an April day is that its glory is so uncertain. On an April day my soul is glowing with imitation. . . .

We are disposed to imitate what we least understand. A wife must often smile to meet people who imitate her husband whom she can read like a book.

The amiable man whom everyone likes no one imitates. . . . What we understand we understand. We imitate the inscrutable. . . .

192

317 W. 29th Street, New York
April 13th, 1918

My dear Willie—I am so glad George is a fisherman—we were all great fishers. I had an Uncle Arthur who was a clerk in the Bank of Ireland and if he got a day off he would think nothing of walking 14 Irish miles away into the mountains for a day's fishing and then the same day at night walk back the whole 14 miles, carrying what fish he caught, and be ready for the bank next morning—he often did that. My cousin old Freddy Beatty lived beside Loch Dan—where he had at the edge of the lake a lovely house and demesne. I spent many a day there for the fishing. He would walk the 12 miles all through a summer night and then, without disturbing the family, sleep as he could *in the green house*—that night he would get a good sleep and the morning after catch the seven o'clock car for Dublin.

Uncle Arthur[1] was always a disappointed man—his three brothers became officers in the army, one of them led the forlorn at the taking of Rangoon and became Governor of Penang. A stutter stopped Uncle Arthur, and so he became a bank clerk, and then the stutter condemned him to remain in the lower ranks. He ought to have been a partner, he really had a remarkable talent. It was a poetical mind that made him a fisherman—he was also a good shot. Every year for a happy fortnight he shot over Wm. Stewart's mountains in Donegal. This obliged him to keep a dog. That dog was his family. He was very irascible and very affectionate. One moment I hated him and the next I would do anything for him. He really could be extraordinarily disagreeable. Then he would stutter out something so laughable that he would win every one. When fishing he was curiously jealous. I remember my father at Loch Dan secretly buying fish of a boy who fished with worms, in order to get the better of Arthur and arouse his jealousy. I think he was jealous of my painting—jealousy is the mark of a man embittered. He read the London *Times* with great assiduity. In his youth he was in great request as second in duels, which he carried out with the rigour of the law.—Yours affectionately—JOHN BUTLER YEATS

[1] His mother's brother, Arthur Corbet.

TO LILY YEATS

193

317 W. 29 St.
May 29, 1918

... No letter from Willie and no word about my play. Are you sure that you sent it to him and that he received it.... Willie I know has a curious idea that he is an extraordinarily wise person, and that I and every-body else are puppets to be moved about hither and thither as his wisdom directs. Possibly therefore he is withdrawing his opinions for reasons connected with the higher diplomacy. Possibly he thinks that if he praised the play I might set about another, and neglect my autobiography....

TO W. B. YEATS

194

June 10, 1918

... It is curious. On all sides I hear the murmuring of many voices, all saying the same thing, like voices out of the darkness and what they say is this, 'What I am doing no longer counts unless it be for the war'. One man in high railway employment assured me that he is unhappy because he does not exactly see how what he does helps the war.

The way to be happy is to forget yourself. That is why Robert Gregory was happy.... Yet there are two ways of forgetting yourself and two ways of being happy. To forget yourself as in the war, seeing nothing but its vastness. 'Remember those that have lived before you and those that will after and be at peace', said Marcus Aurelius. Or to forget yourself in some movement for reform—social reform—or in games of violent self-exertion. I could multiply instances of what I mean—instances of self-devotion and self-forgetfulness. Yet there is another way of self-forgetting which does not require any enormous machinery such as sanguinary war. It is of course that of art and Beauty. The triumph it aims at establishing for ever is to lose yourself while remaining within the vast of your own personality—which is what I understand by Beauty.

Now you see the antagonism between a state of war and the practice of art and literature. (War) offers an easier way of forgetting yourself and willing to be happy we grasp at it with eagerness, and all the poets desert the difficult paths they have been climbing; it is so much easier to carry a rifle and a knapsack than to try to write poetry, Of course the poet with the vision is not seduced, Alan Seeger, for instance. I suppose you have not read his halting verses. (He was killed, and by all accounts extraordinarily brave)—a man to me infinitely more interesting than Brooke. . . .

In everything except art and poetry the loss of self—the oblivion—is not complete. . . . Yet with the people generally war is something so overwhelmingly gregarious that while it lasts it suspends all the movements and the susceptibilities of the solitary man. He is caught into the current. That vast of the inner personality where beauty has her being is deserted, and the external self triumphs. . . .

FROM W. B. YEATS

195

Ballinamantane House,
Gort, Co. Galway, Ireland
June 14, 1918

My dear Father—I have never written to you about your play. You chose a very difficult subject and the most difficult of all forms, and as was to be foreseen, it is the least good of all your writings.[1] I have been reading plays for the Abbey Theatre for years now, and so know the matter practically. A play looks easy, but is full of problems, which are almost a part of Mathematics.—French Dramatists display this structure and 17th century English Novelists disguise it, but it is always there. In some strange way, which I have never understood, a play does not ever read well if it has not this mathematics. You are a most accomplished critic—and I believe your autobiography will be very good, and this is enough for one man. It takes a lifetime to master dramatic form. I am full of curiosity about the memoirs, but of course, I cannot see them until the war is over.

This is a very old house of the usual late eighteenth century or early nineteenth century sort, which the Gregorys have lent us till Ballylee Castle is ready. George is, at this moment, at the Castle, where she has a man digging in front of the cottage that she may plant flowers and be there in a

[1] J. B. Y. must have started the play many years before this. For, in replying to his son, he said, 'when I told Synge that you had discouraged my writing the play and that you spoke a good deal about Rules, etc., he said, "Ask him if he himself obeys these Rules." '

month. She has just come and says all has gone well and that her workman is doing his work. (He had hated the prospect of so much digging!) Last week, we had a fine dish of trout, grey trout and salmon trout, caught, though not by us, in the Ballylee river. The best place is almost under the Castle walls.

I do nothing but write verse, and have just finished a long poem in memory of Robert Gregory, which is among my best works.—Yours affectionately—W. B. YEATS

TO LILY YEATS

196

317 W. 29
June 27, 1918

. . . I wish Willie would take a title. Not a knighthood, but an Earldom or a Dukedom. It would save me a world of embarrassment.

Last night an energetic young Philistine (from Glasgow) said to me, 'I am told Mr Yeats that your son is quite the poet of Ireland. Where is your boy now?' I looked stonily at him and said, 'I don't think "boy" exactly describes my son. I have two sons in Ireland.' A few weeks back a man said to me, 'I see your son has managed to get himself into an anthology', and before that another rascal said to me, 'I am told your son is almost a poet.' 'Yes,' I said, 'almost'. Last night the young Scotch Philistine with his friend talked at length of Carlyle and G. B. Shaw and others—quite at length. They were not carried away, but critical and full of enlightened moderation etc. This is the sort of conversation to which I am constantly exposed, and all because Willie has not a title. . . .[1]

[1] W. B. Yeats wished it to be a secret, but no doubt J. B. Yeats was aware that some years earlier his son had had the refusal of a knighthood. Writing of this to Lady Gregory (Dec. 1st, 1915) W. B. Yeats said:

'. . . I dined with Lady Cunard to meet Balfour. There were 3 men including Balfour and 3 women and I regret to say I did all the talking. I am afraid I can say nothing of Balfour except that he is a most charming and sympathetic listener, so charming and sympathetic that he lures one on into more and more vehemence of speech. The conversation became general at a saying of mine about Carlyle. I was talking to Lady Cunard and I said, "Carlyle was a sheer impostor, *The French Revolution* is now as unreadable as MacPherson's *Ossian*". Lady Cunard repeated this to Balfour who agreed, very pleased with the *Ossian* comparison. I said I spent an evening reading Walpole's letters to get Carlyle out of my head, Balfour then

TO OLIVER ELTON

197

New York
Sept. 17, (?) 1918

You and Great Britain and Ireland must resign yourselves to it—America leads the world. She has been doing it for a long time in several devious ways, unknown even to herself. From now on she will do it openly, and I am glad of it. She has the right ideas and the right methods, in which she is miles ahead of any other nation—more than France. She has the collective mind;—*man himself* in the mass, as a unit in a vast crowd, is destined to be her pupil for years upon years. Hope, the great divinity, is domiciled in America, as the Pope lives in Rome. This all sounds a little eloquent, not to say grandiloquent. America will pay for it a great price. She loses literature and art and poetry—I mean of the great kind, the kind that matters. There the leadership remains with England, if she keeps her presence of mind, her equanimity, her equilibrium, and is not seduced into attempting that for which she has a most blessed incapacity. For England through all the centuries has been the home of the individualistic mind, which is the soul of the *great* poetry and the *great* art. Under English civilization a poet like Willie comes to a natural birth; he is impossible in America.

198

N.Y.
Sept. 24, 1918

Of course all great poets can be both sociable and solitary—Shakespeare for instance. How furiously and madly sociable is Timon, filled with hatred said, "Walpole was just the kind of man Carlyle despised and called insincere, and yet Carlyle himself was the most insincere of all". Then I told tales about George Moore . . . As I came away from the Balfour dinner Lady Cunard said, "The Prime Minister means to be very gracious to you at the New Year, and Mr. Balfour has just said to me that he is in full agreement". I began, "O please not", but Lady Cunard interrupted me with, "Well, you may as well have it offered and you can refuse". I told Bailey about it in confidence, and said in spite of the real satisfaction I would feel at the increased respect of railway porters and spirit mediums I would last night at dinner (my two sisters, Ervine and myself dined with him) Lily said, have to refuse. . . . I told him that if I accepted my family would be shocked and 'They will accuse you next of wanting to be knighted . . .'' '

and rage against people as if he would devour them all! Yet he always ends with the most magnificent bursts of the solitary passion—in soliloquies of the most absolute sincerity, as lonely as if he stood in the centre of Sahara. That is the difference between him and Apemantus—in intellect and intensity they are peers—only Apemantus is not a true solitary—just as the Frenchman is not either.

FROM W. B. YEATS

199

73 Stephen's Green, Dublin
Oct. 17 (1918)

My dear Father—I have often pointed out to George that you and I are in telepathic communication. For instance, your letter about Keats and Shelley came when I had been writing about Keats and Shelley, and except that you put things better once or twice had exactly the same thought. The only difference is that I look on them as two distinct types of men, who could not exchange methods. Each had to perpetuate his own method and neither lived long enough to do so. If you accept metempsychosis, Keats was moving to greater subjectivity of being, and to writing of that being, and Shelley to greater objectivity to consequent break-up of unity of being.

Your last letter however, shows the most curious of all this telepathic exchange.[1] When it came, I said to George (without letting her see the date of your letter), 'When did I write my poem of the Hare?'[2] She said 'about Sept. 20th'. Your letter is dated Sept. 22. My memory is that I was full of my subject for some days before Sept. 20th. I send you the two poems. One line,—'The horn's sweet note and the tooth of the hound,' may have reached you, or the hare's cry—which is to you a symbol of exultation at death. 'The horn's sweet note' might well mean that. Your poem has a fine idea, but I cannot make out whether the symbolizing the joy at death by the scream of the hare is, or is not, too strained an idea. . . . — Yours ever—W. B. Yeats

[1] I have been unable to find this letter.—Editor.
[2] Probably 'The Collar-Bone of a Hare', published in 1919.

After illness

TO JOHN QUINN
200

J. B. Y. had had pneumonia but to the end said it was only indigestion. He remained strong enough to push his nurse out of the room.

Oct. 19, 1918
317 W. 29th Street

My dear Quinn—My will is a sort of haphazard will. What I say in a letter is all a matter of chance. I don't write what I want to write, but something else. In your last letter you slipped in a sentence which I meant to answer but did not. It was to let you know if I wanted anything, for which I give you thanks and say I do not want anything.

I wish my energy would return, but I know by unmistakable signs that it is returning. I have on the stocks a very good article on conversation for the *North American Review*, which but for this illness would have been finished long ago. When you return from your holiday I will send you what I call 'A Suppressed Chapter of My Memoirs'. It is a short account of my life from 1885 till 1900. It was not pleasant to write it nor is it pleasant reading, so it cannot appear in my memoirs. Yet I have a real desire that you see it.

Many thanks for the book on eminent Victorians. There used to be certain Catholics who said that the worst calamity that ever happened to the Catholic church was the death of Mrs. Manning. I think insincerity was the fault of the Victorians.

I have been out twice, yesterday and the day before. The first day I did not dare cross the street altho' I wanted to do so. Yesterday I crossed without thinking about it.

Sloan called the other day. He is a new Sloan every time. He is a progressive man, and therein the best kind of American, tho' even here the progressive man is rare.—Yours very truly—(Sgd) J. B. YEATS

TO OLIVER ELTON
201

N.Y.
Oct. 23, 1918

I have just had a glorious autumn trip from which Quinn and I [have returned]. Winter here is horrible beyond words, but the autumn delightful. *Est facilis descensus Averni* is the motto for the American autumn. It is not pallid as with us, but gorgeous, and is soft-footed—that is, there are no big winds; so that she can keep her soft wrappings of scarlet and gold and orange, while behind her towers and spreads the most intense blue sky I ever saw. . . . The hotel [we stayed in was] like a nobleman's mansion, and our host a nobleman without the insolence, veiled or unveiled; and such a wonderful *raconteur*, as many-travelled and as wise as Ulysses; though his travelling had been altogether in labyrinthine N. York business where he had made his fortune; his hotel, a rich man's hobby; no one received except by invitation. You pay 14 dollars a day and call for what you want. There are a hatchery for fish and a dairy farm and gardens . . . and it does not pay and is not expected to pay. Every[thing] ideal, ideal inn, ideal host, ideal garden—the servants, even, partook of idealism, like family relations—the honour of the house on their minds.

Our waitress (*sketch*) with lovely blue eyes; beautifully fringed with lashes above and below the eyes. I said that she was Scotch, Quinn that she was Irish. She was Irish, from Cavan. Her spinal column straight as a ramrod. She was the prettiest among the waitresses. . . . She is younger than in my picture,—her hair fair with a sparkle in it, and her cheeks like a strawberry just beginning to redden—a contrast to the pale American face.

TO JOHN QUINN

202

317 W. 29th St.
Dec. 14, 1918

My dear Quinn—I have just read your letter and sent off a hurried reply, and in my hurry forgot to thank you for the book you are sending me. I am enjoying my convalescence immensely, reading books that, but for this chance, I would not have read, at any rate with the same attention.

Among other books I have been reading Pliny's Letters. I possess only the first volume. They are extraordinarily interesting. One gets such an insight into the ancient Roman life, and it is so like much of our modern life, even as we see it here in modern America. Only their cruelty; that was appalling. They liked to inflict death. They seemed to enjoy committing suicide. A furiously military people, it had for them a savour, bracing the nerves. They all lived in an atmosphere of mutual adulation. Denied affection by their military puritanism, they turned to its counterfeit—praise. Always when I see a man fond of praise I always think it is because he is an affectionate man craving for affection.—Yours very truly, and no matter what you think, Yours profoundly grateful—(Sgd) J. B. YEATS

203

My dear Quinn—Thanks for your very interesting letter, and again thanks for your book on the Victorians.[1] I read at a single sitting the articles on Manning and Miss Nightingale. When I went to London as a law student, I dined at a very fashionable house where every man, save one who was an admiral, was a colonel, and one had been present at the Crimean war. They said that it was impossible even for the Queen's photographer to obtain a photo on which was not visible a Tommie crouched over a latrine except when a photo was taken for Miss Nightingale. On that occasion the poor soldier boy managed to postpone his necessities.

I did not speak of —— as a man and an individual, only of his intellect. A man may be intellectually one thing and morally another thing. Do we not often meet with men who intellectually are hard as nails and personally soft and tender as women? This, at any rate, was true of my old friend York Powell.

The Irish peasant is one thing, and the young man who has cut all his cables and is out for piracy is another thing. The latter is an unlovely spectacle. He makes war as the German makes war. As was said of Mirabeau, he has 'swallowed all the formulas'. (To all of which my friend Colum is an exception.) The peasant is feudal and his great qualities are gratitude and fidelity. My old Uncle, who had had immense experience as a land agent and who finally threw it all up, refusing most tempting offers, because of the harshness and cruelty of the life, always said, and said it again and again, that gratitude was the great characteristic of the Irish peasant.

I had a letter the other day from my niece in Australia in which she speaks of the appalling commonness of the Australian mind. Whereon I will submit to your superior wisdom my comments: The commonness of

[1] Strachey's *Eminent Victorians*.

the Australian mind means that they have souls shivering in nakedness, spiritual nakedness. Horse racing, card playing, amorous licence, dollar hunting, and all their animal energy notwithstanding, they have dull lives, and some day will perforce wake up and find it out and then, without losing any of their energy, will turn to better things and strive for them. Out of Australian commonness will come progress.

Contrast with this the Irish peasant. His mind is not common but is stored with all manner of rich enjoyment. Give him enough to eat and drink, he is content; indeed so content that he is content even with semi-starvation. The progress that will come out of the commonness of the Australian and Belfast minds will never spring up among Irish peasants.

I think there is a great deal of commonness in the American mind—indeed, everywhere. It is a wide-world characteristic. Artists and poets and their kind are a small oasis in a vast wilderness, and they have a hard struggle to keep their fertility and their freshness. They are constantly threatened by great sand storms, as when one leaves us and goes away to become 'a best seller' or a great journalist.

By the way, do you know that F. Hackett married a few weeks ago a Swedish girl? . . . Colum says Hackett has no philosophy, no connecting ideas, and that is why you cannot read him for long together. He makes a good criticism of Masefield, that he is a stoic and a sentimentalist. Colum came to see me yesterday.—Yours very truly—(Sgd) J. B. YEATS

TO JACK B. YEATS

204

Jan. 4th, 1919

My dear Jack— . . . I believe profoundly in certain people being lucky and others unlucky. Napoleon would never employ an unlucky general—he believed in his own luck. He called it his star—Fanny is lucky—your poor mother was always unlucky—as regards myself I have been lucky and unlucky. It is lucky, I think, to have lived so long, but there are others, the Kaiser for instance, who have lived too long. Did you see what someone said—that the Tzar is still alive and is living with his family in some neutral country and that this is known to one of the Allied Governments. If that is true what a pleasant surprise it will be when it is generally known.

Tolstoi

I have just read with great care and diligence *The Life of Tolstoi* by Maude. If you can scrape the money together I wish you would buy it. I have read it right through again and again—I am certain you and Cottie would enjoy it. If I open it anywhere I go on reading it and the time passes so quickly I am surprised and this though it is some part I have already read several times. The portraits of Tolstoi and his wife and family and · friends are so *intimate*. He thinks and talks and writes with the sympathy of a peasant—or rather he does not think—he describes what he has seen—in this just like a peasant who though he can describe and be fierce or full of pity, cannot really think. In Russia everyone argues—Shakespeare told me that—they are worse than the Americans, and that atmosphere was bad for Tolstoi—leading him to say violent things. Apparently he quarrelled with all because of this verbal combativeness, with every one and yet his heart was brimming with affection. In his old age he became gentler—his wife a great contrast. He wanted to strip himself of his property and own nothing, for that was the way to live—the Countess firmly stopped this for her children's sake—so there was friction between him and her. I don't think she argued—she acted. Somewhere he says that women are inferior to men for a man will sacrifice his family and his principles and a woman won't. She is writing her own memoirs now in her old age. I hope I shall some day read them. She can write and do it well. *There was a real love between them*—so you enjoy reading about this friction—

TO JOHN QUINN

205

Jan. 5, 1919
317 W. 29th St.

My dear Quinn—Many thanks for your kind and vigilant letter, but let me assure your vigilance I am doing all right. When my cough was quite bad and the cough bottle (which the Doctor ordered) in constant requisition, the Doctor sounded me and said of my lungs that it was now all clear.

I am glad you found your old Uncle happy and tranquil. I think as we get older we get fonder of life. In youth we have so many other things to think of and are worried. Yet old age is a mortal sickness. But then I think invalids are always cheerful. It is one of their symptoms.

Tolstoi

Kuhn has in his art desires so different from mine. My object is vivid portraiture, as in Tolstoi's stories. Kuhn aims at a decorative result, a something that will suggest life with the least possible of imitation, and it is of course quite right for him to do so; but it is not my way.

There was no second case of influenza, tho' Mlle. Josephine mentions that she had it before any of us. I remember her having a bad cold, but not influenza, since she never stopped work for an hour. Ten minutes before I was 'taken' with the sickness I was in perfect health. The first symptom was that I staggered.

Many thanks for your kind offers, but I need nothing.

Lately there were two dark days and I spent the time reading Maude's life of Tolstoi. So that my mind is now full of Tolstoi. Bolshevism is Tolstoism. Those practical people who rushed off to start colonies and put his theories to the test, were the plague of his life. Nothing could stop them, altho' he himself said his object was not to reform society, but to find out the meaning of life (page 169 of Life).

Were he alive now he would be in despair. He saw life in pictures as did Christ, and his own peasants. For abstract ideas he had no capacity, at least no inclination. Perhaps that was why he and the Parisian Turgeniev did not get on.

Like Cromwell, he was a Bible Christian, only that he was not a bit interested in the judgment to come, altho' as much interested in personal righteousness as Cromwell himself. It hurt his pride as a man not to be a good man, a perfect man.

It was his misfortune to be, like every Russian in that crude nation, so fond of argument and verbal contention that he could not keep his friends and was left with these foolish adorers, of the sort that started the colonies.

America is afflicted with this same taste for verbal wrangle. It is part of their worship of cleverness. It is shallowness and vulgarity.

I am, as you see, much occupied with Tolstoi. He at any rate was not afraid of death. His soul was like a fountain. Had he lived among an unargumentative people like the English he would have remained an artist and created images of Beauty that would have been more effective in the long run than any of his propaganda. As to the intention and meaning of art he is as far wrong as is G. B. Shaw. Neither can see what Walt Whitman saw when he wrote 'The song is for the singer'.—Yours very truly---
(Sgd) J. B. YEATS

206

Jan. 7th, 1919
317 W. 29

My dear Quinn—I write to you merely because of my uneasiness, the volubility of uneasiness (portrait advancing splendidly).

Roosevelt's death is ill luck for the world, just now especially, and Wilson's proverbial good luck.

I wonder who now will come to the front. Wilson seems to be going about raising hopes that neither he nor any one else can satisfy—as he himself must well know. He is not the man to lead a revolution. All his sonorous verbiage is banality. Roosevelt gone, there is no one to puncture his ballon d'essai. However, the enthusiasm is mostly for the U.S.A. America is a propagandist nation in practical ideas, as France was (and perhaps is) in artistic ideas. England has not that amiability.—Yours very truly—J. B. YEATS

The contrast between Manning and Newman very interesting. Manning had a genius for administration and was consequently an autocrat, ideas merely a part of the machinery he was administrating.

Newman all ideas. These ideas held not because they were true, but because they were agreeable to his artistic nature. As a child he wished that the Arabian Tales were true. Of these men neither cared for truth. They had not Tolstoi's *intensity*.—J. B. Y.

207

317 W. 29th
Jan. 15, 1919

My dear Quinn—I am grateful to you for all the trouble you are taking and have taken on behalf of me and my health and happiness. I don't want to start for home till the days grow warmer. I want once more to see the warm New York days. Besides a sea voyage in winter would be so miserable. . . .

My portrait I think will please you. It is now quite safe. The head is, I think, good. Its merit, a clear intention carried out to the very limit. In it I will live in my habit as I lived and it will hold its own among your masterpieces. It is an honest portrait.

Here is a pretty story that will please you. Willie's wife George, when lately she walked in her sleep and was awakened by the cold, she found herself sitting on a chair with all the baby clothes on her knees. She had not walked in her sleep since her childhood.

Mrs. Roberts of the *Touchstone* has sent back my article on John Sloan. I did not sufficiently praise him. I replied that if she wanted praise she should have gone to a publisher's hack and the less he knew about art the better his qualifications, She replied in anger and I have apologised, saying at the same time that I did not mean to be discourteous and only meant to state my point 'smartly'. Had she been a man I would have laughed at her.

In my article I did find fault but with so much respect and indeed deference that every word breathed a compliment. She complained that the article was about art rather than about Sloan, and that is true. Sloan himself would have enjoyed the article.

It is a great pity that in these days literature has fallen into the hands of women. They are only vehement and are incapable of the suspended judgment and tentative expression of real thought anxious for the truth. Mrs. Foster and Mrs. Bellinger are exceptions.

Did you ever read Brandes' *Reminiscences of Childhood and Youth?* It is good reading. He was in Paris in 1870. He writes most graphically. He tells that when he first went to Paris he came to the conclusion that Denmark was superior. This will remind you of some of my countrymen and countrywomen. He had typhoid in Rome. His account of his illness and its treatment will make you shudder.—Yours very truly—(Sgd) J. B. Yeats

208

317 W. 29th
January 19 (Sunday), 1919

My dear Quinn—If you look at today's *Sun* you will see an article (page 7) entitled 'Ireland and the domestic drama', which will convince you that I am right in thinking Chesterton the greatest of all writers living or dead.[1]

The day after Chesterton's marriage his mother-in-law called on me and said breathlessly (breathless from anxiety) would Gilbert Chesterton ever be able to make a penny, and that his own mother had told her that hitherto he had never made a penny and that the clothes he was married

---

[1] The article on J. B. Yeats in the New York *Sun*, referred to in Memoir.

in were bought by his parents. I perfectly remember that I predicted a brilliant future. Perhaps he heard of it and is grateful in his big-hearted way.

I think I told you that he is a great listener as well as great talker.

In one of the papers I see an article on Strachey's book of the Victorians, written with Catholic malice.—Yours very truly—(Sgd) J. B. YEATS

209

Jan. 26, 1919
317 W. 29th St.

... Your portrait I am working steadily at. It will soon be finished. It once finished, I will get steadily to work at my memoirs. The portrait will please you. It is the child of my old age and ought to be a remarkable infant since it has had such a long gestation. And believe me that an artist's ambition has been a very small part of my zeal. Perhaps years hence you may look at it and bless me and the prayer may help me in Purgatory, that is if I get that far.

I know by innumerable signs that the Petitpas women are in some kind of mess. They give such a good dinner and charge so little. Born inn-keepers, proud of their hospitality, it is a part of the sociable genius of France.

210

Feb. 1, 1919
317 W. 29th Street

My dear Quinn—Whenever a Petitpas approaches I see in her manner a stealthy menace, and I should be frightfully worried but for one thing—the portrait. I am delighted with it. It is like watching a blessed ghost of a long lost beloved slowly materializing. I think of nothing else and I dream of it. My bitter hours are now only notes. When you get it and it is hung on your walls it will have a stark reality that will outweigh all the other portraits, even John's portrait of you. At least that is how it now seems to me, just now immediately after breakfast which with me is always a time of good hope, which, however, often fades away in the evening.

Mrs. Foster came and typewrote for me an article written some time ago which also I am proud of. In fact I am proud all over and in better health and spirits with calmer nerves than I have been for years, and it is all owing to the portrait, I think.

I hope you sometimes look at the last page of the *Tribune* and see Briggs' drawings. He has just broken out into new ground—babies, and they are as good as his boys; better perhaps, for while his boys are deliciously ugly, his babies are deliciously pretty.

I am anxious for news of my grandson. I shall have some, I hope, next Monday. May luck be with them.—Yours very truly—(Sgd) J. B. YEATS

> 'Many a green isle needs must be
> In the deep wide sea of misery.'

FROM W. B. YEATS

2II

96 Stephen's Green [Dublin]
Feb. 4, 1919

My dear Father—I hope you will come back as soon as you can. You will be very comfortable with Lily and you can devote yourself to finishing your autobiography, and if we put you up for the University Club you will not lack conversation. Lily has for a long time been most anxious for your return, and Dublin is I think a more amusing place than it used to be. But perhaps you will have set out before this reaches you and will read my words—sent back to Ireland—at Gurteen Dhas.[1]—Yrs. affectly.—W. B. YEATS

TO LILY YEATS

2I2

This letter was written shortly after the birth of his first grandchild, W. B. Y.'s daughter.

March 19. 1919
317 W. 29 N. York

. . . I enclose you Chesterton's article! I found it in one of my pockets. Also the cable. Anne Butler may like to see it, as her first appearance in correspondence, at present she is better employed, so put both away in a

[1] From now on W. B. Y. wrote frequently to his father in this sense.

safe place. I wonder what the Yeatses will be like 100 years from now, or say ninety, so that Anne Butler may be there. The world lately has been going ahead at such a remarkable speed that to think of years hence makes me quite giddy. I have just done a pencil sketch of myself for Mrs. Winthrop.[1] She may have it reproduced. At any rate my posterity may see it, or some reproduction of it—what will they get out of it! I am glad to have those two little books to my credit, and *I wonder shall I be present.* I have always believed that we are always upon earth. I also believe there is a providence

> Rough hew them how we will
> there is a providence that shapes our ends.

I have no belief ĩ what is called a personal God, but I do believe in a shaping providence—and that this providence is what may be called goodness or love, and that death is only a change in a world where change is a law of existence. . . .

TO JOHN QUINN
213

317 W. 29th
April 4, 1919

My dear Quinn—I have received your letter . . . I marvel now, as always, at the interest you take in other people, myself to wit. I hope God will reward you, for I can only say—thank you; and words are easy, and sometimes worse than easy, and a fraud.

If only I can make this portrait of myself what I hope it will be, you will give me full quittance. Meantime I can only say I am not at all the man you think I am, not at all the happy, indifferent, reckless man with 'healthy' nerves; far otherwise. The fact is we both have nerves, only yours rouse your will into action, and they paralyse my will. Of course, as is evident, you are the better friend to others. Yet my sufferings are real, not that that matters except to myself.

I wrote to Willie some time ago that I was afraid to return to Dublin, afraid as a child dreads the fire. And I may add that New York saved my life, all of which is a dark saying which, however, I could elucidate.

[1] Mrs. Egerton Winthrop, whom Yeats had known since he first came to New York. She was a very kind lady with intellectual curiosities. Yeats did a little portrait of her which was not very good.

I have read your letter, of course, but not yet possessed myself of its contents.

When I say you will give me full quittance, I mean that you will think that you have not wholly wasted yourself, that at any rate I was worth some of your trouble.—Yours very truly—(Sgd) J. B. YEATS

I have the habit of work, and therefore work on whether my will is or is not paralysed. Only it is bad work and has to be done over again.

TO JACK B. YEATS

214

N.Y.
8.7.19

My dear Jack— . . . It is easy to paint a good picture if you have had the industry to acquire the technique. And the English have this industry as also have the German painters—a work of art, that is another matter. Whistler never had the industry to acquire anything except a very limited technique, yet everything he painted or etched is a work of art. He was not really a portrait painter—had not the technique (a portrait demands the utmost reach of technique) and he has not enough sympathy with human nature—his portrait of Carlyle as portrait is nonsense—not a bit like—but as a work of art [it] is decorative and in some degree impressive. J. E. Millais' portrait of the Sage was one of the best portraits ever painted (the [?] destroyed it) and a genuine work of art—a vital expression of the mood in which it was painted. In painting it Millais was alive with puling and sentiment—he revelled in it. It was his way of telling amusing and stimulating things about the irascible old gentleman. There are lots of men painting in England with a wider technique (perhaps) than Millais but their hearts are cold and their painted figures don't tingle with creation and happiness.

I am working on with my Autobiography—30,000 words already typed. I have said a lot about Isaac Butt and have described my old Uncle and Sandymount and the life there. I keep to anecdotes intermingled with reflections, wise or foolish. Quinn says it is not only good but extraordinarily good. I go on working as long as the tap flows—that is till my memory gives out. 'Typing' costs a bit—one dollar for every hour. I have left at the *South American Review*—for their acting Editor to see them, a story and my play. I don't suppose they will accept them in these days so alien from everything which is not war, but my friend the Editor expressed a wish to see them.

Do you ever read Dumas? I find him always delightful. They are his typical novels and I have read a lot of French history of late. In the history I come across Louis XIV and Colbert and Fouquet and then I read about them in Dumas and they are all alive. Andrew Lang says that Dumas is a man 'really of colossal learning'. I believe him. It is interesting to know that Dumas' grandfather was a *negro*. I tell that to my astounded friends who think a negro is only a man to be lynched. There are in America some very stupid things—but they are getting wild about the war.

The weather is positively quite *cool*. . . . —Yours affectionately— JOHN BUTLER YEATS

TO ANDREW JAMESON[1]
215

307 W. 29
July 9, 1919

. . . I send you a magazine with an article by me against prohibition. It is the most audacious magazine in America, and always in difficulties with the authorities. The current number has been suppressed because of obscenities in *Ulysses*. The publisher is a characteristic Child of democracy, and democracy is aristocracy, that is, is as African and powerful and irresponsible as the Sultan of Turkey. The Americans are the least political people I have ever met, hardly anyone ever speaks of politics and *hardly anyone votes*.

TO JOHN QUINN
216

August 8, 1919
317 West 29th Street

My dear Quinn— . . . I hear that Mrs. Beattie[2] was 'caught' and brought before the magistrate. Had I known it at the time I would have written an indignant letter. I relaxed jovially. I did nothing from morning to night.

[1] The Rt. Hon. Andrew Jameson, head of the well-known Irish firm of distillers.
[2] A soothsayer.

I am very busy at my portrait, solving insoluble problems. After all, painting is my real profession. Mrs. —— with characteristic tactlessness writes to me that I write better than I paint, she, mark you, not having seen any of my finished work. Then she wails about herself. I tell her that the natural man hates a sick woman. That gives her to pause. She is clear-headed enough and goodhearted too, but self-love, as Shakespeare calls it, has blinded both her eyes. She is so tactless with me that I have a right to be tactless with her. Some time ago she told me that she had summoned a doctor about her nerves and that he had prescribed, etc., 'but what good to me are his prescriptions?' I then went with her to make a call, and happening to see her going up some stone steps with her dress lifted, I saw her stout legs and I said to her that she had very fine calves for 'a nervous wreck'. She replied sharply that she was not a wreck. She is never cross or malicious, only tactless. She is the most tactless person ever seen outside Germany. [Sketch]

Did you notice in my letter that I wrote that it was only in phantasy that realism came in for its very own. That luminous truth had not shone on Zola. He is an anatomist, not a creative artist. And as to Dickens' characters being 'freaks', that is nonsense. An unimaginative man would call Romeo and Juliet 'freaks'. (*Sketch*)—Yours very truly—(Sgd) J. B. YEATS

217

317 W. 29th
Sept. 9th—Tuesday—1919

My dear Quinn—I did get a shock of pleasure and surprise when I read that marked paragraph. I had not known that you and the French Government were so 'thick' together.[1] I am very sorry now that I could not be present at last Sunday's luncheon when I should have heard all the details and celebrated them. However I could not have gone and for me the day went well.

Mrs. Cleveland stood in front of the portrait in silence for a while and then said solemnly, 'It is very, very like'—an immense relief to me who

[1] Quinn received an honour from the French Government. He had done passionate French propaganda during the war and was enraged because the peace did not give France all and more than all that she wanted. Nothing now was good to him that was not French, and he took to himself a French mistress, much to the annoyance of his Japanese valet.

was prepared for a very different verdict. Afterwards she made suggestions which I carried out, and then she said, 'It is very exciting'. She asked me to dine with her next Wednesday, and I told her that I disliked going anywhere in the evening and that besides there was evening dress, which I abhorred. But I am going; the dressing for dinner is waived aside. I understand the high church mind. It is fraudulent but very human. Protestantism is honest enough but inhuman and censorious and arrogantly conceited in its opinions. My oldest and most intimate friend was a high church Bishop.—Yours very truly—(Sgd) J. B. YEATS

TO ANDREW JAMESON
218

New York
Novr. 14th, 1919

I must bore you with another letter. I remember Spurgeon—he was a great power in the Religious and moral world (and at that time many Englishmen claimed to be 'moral and religious'), and learned Bishops and Archbishops went out of their way to do him homage. And he said *these* words—'I have seen the trail of the theatre on too many ruined homes not to condemn theatres'. At that time the theatre was the special Colossus of wickedness—and had the English been an excitable people or in other words had they all lived on the same [word doubtful] plane, which is the American theory and practice, the theatre would have been abolished by Act of Parliament. For what Spurgeon said and thought was as significant for England as a decree of the Vatican for Papists.

I never drink whiskey or cocktails—alas! I cannot. They disagree with my stomach—miserably and weakly, I imbibe a little California Claret, or used to do. But this prohibition enrages me—it enrages to see the world handed over to people like those in my accompanying sketch, the women leading and the [word doubtful] doing what they are told, while the devil helps. I have no doubt that in mediaeval times it was the women who financed the Inquisition.—Yrs very truly—J. B. YEATS

TO W. B. YEATS

219

329 W. 29
Jany. 9, 1920

Facility in believing marks the poet's difficulty in believing the logician, and in this the philosophers are as the poets, for both philosophy and poetry come out of the heart of belief, Philosophy which is 'not harsh and crabbed as dull fools suppose, but musical as is Apollo's lute and a perpetual feast of nectared sweets' is born of like parentage with poetry.[1] Belief is creation, logic is destruction. The Belfast man consumed and kiln-dried by the fire of logic has opinions, but is far from belief as he is from peace and harmony. Did Sam Butler believe? Does G. B. Shaw? Is Mr. Magee among the logicians? Do the clever lawyers believe? There are writers like Mr. George Moore whose methods are strictly logical, and do they believe? . . . and what about the people of Dublin, so active-minded and clever enough in all conscience . . . do they believe? Is Mr. Joyce a creative artist or the author of the Squinting Windows?

TO JACK B. YEATS

220

Jan. 10 or 18, 1920

My dear Jack—I am greatly pleased with your Xmas present. I am reading it constantly. My grandmother who died in 1861 being then ninety-three often talked of the Ireland of her father, and that must have been about 1792, the date of the Irishman's travel. So you can guess how much I am interested.

When I used to sit in the drawingroom at Sandymount getting up a Greek play for T.C.D., it would have been much better if I had made notes of what my grandmother and her sister Mrs. Clendinning whom we call Sis, would have told me. They were such good talkers with accurate recollection—Sis especially. She was the family chronicle. She knew and remembered everything and had lived all her life with Colonel Young—

---

[1] And so perhaps, as is suggested by Mlle Jeanne Hirsch in her study of the contemporary philosopher Karl Jaspers (*L'Illusion Philosophique*), confuted philosophies retain a value that is not possessed by outmoded scientific works.

and Colonel Young had been looked after and taken care of by Sir John Armstrong who was his uncle also Sis's. The gold watch which you will remember I have was Colonel Young's. Col. Young had been in the Cavalry and was finally in command of the Militia of City of Dublin. All of them, I have no doubt, good Protestants and Royalists.

The watch had been bought out of some war booty of the Col. I don't know which. It was reputed to have cost £80. I showed it to a London watchmaker and he was enthusiastic saying it was made by the best watchmaker of his time. How lovingly its owner must have regarded as he showed it to his friends and told its price.

This is Sunday and I am lunching with Quinns—but it is too cold and the wind being South, my room is very warm—so that I am not enjoying the prospect. I never saw him looking so well and strong, which means that his business is in good shape. I am told that the winter is very severe but as the wind keeps South my room is very warm, so I think it is an unusually mild winter. It is wonderful how every one has settled down to being without drinks—even the topers. I suppose it will go round the world—to some degree—[?] and whiskey and brandy, perhaps will go, but stout and light beers be still permitted. The movement could not have started with such great success anywhere else except America. But here the people are the most lovable and [word indecipherable] in the world. They do not take any interest in their own politics and when a law is passed they are greatly surprised—but that is all—*for every one respects the policeman.* He is the grand man and it is he who tells the people when a law is passed.

Jeanne has presented me with a magnificent top coat so I think I will make a fine appearance before W. B. Yeats and his wife.—Yours affectionately—J. B. YEATS

221

Feb. 12th, 1920
317 W. 29th

... I enclose a drawing of Briggs which may amuse you—art, the progress of Art. Humour still stands in the very front rank—and Shakespeare who lived so long ago has not been approached and there are the Irish poets—and so I am reminded of the singing of larks and other birds. Has the song of the lark improved? The self same song to which Homer listened is heard by us—by superior as by clown. Of course the writer advances *intellectually*—but does human nature advance? It changes but does it advance—the Homeric warriors did things in war not now permitted—but then German warriors did things Achilles would have scorned . . . and Agamemnon would perhaps have been enraged had he seen the slums in modern cities. By all of which I mean that though there has been change there has been no advance—nor what we call progress— while all the time in the sheer matter of poetical beauty Homer stands higher than any of the successors—

Of course lots of new technique has been discovered. We paint in oils and in water colours which give a wider scope. . . . [But] the genius of Art—the soul itself, has it advanced? Perhaps indeed in modern times it has a little shrunken—as much as to say that the lark sings the same song but that it is not so good, just as that there are so many hawks about that it fears to put forth its full strength.

Change is the law of art—not only must the young lady dress differently from her mother and her grandmother but she must constantly vary from herself. But progress, that is another matter—the will may make attention and health and morals correct—and so much is progress. But tho' this kind of progress may restrict or, it may be, enlarge the opportunities of art, it is not itself art—so far as we know change is the law of art, but it knows nothing of progress.

The conditions of art may no doubt improve and as they improve we shall have more artists and a better appreciation of art—just now in the U.S.A. are hundreds of poets where 20 years ago there were only one or two. But the art itself is the same now as before. But tho' we can increase the number of artists and poets, can we make them better?

The fact is art is the expression of unsatisfied human desire—and human desire through all the centuries has never altered—tho' it varies constantly in strength. I think when it is very strong, we have fine toleration and art. Just now in America there is not much unsatisfied human desire. The people are too busy and too happy *and all their desires are satisfied as soon as they arise*. . . .

TO LILY YEATS

222

New York
June 11, 1920

I think I ought in my letter of yesterday to have said a little more about Jack and what would have happened to him had I been the right Honble.

His Book

Judge Yeats. Both he and Willie would have been called to the Bar—of course—and then gone their devious ways—but Jack would·have occasionally returned to his legal association and been the life of every party—and Jack gets that quality from my side of the house. (I met a man here once who had seen a great deal of my brother Willie.[1] He was a dull man—but he said one thing that interested me—he said that Willie 'was *the life of the town*'.) But Jack has an ambition in him or rather a pride and self respect not too easily satisfied, and therefore would not have contented himself with being the wag of the Four Courts—and I wonder what he would have done. It is much easier to write a book than to paint in a distinguished way—so perhaps he would have written.

TO ELIZABETH YEATS

223

317 W. 29 St.
July 5, 1920

I am foolish over my own book.[2] I have a copy which I constantly read and find very illuminating. Swift confesses to something of the sort with his own compositions.

224

Aug. 15, 1920
317 W. 29

. . . Sense of honour is protestant and damn authority. Sense of authority and damn honour is Catholic and for that matter German also: else a naval commander would have refused to torpedo the *Lusitania* and sent to death all those innocent women and children—nor would a French commander have done it for they tho' Catholics have the strongest sense of honour developed by military traditions. Still the general effect of collective teaching is to destroy the sense of personal honour. Could a Jesuit, for instance, whether lay or clerical, have any sense of personal honour, or a schoolboy educated at a Jesuit seminary?

The real object of Protestant teaching is to make a boy behave, even tho' no one is watching him. The whole effort of Catholic teaching is to

[1] His brother, long dead, in Rio.   [2] *Irish and American Essays.*

keep a boy under closest scrutiny night and day, and by the Confessional they can carry their spying into the reaches of the poor lad's soul. The Protestants are more severe than the Catholics because of this respect for human nature. The Catholics are indulgent precisely because they think us angels hopelessly fallen and lost—still in their eyes we are angels, while Protestants regard us as *sturdy criminals*, yet with souls of our own.

TO W. B. YEATS

225

N.Y.

Sept. 10. 1920

The more I think of it the more I feel the importance of your sentence. These thoughts have for so long been my habitual thoughts that I may call them my convictions.

Religion demands that opinions should be proved convictions, absolute truths. Art does not ask this—only that they should be part of the man and become his habit. A religion that praised the Trojan war and its incidents would be a false religion. Yet war and its incidents being Homer's habitual thoughts and part and parcel of his mind and soul they become by infection our thought and so nourishing to our imagination. So that all our dreams and thoughts are fed upon them to all eternity...

226

Sept. 30, 1920

317 W. 29

York Powell used to say that if Todhunter had been of the brand of poets he would have remained a doctor. I think for the poets now there is nothing to do except keep silent, for they must know they are in a vacuum —a great emptiness of all habitual thoughts. Todhunter left doctoring to live in a vacuum.

I have just read Goethe's Herman and Dorothea—such a poem could not now be written, just as no one could write another Homer. And we see what is happening in Ireland. There also the actual has conquered and superseded the habitual. You discovered Ireland which had eluded Dowden and Todhunter, and now where is Ireland? and where are you?

Portrait of Celestine

TO LILY YEATS

227

'Celestine' was the youngest of the Petitpas sisters of 317 W. 29th Street. She married in New York, and Yeats used often to go to her house and lunch with her. When 317 W. 29th Street was taken over by a Madame Jais the management became partly Italian and, if less tidy, far more generous in respect of heating etc. During Yeats' last winter Madame Jais saw to it that his room was always warm and comfortable.

Dec. 20, 1920
317 W. 29

. . . I think I have been neglecting you. The fact is I am all mentally immersed in my portrait of Celestine. It is a masterpiece—a life size portrait of her sitting in her chair. She is a good sitter, always helpful and hopeful and intelligent, and full of keen interest, and her criticism and suggestions most valuable—for tho' she was her sisters' servant she is French and therefore loves a good portrait—[Sketch.]

She wears a dress of light blue. The portrait keeps a steady advance not once has it gone back —and she is already telling of how she will take it with her to France and show it in triumph to her friends in old Brittany. I should like some of those haughty French artists to see it. She is extraordinarily happy. Yesterday she suddenly clapped her hands and said Oh how nice it is to have your own home—she had a dreadful fourteen years under the iron rule of her elder sisters—'They have got the money but I have Henri,' she sometimes says.—It is far and away the best portrait I have painted. . . .

228

New York
Feb. 19th, 1921

. . . I have nothing to give up—except some friendships. I will be sorry to say what will be a last farewell to the Bellingers[1] and to some others, but glad to *escape* from N. York and all it stands for—except one thing that N. York always holds with bountiful hands held out towards me—and

[1] Mr. Bellinger was a musician, and his wife wrote books and plays. Yeats had known them for many years.

that is a chance of work—of employment, Anything may turn up here—a lecture an article a portrait. It is a high gaming table where the poorest has a welcome and a chance. They shall I hope grow with every day that passes.

. . . I sometimes see Boyd and his wife and like *both* greatly—Boyd showed himself amused and *incredulous* when I told him that everybody in Dublin believed I was having an uproarious time of jollity and friendship.

We have had a wonderful winter—only once was it necessary to put on rubbers. When Masefield was asked in England what one should take to America, he said one word, 'rubbers'. You know his silent laconic way.

I am glad Willie has made a speech in Oxford on the Irish situation.

I fancy that Miss W— is spending all her spare time in vilipending Willie, George[1] and myself and that Quinn is listening. A friend of hers tells me that she is greatly disappointed that Willie did not marry her. I replied 'Why she did not meet him except once or twice'. It was rash of me—for I have no doubt this was repeated to Miss W— with *embellishments*. Miss W— is not bad hearted, but she must keep herself somehow or other in the Quinn mind and imagination, and she is most successful in this when she makes mischief between him and his friends.—Yours affectly —J. B. YEATS

TO ELIZABETH YEATS

229

Feb. 20, 1921

My dear Lolly—As you may guess, I am greatly interested in Anne's horoscope. It reads like a description of her father with a foreign blend which of course, is from her mother. How you and Lily will enjoy seeing her unfolding. I think if I were to stay at Oxford my interest would not be so much in the grandchild as in her relations to Willie and George. I would like to see Willie playing with his own child. From the first, whenever American people came up to me in the American way and shouted: 'How you must be interested in your grandchild,' I replied 'No, not a bit, but very much so in seeing my son as a father.'[2] Is it because I shall never see her grown up?

[1] Mrs. W. B. Yeats. [2] At this time W. B. Y. was living in Oxford.

TO LILY YEATS

230

New York
Feb. 26, 1921

... I see in the papers that important people engaged in teaching are making a tremendous 'to do' about the immorality in the schools. I fancy they are right. The cause of this thing is to me quite apparent. It is that the American boy and girl have lost the feeling for *personal pride and honour* and it is all due to democracy. It is undemocratic in America for anyone to have pride. That is why Quinn when he chooses is quite ready to treat me as an office boy, and he treats his clerks in the same way, and that is why George was asked such extraordinary questions about things quite intimate ...[1] There are no proud girls in America. Feminine beauty has not that *touch-me-not quality* which is half the charm of the well-bred girl (of other countries). It is the pride of the democracies and the Americans to have no pride, and it does make life pleasant and easy, but it leaves the American girl naked and defenceless against all these false ideas that are so abundant among socialists.

231

March 13, 1921
317 W. 29

... I wrote to Willie some time ago and said it was as bad to be a poet's father as the intimate friend of George Moore. If you listen to Shelley his father was a monster, in reality his father was a well-intentioned and kind father, however mistaken he may have been in the handling of that rather strange person, his son. He (Shelley) was a rebel against everyone, whether at home, or at College or in the world, and all poets have a tendency to see facts metamorphosed. They will sacrifice anything to a tyrannous need of self-expression. Mirabeau was a man of poetical genius, his father wrote of him, 'What a liar the fellow is and not for any purpose, just for the sake of telling strange histories'. I am rather dreading Willie's forthcoming autobiography which is to appear in the *Dial* .... Lately I have been reading Nietzsche. He says that the people of the North—the English

---

[1] W. B. Yeats and his wife had been on a visit to America.

artisans, for instance, have acquisition for motive. They try to make money in order that they may be independent . . . but that the people of the South just want to be useful to other people. . . . The people now running this house are from the South of France, Marseilles, and their only object is to make people happy and pleased. The Petitpas from the North of France were acquisitors all the time and had no other object. The Petitpas warmed the house the whole winter through with 9 tons of coal. These people in three months used up 25 tons. . . .

232

N.Y.

March 21, 1921

. . . I think lots of men die of their wives and *thousands* of women die of their husbands. But not an American. Here, if there is a little trouble over a hand glass or a tooth brush, they shake hands and part, unless of course, there is a lot of money, when the lawyers take a hand.

TO W. B. YEATS

233

New York

April 9, 1921

. . . I think I myself am fundamentally of the artistic temperament— and I can remember how in discussing real matters with real people, I would sometimes irritate them and be myself embarrassed and covered with confusion—in this way, I would produce in the discussion a phrase or some idea that was purely expressive, and apparently be pleased with myself as if I had made a discovery—while they were seeking a practical result. Perhaps my ultimate desire was just as practical as theirs was, yet they could not forgive me, that I should waste my time and possibly theirs in such irrelevancies—and yet in my effort at expression was a sincerity beyond theirs and quite beyond what they sought, since it was without compromise, whereas the practical result they sought must inevitably be a compromise. Thus I come to my conclusion, that the only sincerity in a practical world is that of the artist. Hence the eternal dispute between them and the rulers of the world. If we speak at all, we must say what we believe otherwise our tongue is palsied. For which reason, artists, in the world's history, *have, when they have been wise, always kept themselves apart*. Napoleon hated Literary men; he said they were merely manufacturers of phrases.

A practical man—and to be practical was Napoleon's genius,—cannot afford to be sincere—cannot afford to see facts in their reality: the fact for instance, that millions of men were being butchered in his wars, for a phantom glory. The phrase maker can see this, and if the writer make good phrases, must see this—unless he is willing to fall in his rank and become like journalists and the manufacturers of banal phrases circulating false coin.

If therefore anyone were to ask me, what is the use of those dreamers poets and artists, I can always reply—that but for them sincerity would perish. Lately I have been reading Keats: he is so young that you can read all his thoughts—he is so transparent—his purpose was against every discouragement to find the truth. Instead of Dostoievsky's angry mood, he has all the appealing ingenuousness of his youthfulness. Both sought truth because of artistic needs and not from ethical or religious ideas.

234

... Without imagination—and of the kind that creates—there is no love, whether it be love of a girl or love of a country or love of one's friend or even of children, and of our wives. Lawyers, mathematicians and practical people, that is the minor sort, have logic and can destroy—and the energy of destruction brings with it its own emotion, which is hatred.

The lawyers here in America directing affairs in Ireland—and all the followers of Parnell, who was a cold logician and politician, are in this element, they are fed full with hatred, hatred of England, and probably have among them a sprinkling of Bolshevists who hate everything and everybody. But—love, there is none, for, poor devils, the imagination which God perhaps gave them, is gone. They have been mutilated perhaps by the rusty knife of some beastly kind of life—but it is gone and therefore they cannot love: all their vehemence is to destroy. That is what makes them the kind of men of action they are—not loving Ireland they don't mind if they destroy a building like the Custom House, built though it was during those 20 years from 1780 to 1800, when Ireland had her own government and held her own course. To every man in Dublin the Custom House was as one of the natural features of the country, it was part and parcel of the 'Old Home'. No one ever crossed that bridge who did not lovingly look towards it.[1] However it is the defeat of the men of destruction and violence. How the English rascals must chuckle with triumph. The Irish heart is full of love, and it is wounded.

235

May 30, 1921
317 W. 29 S.

My dear Willie—Here is a story about Sir Wm. Wilde, that I got from old Mrs. Hime, mother of Maurice Hime, headmaster of Foyle College. When she and her son lived in Monaghan, they had for a neighbour, the Rev. — Wilde, D.D.[2] father of Sir Wm. and with him lived two pretty girls, his nieces, and daughters (illegitimate) of Sir. Wm. There was a dance one evening at the house, to which the Himes went. After Mr. Hime left, one of these girls in her muslin dress and crinoline went too close to the fire and the dress was instantly in flames—after some cries of agony, they died. While they were dying, their mother, who had a small black-oak shop in Dublin, came down and stayed with them. After all was over, even to the funeral, Sir Wm. came down and old Mrs. Hime told me that his groans could be heard by people outside his house. There is a tragedy, all the more intense, because it had to be buried in silence. It is not allowed to give sorrow words. Sir Wm. Wilde's vivacity and stream of talk had its source in this kind of [word indecipherable]—perhaps like the bubbles that appear on the surface when the water begins to boil. Had Oscar known of them, he would not have been so scornful of his poor father—successful, parsimonious and bedevilled, yet Oscar benefited by his parsimony. I wonder what Lady Wilde thought of her husband? I remember the scandalous trial in Dublin when he escaped by the skin of his teeth. On that occasion, Lady Wilde was loyal. When she was Miss Elgee, Mr. Bate found her with her husband when her circumstances were

[1] The Custom House, the finest public building in Dublin, had been set on fire in the endeavour to render English government impossible.

[2] The Rev. Mr. Wilde's Christian name was Ralph. He was the relative but not the father of Sir William. The story told by Yeats is somewhat inaccurate: the curious reader may be referred to the recently published *Life of Sir William Wilde* by Dr. P. G. Wilson.

not doubtful, and told my mother about it—so that she could afford to be wise and tolerant.

Here is the story about Tolstoi. Dillon translated some letters by Tolstoi and made the translation under *his eye and supervision*. (Tolstoi had a perfect knowledge of English) and sent them to the *Daily Telegraph*. These letters were republished in the Russian papers and contained such things as this: 'It is said that if a French noble would by touching a button slay thousands of miles distant, a single Frenchman, he would touch that button, but I say that if a Russian nobleman could slay thousands of Russians thousands of miles away, he would touch that button'. The Tzar, reading the letters, was very angry, and since Tolstoi's wife, a mere ordinary Countess, and of German extraction, being the daughter of an apothecary, was ambitious all her life of a court career, what was Tolstoi to do? He wrote to the papers to say he had never sold his letters to the papers. Dillon, a man of great energy, started on the moment and went to Moscow from St. Petersburg and not finding him there, went on north by sledge journey; well, he found Tolstoi and his wife after three thousand miles of journey. He saw Tolstoi, and what is more to the purpose the Countess, and refusing their urgent hospitality, at once returned to St. Petersburg and telegraphed to the *Daily Telegraph* (who had been alarmed by Tolstoi's denials) Tolstoi's letter taking back his own denial, and this letter of Tolstoi also appeared in the Russian papers. Dillon contented himself by asking that if he had bought a railway ticket by the hands of an agent, not saying himself, would he be justified in saying that he had not bought a railway ticket? This he wrote to the papers and so it ended. He knew Tolstoi well and often stayed with him for weeks together, speaking quite freely the Russian language, but after this he never saw him again—but he received a letter from Tolstoi in which he asked him to try and think as ever of him after this had happened as he had done formerly.

We know how progress is helped and guided in periods of latitudinarian thought.—Perhaps morality grows by a similar laxity and that Shakespeare and Tolstoi, and all such men are victims of their own genius —sympathizing with the wicked as easily as with the good. They have not the same showiness of virtuous endeavour that so nobly characterizes many of our conscientious and right-minded friends and neighbours.

Tolstoi was perhaps a weak husband, and then again so unlike many of us who if we have not genius, have virtue and dignity and can maintain our dignity as husbands and men.—Yours affectionately—J. B. YEATS

Creation out of Love

236

New York
May 31, 1921

... Creation out of love and its innate desire for restfulness, is a woeful business, bringing more tears than smiles; yet it brings smiles—some smiles. And so, if there be a God, He created our woeful existence, And so Tolstoi and Dostoievsky wrote their woeful novels, all out of love and its innate desire for its own particular restfulness.

The English novelists have never so worked, their purpose a moral deduction—Dickens, Thackeray, G. Eliot, all of them—Meredith and Hardy—because of the strength and urgency of this puritan purpose they laboured and made mighty works, knowing that the whole nation would back them and applaud. But theatrical audiences are bent on amusement. There is something about the theatre, something inevitable when people come together *in holiday mood* and *in crowds,* which makes deductive purpose and moral effort an irrelevancy and ridiculous. That is why English writers approach the theatre shorn of half their strength—and that is why we the mere Irish having escaped Puritanism, and so bent on making pleasure a serious concern, succeed where they fail and write the plays. At the theatre moral purpose is a stranger and unwelcome, and love which cares nothing for moral distinctions finds itself at home. There is a lot of love in Bernard Shaw, notwithstanding his long residence in England, and his own conscientious efforts to strangle it, and that is the part of his plays which we like and which we remember: unmoral love which is always whispering its doubts as to the ten Commandments, and as to rules and laws generally, finding its way a potent dissolvent through every hindrance —*its way to the lovable*—where it stops and refuses to be dislodged—and it can put up a strong defence and strike back, even though the people who read the novels are against it. That is why I have a hope for the theatre and prefer it to every other form of Literature. Love striking back can be as fierce as the moralists—in fact having few friends and its situation desperate it will strike *murderously*—and be venomous and obscene—and forgetting all prudence, be more anxious to find enemies than friends— and be in fact love in a temper and write like Ezra Pound and his friends, very shocking to their well wishers, myself for instance, who am old and timid.

237

I have been an unconscionable burden to you and George[1] on your comparatively slender resources and I do assure you that I have sleepless nights thinking of it. Yet from the moment that you invited my burthening of you, I have given all my thoughts to the portrait of myself. So all my sleepless nights only ended in my going on with the painting. When you see my magnum opus, I think you will forgive me. I mean it to be ahead of any portraits Quinn may have and to know this will soothe my last moments. 'Ripeness is all.'. . .

TO LILY YEATS

238

. . . I find that these French servants—high-class maids, etc.—all hate the Catholic Irish. They say that they are all religion and have no sense of duty, and that while they are praying and going to mass, they don't mind leaving the family without breakfast. This girl's uncle is a Priest. She says it is right to be religious, 'but not too far'; and besides I fancy that the Irish give themselves airs and swagger. I know that I hate to meet any of these cold Irish young ladies who are all so untidy and showy, not merely in dress, but in behaviour, etc. . . .

TO W. B. YEATS

239

. . . When is your poetry at its best? I challenge all the critics if it is not when its wild spirit of your imagination is wedded to concrete fact. Had you stayed with me and not left me for Lady Gregory, and her friends and associations, you would have loved and adored concrete life for which as I

---

[1] Mrs. W. B. Yeats.

know you have a real affection. What would have resulted? Realistic and poetical plays—poetry in closest and most intimate union with the positive realities and complexities of life. And that is the world that waits, so far in vain, its poet. I have always hoped and do still hope that your wife may do for you what I would have done. Not idea but the game of life should have been your preoccupation, as it was Shakespeare's and the old English writers', notably the kinglike Fielding. The moment you touch however lightly on concrete fact, how alert you are! and how attentive we your readers become! Whistler was a fine artist, but as a portrait painter a failure. His Carlyle is ridiculous, a mere conventional coat of a prophet, the picture merely a good decorative arrangement. Every artist, poet and painter, should have many visions—first the poem itself or the picture—and with Whistler this included the frame—and then as part and parcel of that the vision of the man or woman or landscape. Da Vinci had his immortal vision of that great lady with the smile. But Whistler was too arrogant or rather too insolent—and insolence I do not love, it makes me think of the nobleman's footman. So he had not the patience to become the student and lover of life itself. Carlyle the man was to him nothing except an occasion for an artistic picture. In Shakespeare's time that kind of insolence was not known among the poets. France had not ennobled and decorated them, they were little better than noblemen's servants or servants to the public—so that there was nothing to prevent their making a close study of life itself—and they had not despised their fellow creatures as did the Puritan and does the modern English gentleman. For this kind of study you have by nature every natural qualification—your conversation shows it. Never are you happier and never more felicitous in words than when in your conversation you describe life and comment on it. But when you write poetry you as it were put on your dress coat and shut yourself in and forget what is vulgar to a man in a dress coat.

Probably you will have a long life, in which will be many revolutions and epochs. It is my belief that some day you will write a play of real life in which poetry will be the inspiration as propaganda is of G. B. Shaw's plays.

Am I talking wildly? Am I senile? I don't think so, for I would have said the same any time these 20 or 30 years. The best thing in life is the game of life, and some day a poet will find this out. I hope you will be that poet. It is easier to write poetry that is far away from life, but it is *infinitely more exciting* to write the poetry of life—and it is what the whole world is crying out for as pants the hart for the water brook. I bet it is what your wife wants—ask her. She will know what I mean and drive it home. I have great confidence in her. Does she lack the courage to say it?

Had you stayed with me, we would have collaborated and York Powell would have helped. We should have loved the opportunity of a poet among us to handle the concrete which is now left in the hands of the humorists and the politicians.

My play which you did have and probably did not read, is a poetical play dealing with the concrete—though of course not very profound, and very demoded, but it is the right sort.

240

New York
July 5, 1921

. . . Lately I have been reading a not very important book, *Le Memorial d'une Famille*, par Emil Sabatier.

It is to be read with much skipping—the art of reading is the art of skipping; but I liked it because it described a side of French life which has always attracted me, when people lived sensitively watching for a happiness made out of affection and of continual sympathy. It is how 'nice' people lived in Ireland, long ago, notably my father's people. My mother's family, of English extraction, worshipped force and so did the Pollexfens and all the English. Force means courage and honesty.

In the 18th century, this kind of preference meant a frank and unbridled animalism, with cock fighting and bull baiting and boxing and every kind of blasphemy. It meant Hogarth and Fielding, and solemn hilarious old Johnson, and the portrait painters like Gainsborough who 'loved' the women they painted, or honoured and worshipped them like Reynolds.

How do we love nowadays? We worship truth. There is to be no more illusion, neither that of sentiment nor that of romance—and liberation has become discipline. It is a world stripped bare of ornament, swept and garnished like a monk's cell—and oh so cold!—and after all is it so very bracing? It seems to me that we have nothing left of that which made our old content, unless it be the pride of intellect. And so the poor poets and artists who do not care much about that kind of vanity, are in dismay— and their courage is gone. How are they to get back their courage?— Please tell me Mr. W. B. Yeats.

241

. . . Life is curious. When I find myself constantly praising anyone and always thinking the nicest things about anyone, it is nearly always because I am contending against a secret dislike within my own mind. On the contrary, when I keep gathering facts and arguments industriously against a man, it is because that man attracts me.

. . . .

We are threatened with a set of opinions which would make the economical situation the basis of society. The esthetical is the basis of society, for in the heart of man, woman and child love is more than logic, though it works so obscurely. Christianity, feudalism, German militarism, patriotism are all of them esthetical. The word itself comes from the Greek verb to perceive, and it is so, for love works by the direct method of intuition, and not as logic does by inference. I love a lord, I love a fine horse, I love banners and trumpets, I love the figure on the Cross, suffering for the sins of the world. . . .

242

In this letter J. B. Y. alludes to the portion of his son's autobiography, entitled 'Four Years (1887–1891)'.

July 23, 1921
317 W. 29

. . . I am reading those chapters by you in the *Dial*. *I am grateful to you* for what you say of Edwin Ellis and of Nettleship. I know the subjects and besides, I have myself written about them, but so inadequately and so wretchedly compared with your few sentences, and I think that the unfortunate phrase 'enraged family' may be thought to mean something different from what I thought. There never has been a moment in my life of meeting you, even though it was by chance in the streets of Dublin, that it did not give me pleasure. As you will find out, there is a feeling that of itself unbidden and of necessity always springs into actuality when a parent meets his offspring, a sort of animalism that defies control, for it is animal and primitive. I think that even in the married state which is the theme of comedy and latterly of philosophical 'high faluting' contempt, there is the same survival of animal feeling; at any rate, if they have lived together long enough for it to be generated. . . .

TO LILY YEATS

243

July 29, 1921

Last night a nice German man dined here, and he told me the great difference in Germany since the war is that now everyone is corrupt, from the Mayor of a town to the tram conductor, and that before the war this was impossible and inconceivable. The fact is that all democracies have always been corrupt,—and for the obvious reason that in a democracy the police are not allowed to carry out their duties. . . . Under a monarchy or an aristocracy the police are powerful. They are the servants of the State, and *the State is not the people.*

TO W. B. YEATS

244

August 24, 1921
317 W. 29

. . . I have just read some stories by Dostoievsky, that is an author who never forgets that he must amuse his readers, whether he wear the cap and bells or the tragic mask he must please. It is the condition under which every artist works and gets not merely his living—which is a matter of small account—but not otherwise can he win intelligent esteem and appreciation. The artist is a solitary man, who has come among us to make himself pleasant. He is a solitary but not a wild man of the woods. He is or he must be a gentleman. It is because Dostoievsky knows this that he stands apart among the tribe of realists who are, at least so many of them, without manners . . . these others sometimes rely on some display of sensual allurement or play to the slums by a propaganda of hatred. . . .

245

MRS. SIMEON FORD TO J. B. YEATS

Rye, N.Y.
September 14, 1921

Dear Mr. Yeats—I have received your kind letter saying you are going home. Your friends will miss you. Monday afternoons will seem strange without you sitting in the big armchair by the fire, but I think it will be very nice for you to be again in your own home with your daughters and your friends about you. ...

It has been a great pleasure to me meeting you, your daughter and your sons. I remember the first time I heard the name of Yeats. A teacher in New York who conducted our literary class for ten years, when the children were babies, said, as I was going to Europe, 'There is a man named Yeats. He has written a book of poems. Get it when you are in London. I can't get it here,' I brought it home to the class and all were delighted with it—enthusiastic—but no other volume was to be found in New York. Scribner's would not send for it, so Mr. Hatch sent for a dozen copies on his own responsibility and the whole class took them. Mrs. Talmage and Mrs. Lamont were two of the members. Then I wrote an article on Mr. Yeats, together with this teacher, in 19—? Miss Moore's article came out a month before mine. They were the first published in New York. Later, as you know, Mrs. Yeats gave a talk for me at the Arts Club, then in 34th Street ...

TO LILY YEATS

246

N.Y.
Sept. 29, 1921

... After three weeks of misery I am now in full possession of myself, and can work and read. It was indigestion and the awful persistent heat. Never before did I suffer from the heat, it sometimes made me giddy—but it did not take away my courage, and then never before was I in New York without a friend. The Bellingers were here and then there were those grim folk, the Petitpas. They were jailers, but a careful and true-hearted jailer is better than no one at all. *This time I was and am all alone.* How glad I shall be to be back among my family. I thought I could live alone. It is impossible. Perhaps I might get married. There are many to choose from. Here are some of them. [Sketches.] all beauties in their circle. Which do you recommend? Consult Jack.

The self-portrait

247

The sketch in the letter is of the portrait of himself on which Yeats had been working for so long. (See Frontispiece). He also had on hand at the end a head and shoulders of himself.

October 10, 1921

... The portrait is now my comfort and no longer my care. Because of it, I was ill, positively ill, all the summer, and I told Quinn and the doctor, who I suppose did not believe me, and I became an old man. My legs were weak under me and my spirits sad coloured, and in the streets I leaned heavily on my stick, and I said to myself: 'this is premature old age'. Now all is changed. I come upstairs with a bounding step (I do hate coming upstairs) and it is only because the portrait looks well, not merely the face but the coat and the body and the hands and the book-case etc. The coat a dark purplish hue, and the waistcoat brown, and I have painted not myself but my image in the looking-glass. So I put in at the bottom of the canvas a foreground of bottles and a palette as you see in my sketch. [Sketch.]

Don't be angry if I am arranging so as to have my passage pushed on into December.

TO W. B. YEATS

248

317 W. 29
Jan. 10, 1922

... It has amused me to read that when Robert Cecil, afterwards Lord Salisbury, was about to marry the Judge's widow and his father told him that if he made such a mis-alliance, he would have to undergo many privations, he said that that could not matter to him, *since he had never enjoyed anything*, and at this time, he was twenty-five years of age.

Years afterwards, when he and Bismarck met at a great Congress to decide the fate of Europe Bismarck said he was a lath painted to look like iron. Lord Salisbury was a man of low vitality, hence the gravity of a lath painted to look like iron. You remember how grave under all circumstances was G. T. Pollexfen. I bet that the gentle Shakespeare was not remarkable for his gravity, and I think that in his plays, he is maliciously always on the watch for grave people as if he did not like them. . . .

TO JOHN QUINN

249

My dear Quinn—Many thanks for the $30. I have been badly wanting underwear and socks. And many thanks also for your hint about the pictures at the American Art Galleries. I was there the other day and saw a very interesting Harpignies.

Induced by Mrs. Becker, who in amazing ignorance praised them, I went to Knoodlers' and saw portraits by Laszlo. That shining cohort of fashionable horrors was amusing. I got from them one good thing. My self-portrait has been facing me for a long time lying against the wall of my room and filling me with despondency. I now see that it is the making of a masterpiece. To know good you must have seen evil. I have seen Laszlo and now I appreciate Yeats.

Last night at the Macdowell Club I was one of ten poets, including Amy Lowell; all of them quite as illustrious as myself; and we read from our works. I read my poem 'Autumn'; it begins

'Great lady of the darkening skies'

and I forgot to mention that the subject was 'Autumn'. So what they made of it I don't know or who they thought the great lady was.

All Sunday I sketched a Miss McCulloch and then went to an At Home where I stayed till after 7 o'clock spending the time in making a sketch of a pretty lady; and coming back here sat with the Courtenays till 11 o'clock. Next Sunday I am to have a final sitting from Miss McCulloch. I have also done for her a drawing of myself.

She is a very clever and pretty young lady, self-supporting, who comes from beyond Chicago and is now writing a book which is to be a history of the actor's tender charms.

I made her acquaintance through her chancing to come here for dinner. Altho' young and pretty, she is versed in all the labour questions. Zimmern seemed to find her interesting when he dined here. Her people are Sabbatarian Scotch people. Naturally she prefers New York to the Far West. But she is a sensible girl and has a high opinion of her parents. She is self-respecting and has the most kindly mind I ever met with. I am glad to say she is coming to live in this house February 1st. Some day you would like to meet her. I would have no hesitation in recommending you to meet her. She has one very rare quality. She always thinks before she speaks. If you speak to her she looks at you gravely for just a second and then replies. And she can talk nonsense with anyone and can be witty. 'I do not take anything at its face value', snorted old Captain Freeman. 'What! Not a pretty girl?' said Miss McCulloch. Captain Freeman was quite nonplussed. These fierce radicals never like to be laughed at. Freeman's own laugh is fiendish and I think he is the most dissuasive man I ever met. Miss McCulloch is persuasive.

I am very sorry to hear you have had a cold. If we knew how to stave off colds we should all live to be a hundred. Willie's had himself inoculated and so, according to his wife, has stopped all colds for two years. It 'took' with him but it is not so with everybody.

The At Home I went to was at 135 West 136th Street, close to Riverside. By mistake I went off to a station at 135th Street, in the Bronx, and had all that distance to walk through that fearful cold, climbing up a big hill as well. The people were very orthodox, Canadians who take in the *Spectator* and admire England. But the hostess sent me into another room and I took with me a pretty and clever American woman whom I sketched. With many thanks, yours very truly—J. B. YEATS

W. B. YEATS TO ELIZABETH YEATS

250

4 Broad Street, Oxford
Feb. 3, 1922

My dear Lolly—I think that things have been for the best. Our father died without ever experiencing the pains and infirmities of age. His letters to me, even those of two or three weeks ago, spoke of his consciousness of well-being. If he had lived longer, he would have grown helpless and known that he was helpless. He had his hopes and ambitions to the last, constantly writing that he was painting his masterpiece. If he had returned home and lived longer, he would not have had that sense of working and thinking, without any touch of enfeebling age. I have of course, a great many letters from him and some of the latest are among the best he ever wrote. He has lived longer than our Sligo grandfather, who was a man of great bodily strength and vitality. And though his life has not been fortunate, he has on the whole, I think, been happy, especially of late years. An

Tribute to J. B. Y.

American publisher, who came to see me a few weeks ago, had promised to sit for him on his return to New York. He lived in hope and I think the past hardly existed for him, and his hopes filled his life. He several times spoke of the pleasure he got from your letters, from what he called 'Lolly's vivid letters'.—Yours affectly—W. B. YEATS

FROM JOHN SLOAN

251

Copy of letter from John Sloan, dated Feb. 7, 1922.

88 Washington Place, New York City
My dear Miss Yeats—That great man your father is no longer with us; we expected him to go—not the mysterious journey into the great beyond —we expected him to go home to Ireland but we had an unformed hope that he would never go. He has gone, gone easily and with serenity and for me the world can never be the same—the great warm glow has gone. But I should have felt about the same had he left for Ireland. He would then have been with you and not with us—now he is with us all.

His was a swift illness—hardly an illness—confined to his room one day, to his bed one day and then away to take first rank among the mighty poets of the past.

We did love him and he loved us. We have the usual regrets—feel that we did not see him enough—appreciate him enough, I think these are the common regrets, moments of realization of how selfish is each part played in the farce of life—some day we may play the drama, I believe that will be nobler.

Let your sister and brothers know how deeply I sympathise with you all.

The church from which he was buried was full of his lovers, about 250 people there (with only 24 hours notice) and they each felt as I did, that they had lost their father—I assure you that my own father's death was not so great a loss to me. I was never as near to him as to John Butler Yeats, we did not understand each other—and had the Puritan standoffishness—no love expressed, all repression.—

A few score men such as your father in the world at any one time would cure its sickness—but our civilization produces other flowers—unsavoury blooms rank and poisonous—John Butler Yeats was one of the rare exceptions.—With etc.—(Signed) JOHN SLOAN

INDEX

Index

Index

Index

Index

Index